Law and Religion

The worlds of law and religion increasingly collide in Parliament and the court-room. Religious courts, the wearing of religious symbols and faith schools have given rise to increased legislation and litigation. This is the first student textbook to set out the fundamental principles and issues of law and religion in England and Wales. Offering a succinct exposition and critical analysis of the field, it explores how English law regulates the practice of religion. The textbook surveys law and religion from various perspectives, such as human rights and discrimination law, as well as considering the legal status of both religion and religious groups. Controversial and provocative questions are explored, promoting full engagement with the key debates. The book's explanatory approach and detailed references ensure understanding and encourage independent study. Students can track key developments on the book's updating website. This innovative text is essential reading for all students in the field.

Russell Sandberg is a lecturer at Cardiff Law School, researching at its Centre for Law and Religion. He has written widely on law and religion, notably as a Specialist Contributing Editior for *Jowitt's Dictionary of English Law*. He chairs the Law and Religion Scholars Network.

Law and Religion

RUSSELL SANDBERG

Lecturer in Law, Cardiff University

CAMBRIDGE
UNIVERSITY PRESS

CAMBRIDGE
UNIVERSITY PRESS

University Printing House, Cambridge CB2 8BS, United Kingdom

Published in the United States of America by Cambridge University Press, New York

Cambridge University Press is part of the University of Cambridge.

It furthers the University's mission by disseminating knowledge in the pursuit of education, learning and research at the highest international levels of excellence.

www.cambridge.org
Information on this title: www.cambridge.org/9780521177184

First published 2011
4th printing 2014

Printed in the United Kingdom by Clays, St Ives plc.

A catalogue record for this publication is available from the British Library

Library of Congress Cataloguing in Publication data
Sandberg, Russell.
Law and religion / Russell Sandberg.
    p.   cm.
Includes index.
ISBN 978-1-107-00379-8 (hardback)
1. Church and state – England.   2. Freedom of religion – England.
3. Religious minorities – Legal status, laws, etc. – England.   I. Title.
KD8600.S36   2011
342.4208'52 – dc22   2010052387

ISBN 978-1-107-00379-8 Hardback
ISBN 978-0-521-17718-4 Paperback

Contents

Preface

The aim of this book is to provide a succinct exposition and critique of the new legal framework concerning religion. It explores the extent to which English law[1] now accommodates religious difference and provides a detailed account of recent legal changes, questioning whether the new laws actually further the protection afforded to religious individuals and groups. It also asks whether it is now possible and desirable to see law and religion as a distinct legal sub-discipline akin to family law or sports law.

Law and Religion furthers many arguments and ideas which I have developed whilst completing my doctorate on 'Religion, Law and Society' at Cardiff University and through teaching the postgraduate master's degree in Canon Law and undergraduate module on Comparative Law of Religion at Cardiff Law School. Interactions with students on these courses have improved the text. This book develops many arguments and ideas that I have previously presented or published elsewhere.[2] The feedback of editors, peer reviewers, readers and conference delegates has been invaluable. A number of these previously published works – indeed many of the better ones – have been co-written and I owe a special debt to my co-writers for helping me to develop the ideas and arguments that follow. This book is designed to complement these earlier publications[3] and other leading works in this field. *Law and Religion* is also complemented by a number of online materials provided on the website of the Centre for Law and Religion at Cardiff.[4] Readers might be particularly interested in the weblinks, lists of recent publications and the Case Database provided on the webpages dedicated to the Law and Religion Scholars Network.[5]

I am indebted to a large number of individuals who have helped develop *Law and Religion*. I owe a special debt to my colleagues at the Centre for

---

[1] This book focuses upon the law of England and Wales, with some comparative references to Scots law. The distinct legal, political and religious situation in Northern Ireland is outside the scope of this work.

[2] The full references to these are provided at the relevant point in the text.

[3] In particular, this book is intended to complement M. Hill, R. Sandberg and N. Doe, *Religion Law: United Kingdom* (The Netherlands: Kluwer Law International, 2010), which provides a comprehensive encyclopaedic elucidation of the law in this area, and the essays published in N. Doe and R. Sandberg (eds.), *Law and Religion: New Horizons* (Leuven: Peeters, 2010).

[4] See www.law.cf.ac.uk/clr/.   [5] See www.law.cf.ac.uk/clr/lrsn.

Law and Religion at Cardiff and to members of the Law and Religion Scholars Network and the Interfaith Legal Advisers Network. In particular, I am beholden to Professor Norman Doe and Honorary Professor Mark Hill QC for their encouragement, advice and friendship. Many of the arguments developed in this book were first stimulated in conversations with them. Frank Cranmer has been especially helpful, keeping me abreast of developments in the field and casting an eye over draft chapters. I am also grateful to a number of other colleagues at the Centre for Law and Religion at Cardiff: Dr Rebecca Catto, Rt Rev. Paul Colton, Eithne D'Auria, John Duddington, Dr Rev. Gerard Garrett, Anthony Jeremy, David Lambert, Professor Peter Luxton, Dr Javier Oliva, Dr Augur Pearce, Rev. Gareth Powell, and Layla Welford have all helped to develop the ideas expressed here. Professor Peter Edge and David Harte, who examined my doctoral thesis, have also offered valuable suggestions.

The support of colleagues at Cardiff Law School has been particularly important to me, especially Professors Gillian Douglas, Nigel Lowe, David Miers, Bob Lee and Dr Urfan Khaliq. I am grateful to Cardiff Law School, the James Pantyfedwen Foundation and the Sidney Perry Foundation for providing funding during my doctoral studies. I am also thankful for the administrative support provided by Sharron Alldred, Sarah Kennedy and Helen Calvert at the Postgraduate Office of Law School and for the research assistance provided by two personal tutees, Anna Mahoney and Jacqueline Trow. I also wish to thank the staff at Cambridge University Press, particularly Sinead Moloney, for their professional commitment to the text. My greatest debt, however, is to my family. This book is dedicated to my parents and to my sister Julia and my brother Marcus for their support, which has been the stuff of legend.

Russell Sandberg
Maesteg, South Wales
August 2010

Table of cases

1

What is 'law and religion'?

Introduction

In twenty-first century Britain the interaction between law and religion is rarely far from the headlines. On 3 September 2002, Shabina Begum, a fourteen-year-old schoolgirl was prevented from wearing her *jilbab* at school. On 8 January 2005, *Jerry Springer: The Opera* was broadcast on BBC2 amid mass protests outside the BBC Television Centre. On 7 February 2008, the Archbishop of Canterbury, Rowan Williams, delivered a lecture on the interaction between English and Islamic law at the Royal Courts of Justice. Each of these events prompted a passionate and wide-ranging debate about the extent to which the law should accommodate religious difference. Moreover, these three events were by no means isolated incidents.

The first decade of the century has witnessed numerous political, social and legal developments concerning religious matters. At the political and social levels, the short- and long-term implications of multiculturalism, religious resurgence and extremism have dominated global and domestic news agendas and public life. The shadow of 9/11 has been cast not only upon the ramifications of the so-called War on Terror, but also upon national debates concerning the extent to which religious difference should be accommodated. These socio-political developments have, of course, impacted upon the law. Debates concerning the wearing of religious symbols and dress in schools and at work, the relationship between religious liberty and free speech and the status of Islamic law and courts are just some of the issues which are symptomatic of an increasingly urgent interest in questions concerning the extent to which State law should accommodate religious difference.

The State legal framework concerning the regulation of religion has changed dramatically over the last decade. Recent years have witnessed a vast number of important legislative developments, most notably in relation to human rights and discrimination law. The Human Rights Act 1998 incorporated the European Convention on Human Rights (ECHR) into domestic law, including the Article 9 right to freedom of religion. Discrimination legislation extended the law to prohibit discrimination on grounds of religion or belief.[1] Moreover, a number of other laws have been enacted

---

[1] Employment Equality (Religion or Belief) Regulations 2003; Equality Act 2006 Part Two. The law is now to be found in the Equality Act 2010.

which affect religion. The most notable changes have included the Anti–Terrorism, Crime and Security Act 2001, the Divorce (Religious Marriages) Act 2002, the Civil Partnership Act 2004, the Racial and Religious Hatred Act 2006, the Charities Act 2006, the Criminal Justice and Immigration Act 2008 and numerous education and immigration statutes. There has also been an unprecedented number of high-profile cases affecting religious freedom.[2] Put simply, there are more laws concerning religion than ever before.

This rise in legislation, litigation and public concern provides the inspiration for this book. The chapters that follow explore the extent to which English law accommodates religious difference in the twenty-first century. They provide a detailed account of the current law, exploring the effect and significance of the recent legal changes. The chapters address three sets of questions:

1. What has been the effect of the new laws? Have they actually furthered the protection afforded to religious individuals and groups?
2. What has been the significance of the new laws? How do they interact with older laws concerning religion?
3. What affect has this had upon the study of law and religion? To what extent can it now be said that law and religion exists as an academic sub-discipline akin to family law or sports law?[3]

This chapter addresses a preliminary question. It asks how 'law and religion' may be defined.

The growth of law and religion

The significant legal changes made in recent years have been responsible in part for the increase in the academic study of law and religion in the United Kingdom. In contrast to many other Western jurisdictions, most notably the United States and continental Europe, the study of law and religion in the United Kingdom is paradoxically a young sub-discipline which focuses on an interaction which has a long history.

It has only been in the last twenty years that the United Kingdom has witnessed a considerable growth in law and religion literature. Although

---

[2] See the Law and Religion Scholars Network Case Database at: www.law.cf.ac.uk/clr/networks/lrsncd.html.

[3] It is possible to conceive of law and religion as a 'subject', 'theme', 'area' or 'branch of law'. For current purposes, law and religion will be regarded as a sub-discipline of law, like criminal law, family law and so on. This conception of law and religion as a sub-discipline follows A. Bradney, 'Some Sceptical Thoughts about the Academic Analysis of Law and Religion in the United Kingdom' in N. Doe and R. Sandberg (eds.), *Law and Religion: New Horizons* (Leuven: Peeters, 2010), p. 299 and, more generally, A. Bradney, 'The Rise and Rise of Legal Education' (1997) 4 *Web Journal of Current Legal Issues*, http://webjcli.ncl.ac.uk/1997/issue4/bradney4.html.

a number of key legal works were produced much earlier,[4] most of these were concerned exclusively with the law of the Church of England or the Church of Scotland[5] and were often practical guides aimed at the 'black letter' practitioner rather than academic monographs. Law and religion could not be said to exist as a separate academic discipline.[6] There were no specialist journals, no research clusters and very few, if any, academics who exclusively specialised in the area.[7]

The academic study of law and religion in the United Kingdom blossomed in the last decades of the twentieth century. In 1987 the Ecclesiastical Law Society was formed, providing a journal[8] and a forum[9] for issues of law and religion to be discussed, with emphasis placed upon both academic rigour and practical application. Although the society's prime focus is upon the law of the Church of England,[10] its scope has widened as time has passed. Its journal now regularly includes pieces on state law on religion, comparative religious law and the regulation of religion overseas.[11] In 1991, the Ecclesiastical Law Society supported the establishment of a Masters Degree programme in Canon Law at Cardiff University. The LLM, the first of its type in the United Kingdom since the Reformation,[12] provided the opportunity for the postgraduate study in the canon law of the Anglican churches of the United Kingdom, particularly that of the Church of England, as well as the study of the law of the Roman Catholic Church and State law affecting religion. The LLM led to the development of the Centre for

---

[4] See, e.g. W. Dale, *The Law of the Parish Church* (London: Butterworths, 1932); G. Moore, *Introduction to English Canon Law* (Oxford: Clarendon Press, 1967); J. Pitchford, *An ABC for the PCC* (London: Wyche, 1980); and G. Moore, T. Briden and K. MacMorran, *Handbook for Churchwardens and Parochial Church Councillors* (London: Mowbray, 1989).

[5] See, e.g. A. Taylor Innes, *The Law of Creeds in Scotland Laws* (Edinburgh: Wm Blackwood, 1867); W. Mair, *Digest of Church Laws* (Edinburgh: Wm Blackwood, 1887); J. T. Cox, *Practice and Procedure in the Church of Scotland* (Edinburgh: Wm Blackwood, 1934); and F. C. Lyall, *Of Presbyters and Kings: Church and State in the Law of Scotland* (Aberdeen: Aberdeen University Press, 1980).

[6] A. Pearce, 'England's Law of Religion – The History of a Discipline' in N. Doe and R. Sandberg (eds.), *Law and Religion: New Horizons* (Leuven: Peeters, 2010), p. 13.

[7] See K. Counsell, 'The Teaching of Canon Law in England and Wales: 1400–1996' (University of Wales, Cardiff: LLM in Canon Law Dissertation, 1997).

[8] The *Ecclesiastical Law Journal*, published now by Cambridge University Press.

[9] The Society holds a bi-annual conference and a series of lectures. See www.ecclawsoc.org.uk/.

[10] According to its website, the society was formed 'to promote the study of ecclesiastical and canon law particularly in the Church of England and those churches in communion with it'. The Archbishop of Canterbury and York serve as Patrons.

[11] This is reflected in the composition of the Journal's Editorial Advisory Board, which includes respected practitioners and academics from across the globe.

[12] Some canon law was taught before 1991. From the late 1960s to 1981 Garth Moore offered a half paper on the canon law of the Church of England as part of the law degree at Cambridge. At Oxford, seminars in canon law were conducted by Eric Kemp in the 1950s. See M. Kotiranta, 'The Teaching and Study of Church-State Relations in the Nordic Countries, in the United Kingdom and in Ireland' in J. Valle and A. Hollerbach (eds.), *The Teaching of Church-State Relations in European Universities* (Leuven: Peeters, 2005), pp. 105, 153.

Law and Religion at Cardiff University, the first such research cluster at a university in the United Kingdom,[13] numerous publications,[14] and national and international conferences.[15] Moreover, in 2000 Cardiff launched the undergraduate LLB module Comparative Law of Religion, a course which largely examines the interaction between State law and religion.

At the same time, a number of law academics and practitioners from outside Cardiff began writing in this field and, as Anthony Bradney has pointed out, 'in some cases, this writing constitutes not just an occasional interest but is, rather, central to their research careers'.[16]

Recent years have seen several important publications[17] and the setting up of research clusters and research centres at Bristol and Oxford Brookes. Moreover, numerous law and religion courses have been set up in law schools at both undergraduate and postgraduate levels. In 2008 the Law and Religion Scholars Network (LARSN) was launched. This initiative, led by the Centre for Law and Religion at Cardiff, was designed to bring together for the first time academics from across the United Kingdom interested in all dimensions of the study of law and religion. LARSN organises an annual conference on law and religion and at the time of writing has over 160 members, most of whom are based at UK law schools. Law and religion is fast becoming an established legal sub-displine in the United Kingdom. As Edge commented upon the first meeting of LARSN:

> There have long been members of British law schools who have contributed to this field – although sometimes not in frank terms. But there are more of us than ever before and the time is ripe to develop a community of scholars.[18]

---

[13] See N. Doe, 'The First Ten Years of the Centre for Law and Religion, Cardiff University' (2008) 10(2) *Ecclesiastical Law Journal* 222.

[14] Most notably, N. Doe, *The Legal Framework of the Church of England* (Oxford: Clarendon Press, 1996); N. Doe, *Canon Law in the Anglican Communion: A Worldwide Perspective* (Oxford: Oxford University Press, 1998); and M. Hill, *Ecclesiastical Law*, 3rd edn, (Oxford: Oxford University Press, 2007).

[15] The centre co-founded the Colloquium of Anglican and Roman Catholic Canon Lawyers and contributes to the European Consortium for Church and State Research. In 2007 the centre founded the Interfaith Legal Advisers Network (ILAN), designed to bring together for the first time advisers to a wide range of religious groups to share their experiences and address contemporary themes at the interface between religious law and State law.

[16] A. Bradney, 'Politics and Sociology: New Research Agenda for the Study of Law and Religion' in R. O'Dair and A. Lewis (eds.), *Law and Religion* (Oxford: Oxford University Press, 2001). p. 66.

[17] Monographs include: J. A. Robillard, *Religion and the Law* (Manchester: Manchester University Press, 1984); A. Bradney, *Religions, Rights and Laws* (Leicester: Leicester University Press, 1993); A. Bradney, *Law and Faith in a Sceptical Age* (Oxford: Routledge Cavendish, 2009); P. W. Edge, *Legal Responses to Religious Difference* (The Hague: Kluwer Law, 2002); P. W. Edge, *Religion and Law* (Aldershot: Ashgate, 2006); C. Hamilton, *Family, Law and Religion* (London: Sweet and Maxwell, 1995); R. Ahdar and I. Leigh, *Religious Freedom in the Liberal State* (Oxford: Oxford University Press, 2005); N. Addison, *Religious Discrimination and Hatred Law* (Oxford: Routledge, 2006); L. Vickers, *Religious Freedom, Religious Discrimination and the Workplace* (Oxford: Hart, 2008); and J. Rivers, *The Law of Organized Religions* (Oxford: Oxford University Press, 2010).

[18] P. W. Edge, 'Law and Religion Scholars Network' (2008) 10(3) *Ecclesiastical Law Journal* 360, 361.

Defining law and religion

The term 'law and religion' has become the term most frequently used to describe this community of scholars in the United Kingdom. The term has been utilised in the titles of numerous edited collections,[19] in the names of research centres and groupings[20] and, perhaps most importantly, in the name of the association which scholars have set up, the Law and Religion Scholars Network. However, little attention has been paid to the definition and scope of 'law and religion'.[21] Most books which use the two words in their title do not provide a definition of their subject-matter, but rather implicitly accept an underlying theme. Most embrace what may be described as the 'relationship thesis': to study law and religion is to study the relationship between these two social phenomena.[22] Other works, typically those examining religion in the context of international human rights laws,[23] state that their theme is 'religious freedom'.[24] However, such statements reveal very little about the subject-matter and purpose of law and religion as a legal sub-discipline.

The external and internal aspects of law and religion

Some academics, however, have attempted to define the sub-discipline by means of content. Doe, for instance, has defined 'law of religion' as 'the study of the laws of States on religion and the laws or other regulatory instruments of religious organisations'.[25] The sociologists of religion

---

[19] E.g. R. O'Dair and A. Lewis (eds.), *Law and Religion* (Oxford: Oxford University Press, 2001); P. W. Edge and G. Harvey (eds.), *Law and Religion in Contemporary Society: Communities, Individualism and the State* (Aldershot: Ashgate, 2000); R. J. Ahdar (ed.), *Law and Religion* (Aldershot: Ashgate, 2000); P. Cane, C. Evans and Z. Robinson (eds.), *Law and Religion in Historical and Theoretical Context* (Cambridge: Cambridge University Press, 2008); R. Mehdi *et al.* (eds.), *Religion and Law in Multicultural Societies* (Denmark: DJOF Publishing, 2008); and N. Doe and R. Sandberg (eds.), *Law and Religion: New Horizons* (Leuven: Peeters, 2010).

[20] Such as the Centre for Law and Religion at Cardiff, the Centre for the Study of Law and Religion at Bristol and the Applied Study of Law and Religion Group at Oxford Brookes.

[21] The main exceptions are A. Bradney, 'Politics and Sociology: New Research Agenda for the Study of Law and Religion' in R. O'Dair and A. Lewis (eds.), *Law and Religion* (Oxford: Oxford University Press, 2001), p. 65 and the essays published in N. Doe and R. Sandberg (eds.), *Law and Religion: New Horizons* (Leuven: Peeters, 2010).

[22] See, e.g. A. Bradney, *Religions, Rights and Laws* (Leicester: Leicester University Press, 1993), pp. 3, 8; P. W. Edge, *Legal Responses to Religious Difference* (The Hague: Kluwer Law, 2002), p. 3.

[23] Most notably C. Evans, *Freedom of Religion and the European Convention on Human Rights* (Oxford: Oxford University Press, 2001); M. Evans, *Religious Liberty and International Law in Europe* (Cambridge: Cambridge University Press, 1997); and P. M. Taylor, *Freedom of Religion – UN and European Human Rights Law and Practice* (Cambridge: Cambridge University Press, 2005).

[24] See also, e.g. C. Hamilton, *Family, Law and Religion* (London: Sweet Maxwell, 1995) vii; and R. Ahdar and I. Leigh, *Religious Freedom in the Liberal State* (Oxford: Oxford University Press, 2005).

[25] N. Doe, 'A Sociology of Law on Religion – Towards a New Discipline: Legal Responses to Religious Pluralism in Europe' (2004) 152 *Law and Justice* 68. This definition was adopted by M. Hill and R. Sandberg, 'Is Nothing Sacred? Clashing Symbols in a Secular World' [2007].

Beckford and Richardson have similarly noted that religion 'is an object of regulation by internal and external agencies'.[26] They distinguish between 'two sides' of the regulation of religion: first, how 'religion is subject to control by external agencies'; and secondly 'the capacity of religious ideas and organisations to regulate thought and action'. They stress that this second side not only includes the role of religion as an agency of socialisation, but also what they refer to as the '"internal" self regulation of religions', which may be understood as including the laws or other regulatory instruments of religious groups.

From these definitions it may be argued that the study of law and religion includes the study of two complementary and overlapping elements.[27] The first of these are the 'external' temporal laws affecting religious individuals and groups. This consists of laws made by the state, international bodies[28] and sub-State institutions.[29] The second of these are the 'internal' spiritual laws or regulations made by religious groups themselves which affect the members of those groups and how those groups interact with the secular legal regime. For convenience, these external laws affecting religion may be termed 'religion law', whilst the internal laws made by religious groups may be termed 'religious law'. Law and religion may thus be understood as including both the study of religion law and religious law.

However, a note of caution must be sounded before developing this argument further. This conceptualisation does not mean that the study of law and religion is *only* the study of religion law and religious law. Rather, it means that the study of law and religion is *at least* the study of religion law and religious law. Law and religion also includes the study of the relationship between law and religion. This may be underlined by reference to the work of the late American writer Harold Berman, whose writings on the relationship between law and religion have been hailed as 'a *sine qua non* to contemporary discourse on the subject'.[30] Berman's *The Interaction of Law and Religion*, based on his 1971 Lowell Lectures on Theology, includes chapters on the religious dimensions of law, the

---

Public Law 488: law and religion is 'both the study of state law on religions and of the internal laws or other regulatory instruments of religious organisations'.

[26] J. A. Beckford and J. T. Richardson, 'Religion and Regulation' in J. A. Beckford and N. J. Demerath (eds.), *The Sage Handbook of the Sociology of Religion* (London: Sage, 2007), p. 396.

[27] The following develops arguments first made in R. Sandberg, 'Church-State Relations in Europe: From Legal Models to an Interdisciplinary Approach' (2008) 1(3) *Journal of Religion in Europe* 329.

[28] Examples can be found not only in global and regional human rights guarantees, but also in the law of the European Union: on which see N. Doe, 'Towards a Common Law on Religion in the European Union' (2009) *Religion, State and Society* 147.

[29] Examples include laws affecting religion made by devolved bodies, on which see J. Oliva and D. Lambert, 'Regional Ecclesiastical Law: Religion and Devolution in Spain and Wales' in N. Doe and R. Sandberg (eds.), *Law and Religion: New Horizons* (Leuven: Peeters, 2010), p. 279.

[30] R. J. Ahdar, 'The Inevitability of Law and Religion: An Introduction' in R. J. Ahdar (ed.), *Law and Religion* (Aldershot, Ashgate, 2000), p. 2.

influence of Christianity on the development of Western law and law as a dimension of religion.[31] All of these topics may also be seen as part of law and religion. Similarly, the American academic John Witte Jr has elucidated how law and religion exist as 'two great interlocking systems of ideas and institutions, values and beliefs'[32] and has explained how law and religion can serve as a 'binocular' in order 'to view afresh many familiar ideas and institutions that have been studies principally through the "monocular of law" or the "monocular of religion" alone'.[33] The study of law and religion thus includes what Berman referred to as the study of 'law and religion in the broadest sense'.[34] In studying law and religion, it is important not to be limited by the same preoccupations of some of Berman's listeners who were apparently 'concerned that more emphasis was not placed on the conflicts between law and religion'.[35] The conceptualisation of law and religion as including both the study of religion law and religious law is not intended to be confining. Rather, as will be shown below, the conceptualisation is designed to be broadening, suggesting that law and religion is *at least* the study of religion law and religious law.

The inadequacy of other terms

Before further explaining the terms 'religion law' and 'religious law' and how the two necessarily overlap, it is important to explain why these terms are preferable to other labels, such as ecclesiastical law, canon law and law on religion, which are often used to describe all or part of the study of law and religion.

The most popular alternative label is 'ecclesiastical law'. This is particularly true on the Continent: in France, the sub-discipline is known as *droit ecclésiastique*; in Italy, *diritto ecclesiastico*; and in Spain, *derecho eclesiástico*.[36] However, as Doe has explained, the inconsistent use of this expression and the lack of any agreed definitional criteria have rendered its use 'extremely problematic'.[37] The term has a clear Christian connotation. Moreover, its usefulness is undermined by various different and contradictory meanings

---

[31] H. J. Berman, *The Interaction of Law and Religion* (London: Bloomsbury Press, 1974), p. 11.

[32] J. Witte Jr, *God's Joust, God's Justice: Law and Religion in the Western Tradition* (Michigan: William B., Eerdmans Publishing Company, 2006), p. 461.

[33] *Ibid.*, 5. See also J. Witte Jr, 'Introduction' in J. Witte Jr and F. S. Alexander (eds.), *Christianity and Law* (Cambridge, Cambridge University Press, 2008), p. 1.

[34] H. J. Berman, *The Interaction of Law and Religion* (London: Bloomsbury Press, 1974), p. 11.

[35] *Ibid.*

[36] There are some exceptions: in Germany the sub-discipline is called *Staatkirchenrecht*. See B. Basdevant-Gaudemet, 'Historie du Droit ecclésiastique en Europe' in J. Valle and A. Hollerbach (eds.), *The Teaching of Church-State Relations in European Universities* (Leuven: Peeters, 2005), pp. 1, 19.

[37] N. Doe, *The Legal Framework of the Church of England* (Oxford: Clarendon Press, 1996), pp. 12–15.

that it has been understood to have. 'Ecclesiastical law' has been used as a synonym for religious law. The term has been used to describe all of the law created for the Church by God and by the Church: for example, Georg May has contended that the term 'ecclesiastical law' describes religious law: it is 'entirety of the norms of the law laid down by God and by the Church', but does not include laws regulating Church affairs that are made by the State.[38] In contrast, in the continental literature,[39] the term 'ecclesiastical law' is used as a synonym for religion law. It has been used to refer exclusively to law created by the State for the Church. However, even in this sense 'ecclesiastical law' does not seem to include law created by the State that *affects* the Church rather than only laws created for the Church and it is uncertain whether the reference to 'the Church' includes all Christian denominations, other faiths and individual forms of religiosity.[40]

Furthermore, the term 'ecclesiastical law' has taken on a technical meaning in relation to the Church of England, being defined as 'the law of the Church of England to the exclusion of all other law applicable to other churches'.[41] This definition has been used by both the legislature[42] and the judiciary.[43] The term is used to label a learned society,[44] a leading journal[45] and a major text.[46] Hill notes that 'the term ecclesiastical law is used to denote the law of the Church of England, howsoever created'.[47] This includes both religion law and religious law. This notion that the Church of England is regulated by both internal and external laws is articulated by Huizing, who distinguishes between the 'internal public ecclesiastical law or the basic juridical relations within the Church' and the 'external public ecclesiastical law or the juridical relations between Church and State'.[48] The term 'ecclesiastical law' cannot therefore be seen as a synonym for law and religion in England since it covers only the law of the Church of England.

Nevertheless, the recognition that the ecclesiastical law of the Church of England includes internal and external laws may be usefully applied to

---

[38] G. May, 'Ecclesiastical law' in K. Rahner, *Encyclopaedia of Theology* (Edinburgh: T & T Clark, 1981), p. 395, quoted by N. Doe, *The Legal Framework of the Church of England* (Oxford: Clarendon Press, 1996), p. 14.

[39] See, for instance, the essays in J. Valle and A. Hollerbach (eds.), *The Teaching of Church-State Relations in European Universities* (Leuven: Peeters, 2005).

[40] This is why the phrase 'Church-State relations' is also problematic. Moreover, that term often gives the erroneous impression that religion is only affected by constitutional laws.

[41] N. Doe, *The Legal Framework of the Church of England* (Oxford: Clarendon Press, 1996), p. 14.

[42] See, e.g. the Welsh Church Act 1914. See Chapter 4.

[43] See, e.g. the *dicta* of Sedley LJ in the Court of Appeal decision in *Aston Cantlow* v. *Wallbank* [2001] EWCA Civ 713: 'Ecclesiastical law is a portmanteau term which embraces not only the canon law but [also] both secular legislation and common law relating to the church' (para. 8).

[44] The Ecclesiastical Law Society, which is discussed above.   [45] The *Ecclesiastical Law Journal*.

[46] M. Hill, *Ecclesiastical Law*, 3rd edn (Oxford: Oxford University Press, 2007).

[47] *Ibid.*, para. 1.02.

[48] P. Huizing, 'Church and State in Public Ecclesiastical Law' (1970) 86 *Concilium* 126, quoted by N. Doe, *The Legal Framework of the Church of England* (Oxford: Clarendon Press, 1996), p. 14.

other religious communities and individuals. If ecclesiastical law (in an English sense) is defined as the study of both the external and internal laws applicable to the Church of England, then this supports the argument that law and religion may be defined as the study of both external and internal laws applicable to all religious groups and individuals. This supports the definitions of religion law and religious law given above.

Other labels often used to describe all or part of law and religion are also problematic. The term 'canon law' is not an adequate substitute for 'religious law' because of its clear Christian association.[49] Moreover, even within Christianity, the use of the term is problematic.[50] For instance, while some commentators on the law of the Church of England interpret the term narrowly just to refer to one source of law (the canons of the Church of England),[51] others use the term widely as a synonym for ecclesiastical law.[52] The term 'law on religion' is also insufficient since it may exclude the study of the general relationship between law and religion or the study of laws of general applicability that happen to affect religious individuals or groups. For example, while the provisions in the Equality Act 2010 which prohibit discrimination on grounds of religion are clearly part of a 'law on religion', it is difficult to see how the provisions prohibiting discrimination on grounds of sexual orientation fall into this category, apart from possibly the specific exceptions to religious groups provided in the legislation.[53] However, the law prohibiting discrimination on grounds of sexual orientation clearly affects religious groups. So those legal provisions (as well as, for example, the Civil Partnership Act 2004) may be understood quite properly to be part of the study of religion law.[54]

The term 'law and religion' is also problematic. In the context of the legal regulation of sport, a number of academic writers have argued that the term 'sports law' is preferable to 'sport and the law' on the basis that while the term 'sport and the law' simply describes the interactions between sport and national law, the term 'sports law' refers to an identified legal subject:[55]

> 'Sports law' attempts to provide an underlying explanation of why sports as a group of related activities are, and should continue to be, treated differently by

[49] See further Chapter 9.
[50] See N. Doe, *The Legal Framework of the Church of England* (Oxford: Clarendon Press, 1996), pp. 12–13.
[51] M. Hill, *Ecclesiastical Law*, 3rd edn (Oxford: Oxford University Press, 2007), p. 2.
[52] T. Briden and B. Hanson, *Moore's Introduction to English Canon Law*, 3rd edn (London: Mowbrays, 1992), p. 4.
[53] See Chapter 6.
[54] These topics are regularly examined by law and religion writers. See, e.g. M. Hill, 'Church, State and Civil Partners: Establishment and Social *Mores* in Tension' in N. Doe and R. Sandberg (eds.), *Law and Religion: New Horizons* (Leuven: Peeters, 2010), p. 57; and R. Sandberg, 'The Right to Discriminate' (2011) 13 *Ecclesiastical Law Journal* (forthcoming).
[55] See M. James, *Sports Law* (London: Palgrave Macmillan, 2010), p. 19; and S. Gardiner *et al.*, *Sports Law*, 3rd edn (London: Cavendish, 2006), pp. 88–91.

the law; it is the development of an underlying theory that draws together cases using disparate legal principles into a single coherent subject.[56]

This distinction may also be applied to the regulation of religion. One of the key questions which this book seeks to answer is whether laws affecting religion can now be understood as forming a single coherent sub-discipline: in short, whether it is now possible to speak of something particular called 'religion law' as well as a general interaction called 'law and religion'.

It follows that law and religion – the general study of how law and religion interact – may be best understood as including both the study of two complementary and overlapping elements. The first is religion law, the 'external' temporal, spiritual laws made by the State (and international bodies and sub-State institutions) which affect religious individuals and groups. The second is religious law, the 'internal' laws or other regulatory instruments made by religious groups themselves which affect not only the members of those groups, but also how those groups interact with the State. The remainder of this chapter will develop these categories and show why the study of law and religion necessarily involves both the study of religion law and religious law.

Religion law

Religion law can be seen as an area of law akin to education law, sports law or media law.[57] For current purposes it may be defined by analogy with family law.[58] As Douglas notes, there is a 'problem of boundary-setting' in relation to family law since the branch of law does not correspond with a certain legal action, like the law of trusts and the law of tort. Instead, family law 'relates in some way to an entity – the family – which has meaning ... outside the legal domain'.[59] For Douglas, 'the essence of family law is that part of the law which is concerned with the recognition and regulation of certain family relationships and the implications of such recognition'.[60] The same is true of religion law: 'religion' certainly has meaning outside the legal

---

[56] M. James, *Sports Law* (London: Palgrave Macmillan, 2010), p. 19. See further Chapter 10.

[57] The only use of this term 'religion law' at the moment is the title for Neil Addison's webpage www.religionlaw.co.uk, the contents of which coincide with the concept of external law affecting religion identified above. An *Encyclopaedia of Religion Law* – edited by Rik Torfs – has been published as part of the International *Encyclopaedia of Laws* series. Its focus is also national and international law affecting religion. See, e.g. the monograph on the United Kingdom: M. Hill, R. Sandberg and N. Doe, *Religion Law: United Kingdom* (The Netherlands: Kluwer Law International, 2010).

[58] For a different approach to the definition of family law, which focuses upon the functions that the law seeks to fulfil, see M. Freeman, *Understanding Family Law* (London: Sweet & Maxwell, 2007), pp. 5–9.

[59] G. Douglas, *An Introduction to Family Law*, 2nd edn (Oxford: Clarendon Press, 2004), p. 3.

[60] She points out that 'non-recognition is equally important to the discussion': *ibid.*

domain and 'religion law' is concerned with the recognition and regulation of certain religious relationships.

Further, Douglas' understanding of family law may assist an elucidation of religion law in three respects. First, Douglas notes that the goal of family policy – a 'stable family life' – is recognised by both domestic and international law and that the right to family life is protected as a human right.[61] The same is true of religion and religion law: 'religious freedom' is now regarded as a human right in both domestic and international law.[62] Secondly, she points out that family law 'has grown piecemeal in response to perceived social change – often presented as a problem to be tackled'.[63] The same is true of religion law, and scholars in this field should be aware of this and – as Bradney has argued[64] – should ensure that this conceptualisation does not inhibit scholarship. Thirdly, Douglas notes that although many different fields of law (such as tax law and housing law) impact upon family members and family life, these 'peripheral laws' are not automatically regarded 'as aspects of something called family law', but equally should not be ignored since they interact with the body of family law. This may be useful in terms of constructing a category called religion law: religion law does not need to be an all-encompassing category; we may choose to see asylum and immigration law, for example, in the same manner as Douglas in the context of family law sees tax and housing laws.

The work of Douglas is thus valuable in beginning to determine how religion law can be understood as a legal sub-discipline. As is the case with many other legal sub-disciplines, defining religion law is problematic.[65] However, it is important since the definition we use (whether explicitly or implicitly) serves as a means of inclusion and exclusion.[66] For instance, one result of current understandings of what religion law includes is that much of the literature on ethnic minority rights and legal pluralism[67] is often excluded.[68] This has meant, for example, that the work of the late Sebastian

---

[61] *Ibid.*, 4.   [62] See further Chapters 2 and 5.

[63] G. Douglas, *An Introduction to Family Law*, 2nd edn (Oxford: Clarendon Press, 2004), p. 4.

[64] A. Bradney, 'Politics and Sociology: New Research Agenda for the Study of Law and Religion' in R. O'Dair and A. Lewis (eds.), *Law and Religion* (Oxford: Oxford University Press, 2001), pp. 65, 80–1.

[65] And it is easy to abandon the task deriding the quest for definition as being a positivist pipedream: see L. Farmer, 'The Obsession with Definition: The Nature of Crime and Critical Legal Theory' (1996) *Social and Legal Studies* 57; and R. Sandberg, 'A Whitehall Farce? Defining and Conceptualising the British Civil Service' [2006] *Public Law* 653, 663.

[66] This argument is developed further in relation to the definition of religion in Chapter 3.

[67] See, e.g. P. Shah, *Legal Pluralism in Conflict: Coping with Cultural Diversity in Law* (London: Routledge, 2005). For a rare example of a work in law and religion which uses a pluralist perspective, see D. Harte, 'Structures of Religious Pluralism in English Law' in N. Doe and R. Sandberg (eds.), *Law and Religion: New Horizons* (Leuven: Peeters, 2009), p. 159.

[68] For an example of a work that extends religion law, see Samantha Knight's practitioner text *Freedom of Religion, Minorities and the Law*. It introduces a number of legal areas hitherto neglected by religion law academics, such as health and safety regulations, animal rights, planning law, prison law and perhaps most notably immigration and asylum law, which is

Poulter[69] has tended to be regarded as being on the margins of law and religion since it focused on the concept of ethnicity rather than of religion in order to include discussion of non-religious customs and practice (as well as religious practice).[70] Attention to the question of definition may allow us to question the borders that have been drawn.

Determining the correct ambit of religion law is perhaps an impossible task. For example, it might be thought that breaches of the general law by ministers of religion would not be understood as part of religion law. If a cleric commits theft, then that is clearly part of the criminal law; the fact that the defendant is a minister of religion adds nothing. However, the decision in *Maga* v. *The Trustees of the Birmingham Archdiocese of the Roman Catholic Church*[71] undermines this conclusion. The Court of Appeal held the Church vicariously liable for the sexual abuse committed by a priest against a boy who was not involved in the activities of the Church. The judgment also suggested that churches are more likely to be vicariously liable in such cases than secular employers.[72] This differential treatment might suggest that cases like *Maga* can and should be seen as part of religion law. A careful balancing act needs to be performed. Whilst a restrictive conception of the sub-discipline may exclude important aspects of the interaction between law and religion, an all-encompassing conception may equally be problematic, bringing together laws which have little in common. There is a need to extrapolate the trends and themes which underline the sub-discipline and draw together 'disparate legal principles into a single coherent subject'.[73] This would seem to support the use of the label 'religion law' over the more general 'law and religion' and the drawing of analogies with family law, sports law, media law and so on.

Religious law

Religious law may be defined as the study of the 'internal' laws or other regulatory instruments created by religious collectives themselves. It includes

given its own chapter. S. Knights, *Freedom of Religion, Minorities and the Law* (Oxford: Oxford University Press, 2007).

[69] S. Poulter, *Asian Traditions and English Law: A Handbook* (Staffordshire: Runnymede Trust, 1990); and S. Poulter, *Ethnicity, Law and Human Rights: The English Experience* (Oxford: Clarendon Press, 1998).

[70] See A. Bradney, 'Politics and Sociology: New Research Agenda for the Study of Law and Religion' in R. O'Dair and A. Lewis (eds.), *Law and Religion* (Oxford: Oxford University Press, 2001), pp. 65, 69.

[71] [2010] EWCA Civ 256.

[72] As Smith LJ put it at para. 95: 'It will be necessary to examine with what ostensible authority the church clothes its priests or pastors and for what legitimate purposes. ... If those legitimate purposes clothe the priest or pastor with the ostensible authority to create situations which the priest or pastor can and does then subvert for the purposes of abuse, I see no reason why that church should not be vicariously liable for the abuse'.

[73] Cf. M. James, *Sports Law* (London: Palgrave Macmillan, 2010), p. 19. See further Chapter 10.

not only the rules found in sacred texts, but also the more practical rules developed by religious groups themselves.

Chapter 9 will examine how religious law can be defined by reference to its purposes, sources, subject-matter and the way in which it is studied. Although the label 'religious law' is by no means unproblematic,[74] the term is in frequent use and, as Chapter 9 will discuss, can be useful.

The important point is that 'religion law' and 'religious law' are two complementary and overlapping entities. Religious groups are regulated by both religion law and religious law and it is often difficult to draw a line between the two. This is well illustrated by reference to the Church of England.[75] The Church of England is regulated by general sources of religion law applicable to all religious groups[76] and specific pieces of religion law applicable only to the Church of England.[77] It is also regulated by its own religious law.[78] However, as will be discussed later in this book,[79] the fact that the Church of England is established by law means that some of its legal instruments cannot easily be classified as either religious law or religion law. This is especially true of Measures. These legal instruments are created by a religious body (the General Synod of the Church of England), but are then considered by the Ecclesiastical Committee of the UK Parliament. Once given Royal Assent they have the same effect as an Act of Parliament and are bound with the Statutes.[80] It is difficult to classify Measures – and much of the law affecting the Church of England – as being either religion law or religious law.[81] The study of the law of the Church of England thus necessarily requires the study of both religion law and religious law.

The fact that the study of the law of the Church of England requires the study of both religion law *and* religious law has important repercussions for the study of law and religion in the United Kingdom. If the study of the law affecting the Church of England is part of the study of law and religion, then it follows that the study of law and religion *necessarily* includes the study

---

[74] See the comments of A. Huxley, 'Introduction' in A. Huxley (ed.), *Religion, Law and Tradition: Comparative Studies in Religious Law* (London: Routledge, 2002), p. 6 (although he does use the term in the subtitle of his collection), discussed in Chapter 9 below.

[75] See further Chapters 2 and 4.

[76] Such as Acts of Parliament (e.g. Marriage Act 1949), secondary legislation (e.g. Employment Equality (Sexual Orientation) Regulations 2003), EU law (e.g. Directive 2000/78/EC) and case law (e.g *Aston Cantlow* v. *Wallbank* [2003] UKHL 37).

[77] These also include Acts of Parliament (e.g. Church of England Assembly (Powers) Act 1919) and case law (e.g. *R* v. *Chancellor of St Edmundsbury and Ipswich Diocese, ex parte White* [1948] 1 KB 195).

[78] For example, as Doe points out: 'The central doctrinal and liturgical documents of the Church of England, the Thirty Nine Articles of Religion, the Book of Common Prayer and other service books, contain rules and rubrics imposing obligations and conferring rights': N. Doe, *The Legal Framework of the Church of England* (Oxford: Clarendon Press, 1996), pp. 18–19.

[79] See Chapter 4.

[80] Church of England Assembly (Powers) Act 1919, s.1(5). See *R* v. *Archbishops of Canterbury and York Ex parte Williamson* (1994) *The Times* 9 March. See further Chapter 4.

[81] See further Chapter 9.

of both halves of law and religion and how they interact with each other. There is no watertight distinction between religion law and religious law. The distinction between them is made to highlight the fact that the two are interconnected. It is made to stress the importance of including the study of religious law alongside religion law. This is a concern because scholarship on religion law and religious law has tended to become isolated. Many works on religious law have been written as if those laws exist in isolation from wider society. And many works on religion law often exclude any analysis of the laws of religious organisations themselves. This seems strange: how can one hope to understand further the relationship between law and religion if it is not recognised that religious bodies formulate their own systems of law and that these systems interact with State law?

The conceptualisation of law and religion as *at least* the study of both religion law and religious law also counters a criticism of existing law and religion literature made by Bradney, who contends that 'to date research into religion and law has mainly concerned itself with identifying instances where law hampers the free exercise of religion or areas where it is argued legal rules can be created so as to allow free exercise'.[82] Although, as the complaints of some of Berman's listeners show,[83] this may be the preoccupation of some writers on religion law, but it is not, as Bradney recognises,[84] a preoccupation of writers on religious law. Recognition of the importance of the study of religious law to law and religion would redress this, providing a broader approach to the study of law and religion. The study of law and religion may be seen as *more than* the study of religion law and religious law, but the study of law and religion must be seen as *at least* the study of religion law and religious law.

Conclusions

This book seeks to tell the story of how law and religion interact in twenty-first-century Britain. The chapters that follow will provide a succinct exposition and critique of the new legal framework concerning religion. They attempt to map out some of the key areas of religion law, assessing the changes made by the new laws as well as exploring the extent to which English law recognises religious law.[85]

---

[82] A. Bradney, 'Politics and Sociology: New Research Agenda for the Study of Law and Religion' in R. O'Dair and A. Lewis (eds.), *Law and Religion* (Oxford: Oxford University Press, 2001), pp. 65, 67.

[83] H. J. Berman, *The Interaction of Law and Religion* (London: Bloomsbury Press, 1974), p. 11.

[84] A. Bradney, 'Politics and Sociology: New Research Agenda for the Study of Law and Religion' in R. O'Dair and A. Lewis (eds.), *Law and Religion* (Oxford: Oxford University Press, 2001), pp. 65, 67, fn. 10.

[85] The coverage is not exhaustive. Some of the other areas are discussed in M. Hill, R. Sandberg and N. Doe, *Religion Law: United Kingdom* (The Netherlands: Kluwer Law International, 2010).

Chapters 2 to 4 provide an introduction to how English law generally deals with religion. Chapter 2, 'Historical Development', seeks to place the legal changes that have occurred in the twenty-first century into their historical context. It provides a historical sketch of how the interaction between law and religion has developed in England. Chapter 3, 'Legal Definitions of Religion', examines the main ways in which English law now recognises religion. It examines the definitions of religion currently found in key areas of English law – charity and registration law, human rights law and discrimination law – discussing the definitions of religion currently used and the effect of these definitions. Chapter 4, 'The Legal Position of Religious Groups', explores how English law recognises and regulates religious groups. It questions how the legal status of the established Church of England continues to differ from other religious groups (both disestablished and non-established).

Chapters 5 and 6 deal with the two most significant changes that have occurred in religion law in the twenty-first century. Chapter 5, 'Religious Freedom as a Human Right', explores the effect that the Human Rights Act 1998 has had upon religious freedom. Analysing the case law, it contends that English courts are increasingly adopting a stricter line than their counterparts in Strasbourg. Chapter 6, 'Discrimination on Grounds of Religion', scrutinises the effect of new laws prohibiting discrimination on grounds of religion or belief. It questions whether the new laws have actually promoted the protection afforded to individuals.

Chapters 7 and 8 focus upon areas where law and religion have long interacted and examines how these older laws concerning religion interact with newer pieces of religion law and societal change. Chapter 7, 'Religious Offences', explores the changing ways in which English criminal law interacts with religion. It examines the recent abolition of the offence of blasphemy and the extent to which criminal offences continue to protect religion, including religiously aggravated offences. Chapter 8, 'Religion in Schools', looks at the law concerning religious education and worship in schools and the legal status of faith schools. It questions whether the current laws are sustainable in light of changing social norms, the increased legal protection of the rights of the child and the new legal framework concerning religion addressed in previous chapters.

Although there will be some reference to religious law throughout these chapters, Chapter 9 will explore the topic in depth. 'Religious Law' addresses themes that came to the fore in the reaction to the Archbishop of Canterbury's 2008 lecture.[86] The chapter questions the usefulness of religious law as a label and examines the extent to which English law recognises and enforces religious law, with special reference to the Arbitration Act 1996.

---

[86] R. Williams, 'Civil and Religious Law in England – A Religious Perspective' (2008) 10 *Ecclesiastical Law Journal* 262.

Chapter 10, 'The Clash of Arms', returns to the main questions laid out in this chapter. It draws upon the previous chapters to explore the main trends underlying the legal regulation of religion in England and Wales today, identifying the main problem areas and suggesting ways forward. It also returns to the question of whether law and religion can and should now be seen as a distinct legal sub-discipline.

This chapter has suggested that the significant number of new laws and noteworthy cases concerning religion, together with the development of a community of scholars, indicates that law and religion can now be conceived of as an academic sub-discipline akin to family law, education law or media law. The remainder of this book will seek to test this claim. The next chapter will begin this by attempting to understand the legal developments of recent years within a wider historical context. This will allow us to ask whether the legal changes of the twenty-first century should be seen as a substantial shift in the way in which law and religion interact.

2

Historical development

Introduction

In order to know where you are going, you need to know where you have come from. This chapter reflects this truism, providing an overview of the ways in which law and religion have interacted throughout English history. It is illustrative rather than exhaustive, seeking to place the significant legal changes that have occurred in the twenty-first century into their historical context. The question is whether these new laws are best seen as providing historical continuity to what went before or a substantial shift in the way in which law and religion interact.

The following provides a brief summary of a complex historical process, focusing upon the general direction of the law.[1] It contends that the relationship between law and religion in England[2] has developed through four broad overlapping but conceptually distinct phases: firstly, the temporal–spiritual partnership which followed the Norman Conquest; secondly, the era of discrimination and intolerance which resulted from the Reformation of the sixteenth century; thirdly, the epoch of toleration which followed from the Glorious Revolution of 1688–89; and fourthly, the current age of positive religious freedom which may be dated back to the Human Rights Act 1998.[3]

---

[1] For a fuller analysis, see generally *The Canon Law of the Church of England being the Report of the Archbishops' Commission on Canon Law* (London: SPCK, 1947); R. H. Helmholz, *The Canon Law and Ecclesiastical Jurisdiction from 597 to the 1640s*, Oxford History of the Laws of England (Oxford: Oxford University Press, 2004), vol. 1; R. H. Helmholz, *Roman Canon Law in Reformation England* (Cambridge: Cambridge University Press, 1990); J. Gunn, 'Religious Liberty (Modern Period)' in E. Fahlbusch *et al.* (ed.), *Encyclopaedia of Christianity* (Michigan: Wm. B. Eerdmans, 2005), vol. 4, 605–17; A. Pearce, 'England's Law of Religion – The History of a Discipline' in N. Doe and R. Sandberg (eds.), *Law and Religion: New Horizons* (Leuven: Peeters, 2010) 13; and J. Rivers, *The Law of Organized Religions* (Oxford: Oxford University Press, 2010), ch. 1.

[2] This chapter focuses solely upon the position of England. For an examination of Wales, see T. G. Watkin, *The Legal History of Wales* (Cardiff: University of Wales Press, 2007).

[3] The typology discussed here is largely derived from N. Doe, 'National Identity, the Constitutional Tradition and the Structures of Law on Religion in the United Kingdom' in *Religions in European Union Law* (Luxembourg: Proceedings of the European Consortium of Church and State Research, 1997), pp. 93, 109–10.

The temporal–spiritual partnership

There are a few dates in English history that are as ingrained upon the national consciousness as 1066. The Norman Conquest provided a water-shed moment which had long-term implications upon the nation's laws and the regulation of religion. At the Battle of Hastings, the Duke of Normandy, William the Conqueror, rode with the banner of the Pope. His victory not only led to a connection between England and Normandy, but also strength-ened the connection between Britain and Rome. 1066 was to change the face of English law, leading to the development of the common law as we now know it today.[4] Moreover, a distinction was to develop between the English royal common law and the Western papal canon law. Broadly speaking, the common law and the royal courts were to deal with 'temporal' matters applying the King's common law, while the 'Courts Christian' were to deal with 'spiritual matters' applying Roman Catholic canon law. However, it is important not to overstate this trend. Numerous intersections between secular and church life and government existed. The following seeks to sketch the true effect of the events of 1066, by looking at the development of the King's Courts and the Courts Christian and the relationship between them.

The effect of the Norman Conquest

It is important to begin, however, with a brief mention of the situation which existed in Anglo-Saxon England prior to the Norman Conquest. Christianity originally came to England when it had eventually become accepted by the Roman Empire.[5] However, by AD 410 the Roman troops had left Britain. As the Roman Empire collapsed, pagan religion once again asserted its supremacy. The following centuries witnessed the slow re-emergence of Christianity. In the late sixth century, Celtic and continental missionaries came to share their faith with the English. By the time of the Anglo-Saxons, a strong Christian influence had taken hold. After the Synod of Whitby in 663, England became fully a part of the worldwide Catholic Church, which was led from Rome. Although the canon law of the Church was formed in Rome,[6] spiritual matters were still dealt with domestically. Tithes taxed the people to pay for the Church, while the bishops in particular had a key role in governing the Kingdom. However, that governance tended

---

[4] This common law quickly became entrenched, so much so that in *Wallyng* v. *Meger* (1470) 47 SS38 Catesby Sjt said that the English common law had been in existence 'since the creation of the world'. See J. H. Baker, *An Introduction to English Legal History*, 4th edn (London: Butterworths, 2002), p. 1.

[5] T. G. Watkin, 'Church and State in a Changing World' in N. Doe *et al.* (eds.), *English Canon Law – Essays in Honour of Bishop Eric Kemp* (Cardiff: University of Wales Press, 1998), pp. 82, 84.

[6] See M. Hill, *Ecclesiastical Law*, 3rd edn (Oxford: Oxford University Press, 2007), paras. 1.07–.11.

to occur at a local level. There was no national legislature[7] or judiciary, but matters were adjudicated, administered and legislated at a local level in 'moots'.[8]

As Baker has put it, 'England was still governed more by unwritten and variable custom than by uniform and settled law'.[9] The moots reached their decisions without reasoned explanation, and neither followed nor laid down binding rules in a sense understandable in modern times. Government was largely a local matter. Each shire (roughly analogous to a county today) had its own moot to which all the free men were called to attend. Each shire was divided into smaller units, called hundreds,[10] which had their own moots. Both the shire and the hundred courts were sovereign within their geographical limits. There was no hierarchical relationship between the two; but troublesome disputes were commonly reserved for the shire moot. A King's Court, known as the Witenagemot or Witan,[11] did exist, but this functioned as a meeting of royal advisers rather than a court of law.[12] That said, the shire courts were accountable to the Witan and the King would preside over the shire court when he was in that region.

The Norman Conquest led to the strengthening of the King's Court and the centralisation of government. Whereas the Witan had been a collection of great men who advised the King, by the thirteenth century the members of William's King's Court – the *Curia Regis* – were no longer politicians, but judges.[13] The *Curia Regis* was intimately linked into the feudal system that William developed from his experiences in Normandy.[14] This meant that over time the *Curia Regis* became supreme.[15] As Baker points out, the shift is well shown by the treatise 'On the Laws and Customs of England', questionably attributed to Glanville (who was the Justiciar of England between 1180 and 1189). Unlike earlier works, the treatise made reference to the fixed customs of the King's Court and stated that the King had the ultimate authority.

---

7   The Anglo-Saxon codes did not 'codify existing customs, let alone make new law': J. H. Baker, *An Introduction to English Legal History*, 4th edn (London: Butterworths, 2002), pp. 2–3.

8   See *ibid.* ch. 1 and S. F. C. Milsom, *Historical Foundations of the Common Law*, 2nd edn (London: Butterworths, 1981), ch. 1.

9   *Ibid.*, p. 3.

10   A hundred was comparable to a village or group of small villages. It consisted usually of either one hundred households or one hundred acres of land.

11   Strictly speaking, the 'Witan' were the members and the 'Witenagemot' was the council.

12   It was the predecessor of Parliament and the Privy Council.

13   H. G. Hanbury and D. C. M. Yardley, *English Courts of Law*, 5th edn (Oxford: Oxford University Press, 1979). p. 21.

14   As Milsom notes, these changes did not occur immediately after the conquest. Indeed, a case can be made that the development of this system was interrupted by the Conquest: S. F. C. Milsom, *Historical Foundations of the Common Law*, 2nd edn (London: Butterworths, 1981), p. 19.

15   J. H. Baker, *An Introduction to English Legal History*, 4th edn (London: Butterworths, 2002), pp. 12–13.

The Courts Christian

The separation of the lay and spiritual jurisdictions was one of the clearest legal changes that occurred as a result of the Norman invasion.[16] The common view is that before 1066 the shire and the hundred moots heard both temporal and spiritual cases. The bishop presided, with the earl, over the shire moot. Spiritual cases were also heard by the hundred moots and by synods within the Church. The Ordinance of William I, issued some time before 1085, changed this. The Ordinance removed spiritual cases from the shire and hundred moots.[17] Those spiritual cases previously heard by the shire moots were now heard by the bishop; those previously heard by the hundred moot were now heard by the archdeacon.

By the twelfth century, a system of ecclesiastical courts had crystallised.[18] These 'Courts Christian' had an extensive jurisdiction, including clergy misconduct cases, matters concerning church fabric and consecrated land, the payment of tithes, offences against religion and morality (including blasphemy, heresy, drunkenness, contempt of clergy and defamation), the validity of marriage, the determination of the legitimacy of children and the validity and enforcement of will insofar as they related to personal property. As Milsom has noted:

> The Courts Christian in England were part of a European system subject to the Papal *Curia*, administering a sophisticated and in principle uniform law based on the Roman.... All lawful men were Christian and important areas of their lives were subject to the law of the Church and no other.[19]

Moreover, it can be claimed that the Courts Christian were the earliest courts in England that looked like courts of law. A single judge considered and compared the evidence of witnesses and applied the rules of law to the facts. The rules of law could even be looked up in books.[20] Unlike the royal common law, which was to be found in the forms of action (writs),[21] the Church had a substantive law in the modern sense.

The Courts Christian applied law that was both external and internal to the Church. External laws included the Western canon law, which from

---

[16] A. Carter, *A History of the English Courts*, 7th edn (London: Butterworth, 1944), p. 9.

[17] J. H. Baker, *An Introduction to English Legal History*, 4th edn (London: Butterworths, 2002), p. 127.

[18] The Courts Christian operated on the same levels as the other courts, apart from the fact that its highest authority was not the King, but the Pope in Rome. The equivalent to the hundred levels was the Archdeacon's court. The Consistory court was analogous to the shire; whilst the Provincial court acted on a level loosely parallel to that of the kingdom.

[19] S. F. C. Milsom, *Historical Foundations of the Common Law*, 2nd edn (London: Butterworths, 1981), p. 23.

[20] *Ibid.*, p. 25.

[21] See J. H. Baker, *An Introduction to English Legal History*, 4th edn (London: Butterworths, 2002), ch. 4.

around 1140 onwards began to be organised into collections,[22] and the
Ius Commune of Western Christendom;[23] whilst internal laws included the
native and provincial laws of the Church in England as created by assemblies
of bishops and clergy known as synods and convocations.[24] The relationship
between these two sources of law has been the subject of a long-running
exchange, which may be described as the 'Stubbs–Maitland debate' after
the two main protagonists.[25] In the nineteenth century, William Stubbs,
the Bishop of Oxford and historian, contended that although the papal law
of Rome was of great authority in the medieval period, it was not binding
upon the English Church.[26] He asserted that the Courts Christian applied
the native law even where it was in conflict with the papal law. By contrast,
Frederic Maitland, the agnostic legal historian, claimed that 'large portions'
of Western canon law were 'regarded as absolute binding statute law' and
that Stubbs' evidence related only to cases where royal law forced ecclesiastical practice to depart from canon law.[27] He argued that the evidence
indicated that the English church courts accepted and applied Western
canon law.

Modern scholarship has broadly supported the view of Maitland, but has
qualified it in certain respects. Research has indicated that both Stubbs and
Maitland thought in positivist terms which were not shared by medieval litigants and court personnel. The Stubbs–Maitland choice, either that Western
canon law was binding statute law or that the English Church enjoyed an
unfettered discretion, does not need to be made. As Helmholz has written,
in practice there was little conflict. The judges 'tacitly accepted a restriction
of ecclesiastical jurisdiction based in subject matter'.[28] Indeed, the relationship between the common law and Western canon law was much more
fluid than either Stubbs or Maitland suggested. Canonical jurisprudence
'shaped the English practice at many points',[29] not least in its allowance
of flexibility. The English Courts Christian 'tolerated a disparity between

---

[22] *The Canon Law of the Church of England, Being the Report of the Archbishop's Commission on
     Canon Law* (London: SPCK, 1947), pp. 5–6.
[23] 'The English Church recognized the same law as the rest of the Church': Z. N. Brooke, *The
     English Church and the Papacy*, 2nd edn (Cambridge: Cambridge University Press, 1931),
     p. 113.
[24] See *The Canon Law of the Church of England, Being the Report of the Archbishop's Commission
     on Canon Law* (London: SPCK, 1947), pp. 37–8.
[25] See R. H. Helmholz, *Roman Canon Law in Reformation England* (Cambridge: Cambridge
     University Press, 1990), pp. 4–20. and C. Donahue Jr, 'Roman Canon Law in the Medieval
     English Church: Stubbs vs. Maitland Re-Examined After 75 Years in the Light of Some Records
     from the Church Courts' (1974) 72 *Michigan Law Review* 647–708.
[26] W. Stubbs, 'Historical Appendix', *Report of the Commissioners into the Constitution and
     Working of the Ecclesiastical Courts* (London: 1883), vol. I.
[27] F. Maitland, *Roman Canon Law in the Church of England* (London: Methuen, 1898).
[28] R. H. Helmholz, *Roman Canon Law in Reformation England* (Cambridge: Cambridge
     University Press, 1990), p. 7.
[29] *Ibid.*, p. 11.

formal rule and local customary practice'.[30] The system was characterised by cooperation. As Donahue notes, litigants did not regard the choice of one forum as precluding recourse to the other.[31]

This is not to say that conflicts did not arise. As Donahue notes, the Courts Christian depended upon the King to support their jurisdiction and sanctions.[32] As the medieval period continued, there were a number of jurisdictional clashes such as the dispute between Henry II (1154 to 1189) and Becket, the Archbishop of Canterbury, over whether clergy who had broken the King's peace should be tried in the King's Court as well as the Courts Christian.[33] However, as a general rule, the jurisdictional boundaries remained stable and broadly settled.[34] The matter was policed by the writ of prohibition. These royal writs were issued against the exercise of jurisdiction in a particular case by a church court, bringing the matter to the common law courts. By the fourteenth century, applications for these writs became regulated by a process known as a consultation. This enabled the writ to be withdrawn if a party satisfied the royal judges that the matter was spiritual. The decision as to what matters were spiritual or temporal therefore lay with the common law courts.[35]

Although the medieval period was by no means heterogeneous, several general trends can be identified. The period saw the steady growth of courts, including the courts of the Church. Their jurisdictional boundaries were generally stable and the relationship between the two was largely characterised by cooperation. However, it would be artificial to speak of a distinction between the common law and religious law in this context.[36] The jurisdiction of the different courts overlapped. It is also not meaningful to speak of 'religion law' in the medieval period. Although the term could be used to describe the jurisdiction of the Courts Christian, this would have

---

[30] *Ibid.*, pp. 11–12.

[31] C. Donahue Jr, 'Roman Canon Law in the Medieval English Church: Stubbs vs. Maitland Re-Examined After 75 Years in the Light of Some Records from the Church Courts' (1974) 72 *Michigan Law Review* 647, 700.

[32] *Ibid.*

[33] The dispute concerned Clause 3 of the Constitutions of Clarendon 1164, which laid out the definition of the relationship between royal and ecclesiastical justice. See J. H. Baker, *An Introduction to English Legal History*, 4th edn (London: Butterworths, 2002), p. 128; and H. Berman, *Law and Revolution* (Cambridge: Harvard University Press, 1983), ch 7.

[34] In 1215 *Magna Carta* expressed the general autonomy of the Church, including the free election of bishops.

[35] The jurisdictional boundaries were further clarified by the writ *Circumspecte agatis* (1285) and the *Articuli cleri* (1315). These stated that the Courts Christian had an unquestioned jurisdiction over marriage, illegitimacy, succession to personal property and punishment of moral sin. The appointment of clergy to benefices was for the bishop, while tithes were the subject of a complicated division of authority. See J. H. Baker, *An Introduction to English Legal History*, 4th edn (London: Butterworths, 2002), pp. 128–30.

[36] See N. Doe, *Fundamental Authority in the Late Medieval English Law* (Cambridge: Cambridge University Press, 1990) for an analysis of how the common law used religious law concepts and divine law.

the effect of giving the term a very wide meaning. It would also be inaccurate. Many areas upon which the Courts Christian adjudicated were not especially religious because there was no real distinction between religious and temporal matters either in law or in society at large. England was virtually a mono-credal society. People were Christian in the same way that they were English. However, at all times, there was an implicit tension between these two identities. Although the Courts Christian looked to Rome, their jurisdiction depended upon the support of the King.

Discrimination and intolerance

The next turning-point was the English Reformation of the 1530s. As is well known, the English Church broke away from Rome because of the marital problems of Henry VIII (1509 to 1547). The King, desperate for a male heir, was frustrated by the Pope in his quest for an annulment. The result was the end of Catholic England as a matter of law. The English Church split from Rome and authority was shifted from the Pope to the King. However, the matter was not simply about Henry VIII's marital problems. The English reformation was part of a much larger Western Reformation, whereby the Catholic monopoly was challenged by the advent of Protestantism and the supra-national role of Rome gave way to the supremacy of individual states.[37] The catalyst may have been different in England, but the general trend was the same.

The English Reformation led to the ousting of papal jurisdiction, the liberation of the Church of England from 'foreign' jurisdiction and religious intolerance towards all other religious groups.[38] However, it was by no means a uniform process. While the reign of Henry VIII saw significant constitutional change and the dissolution of the monasteries, the rejection of Catholic doctrines and practices only really occurred during the brief reign of his son Edward VI (1547 to 1553). This was followed, however, by the restoration of papal authority during Mary's reign (1553 to 1558). The reign of Elizabeth I (1558 to 1603) undid this, reinstating and developing the Protestantism which existed under Henry and Edward. With the exception of the period of the Commonwealth (1648 to 1660) when there was a 'toleration' of dissenting Protestant groups, this general trend continued throughout the seventeenth century. The following seeks to sketch the effect of the Reformation upon the Church of England on the one hand and alternative religion on the other. The dividing line drawn here between the

---

[37] See H. Berman, *Law and Revolution II* (Cambridge: Harvard University Press, 2003), Pt I; and J. Witte, *Law and Protestantism* (Cambridge: Cambridge University Press, 2002).

[38] See E. Duffy, *The Stripping of the Altars* (New Haven: Yale University Press, 1992).

Church of England as the norm and other religious groups continues to be seen in the current law.[39]

The English Church

The Reformation statutes of the 1530s[40] terminated papal jurisdiction in England with the King replacing the Pope as head of the English Church.[41] The Ecclesiastical Appeals Act 1532 declared that England was an 'empire' which was governed by 'one Supreme head' covering matters both spiritual and temporal 'without the intermeddling of any exterior person or persons'.[42] This assertion of royal supremacy was seen as a restoration, simply declaring the truth according to the 'ancient laws of the realm'.[43] The kingdom of England was now seen as being synonymous with the Church of England. As Watkin has put it: 'To be a subject of the King of England enacted acceptance of the reformed faith as part and parcel of loyalty to the sovereign.'[44] This entanglement with the State can still be seen in the 'incidents of establishment' which continue to apply to the Church of England today.[45]

However, the effect of the Reformation statutes upon the law of the Church was gradual rather than systematic.[46] Although the Submission of the Clergy Act 1533 provided for a Commission to be set up to review the existing canon law, no code was enacted until the Canons Ecclesiastical 1603/04.[47] Instead, the 1533 Act provided that Papal canon law was to continue to apply, unless it was 'contrariant or repugnant to the law, statutes or custom' of the realm or to the King's prerogative. This meant that the canon law of the 1530s remained in force not because of papal authority, but

---

[39] See Chapter 4.

[40] Important legislation included the Act in Restraint of Appeals 1532, Appointment of Bishops Act 1533, Submission of the Clergy Act 1534, Act of Supremacy 1534, Act in Restraint of Annates 1534 and the Ecclesiastical Licences Act 1534. Other legislation followed, such as the Sacrament Act 1547 and Act of Supremacy 1558.

[41] See J. H. Baker, *An Introduction to English Legal History*, 4th edn (London: Butterworths, 2002), pp. 130–3.

[42] Preamble.

[43] *Caudrey's Case* (1591) 5 Co Rep 1 at 7a. See A. Pearce, 'England's Law of Religion – The History of a Discipline' in N. Doe and R. Sandberg (eds.), *Law and Religion: New Horizons* (Leuven: Peeters, 2010), p. 13.

[44] T. G. Watkin, 'Church and State in a Changing World' in N. Doe *et al.* (eds.), *English Canon Law – Essays in Honour of Bishop Eric Kemp* (Cardiff: University of Wales Press, 1998) p. 87.

[45] See Chapter 4.

[46] M. Hill, *Ecclesiastical Law*, 3rd edn (Oxford: Oxford Univeristy Press, 2007), para. 1.12. See *The Canon Law of the Church of England, Being the Report of the Archbishop's Commission on Canon Law* (London: SPCK, 1947), ch. IV; and G. Arthur, *Law, Liberty and Church* (Aldershot: Ashgate, 2006), ch. 5.

[47] For an overview of the attempts made to create a new code, see M. Hill, *Ecclesiastical Law*, 3rd edn (Oxford: Oxford Univeristy Press, 2007), para. 1.13.

by virtue of statute.[48] The Submission of the Clergy Act 1533 remains on the statute book to this day, meaning that unless affected by later legislative Act or custom, the pre-Reformation canon law remains a source of law for the Church of England.[49]

The situation was characterised by both change and continuity. The Convocations of Canterbury and York retained their ancient power to promulgate canons, but now Royal Assent was required for their execution.[50] Although appeals to Rome were now forbidden,[51] the jurisdiction[52] and hierarchy of the church courts remained largely intact. Modern scholarship has shown that the lawyers practising in the courts of the Church still appealed to Roman jurisprudence and practice.[53] Although the Canon Law Faculties at Oxford and Cambridge were dissolved in order to prevent the influence of 'foreign' laws, this only meant that expertise in church law was now gained through practice in the courts.[54] A learned society, known as Doctor's Commons, filled the gap for a time, but eventually the Church Courts became more and more influenced by the common law.[55]

The disadvantaging of alternative religion

The identification of Church and State was at its peak during this period. The law mirrored the view of the character Parson Thwackum in Henry Fielding's novel *Tom Jones*, originally published in 1749: 'When I mention religion, I mean the Christian religion; and not only the Christian religion, but the Protestant religion; and not only the Protestant religion, but the Church of England'.[56] This not only meant that the Church of England was protected as the norm, but also that any other religious practices were

---

[48] *Ibid.*, para. 1.14.

[49] In *Bishop of Exeter* v. *Marshall* (1868) LR3 HL 17, it was held that to become part of customary law a rule or usage of pre-Reformation canon law must be pleaded and proved to have been recognised, continued and acted upon in England since the Reformation. See also *R* v. *Archbishop of Canterbury* [1902] 2 KB 503.

[50] Submission of the Clergy Act 1533. The need for royal assent remains to this day in relation to both Canons and a newer source of law called Measures. See Chapter 4.

[51] The appeal to the papal *curia* was replaced by appeals to the Court of Delegates, which existed until the nineteenth century.

[52] Jurisdiction over such matters as contract, some forms of defamation and trusts had already been transferred to the common law courts from the church courts by the end of the fifteenth century.

[53] See R. H. Helmholz, *Roman Canon Law in Reformation England* (Cambridge: Cambridge University Press, 1990).

[54] *The Canon Law of the Church of England, Being the Report of the Archbishop's Commission on Canon Law* (London: SPCK, 1947), p. 53.

[55] See G. D. Squibb, *Doctors' Commons: A History of the College of Advocates and Doctors of Law* (Oxford: Clarendon Press, 1977); P. Barber, 'The Fall and Rise of Doctors' Commons' (1996) 4 (18) *Ecclesiastical Law Journal* 462.

[56] H. Fielding, *The History of Tom Jones, A Foundling* (London: Dent, 1998), p. 98, discussed by P. J. Griffiths, *Problem of Religious Diversity* (London: Blackwell, 2001) p. 6.

unlawful. Since 'subject of the Crown' was synonymous with 'member of the church', adherents to other religions, most notably Catholics and extreme Protestant dissenters, suffered severe legal disabilities. Oaths were to be taken acknowledging the royal supremacy[57] and those who failed to attend church were penalised.[58] Alternative worship was unlawful and those who were wilfully present at such worship were liable to fines and/or imprisonment.[59] Laws made religious conformity a precursor of taking public office.[60] This included the Crown. The Coronation Oath Act 1688 required that the monarch had to promise to 'maintain the laws of God, the true profession of the gospel and the Protestant reformed religion established by law'. As the historian Simon Schama has put it, within two generations 'Catholic England' went from being a truism to being treason.[61]

The Reformation dramatically altered the course of English history and resulted in a relationship between Church and State which remains identifiable today. The distinction between the established Church of England as the norm and all other religious groups remains with us.[62] Moreover, much of the legal framework remains unchanged. It could be said that the statutes of the 1530s are the base of the modern law of the Church of England. Moreover, they remain important pieces of religion law, laws made by the State for a religious group. However, as we have seen, the English Church also continued to be regulated by religious law, adopting many of the canon laws that had applied to the Church prior to the Reformation. It also created laws and adjudicated on them chiefly in the Convocations and in the church courts. However, in both contexts, the State was far from benign. The Canons created by the Church required Royal Assent, while the abolition of the teaching of canon law in the universities meant that the church courts were increasingly influenced by common law practice. In both cases we see the fusion of religion law and religious law, a fusion which continues to this day. The laws declaring other religious practices unlawful can also be seen as pieces of religion law. They represent the start of the acceptance that laws were needed to deal with religions other than the Established Church. However, by modern standards those laws were crude. They recognised the existence of alternative religion, but not its lawfulness. For the time being at least, dissent was not to be tolerated.

Religious toleration

It is difficult to pinpoint the precise date when this changed. Over the course of the seventeenth, eighteenth, nineteenth and twentieth centuries,

---

[57] Act of Supremacy 1534.   [58] Act of Uniformity 1551; Act of Uniformity 1558.
[59] Religion Act 1592; Act of Uniformity 1662; Conventicle Act 1664; Conventicle Act 1670.
[60] Test Act 1672; Corporation Act 1661.
[61] S. Schama, *A History of Britain* (London: BBC Books, 2000), vol. 1, p. 233.
[62] It is the basis for Chapter 4.

most of the legal disabilities against alternative religions were removed. The
process was slow, piecemeal, uneven and sometimes contradictory. However, the Glorious Revolution of 1688 to 1689, when the two Parliaments
invited the Protestants William III (1689 to 1702) and Mary II (1689 to
1694) to take the throne in place of the Roman Catholic James II (1685
to 1688),[63] may be regarded as the starting point of limited and piecemeal
toleration.

Upon accession, William and Mary issued a decree abolishing legal
requirements which made religious conformity a precursor of taking public office.[64] They also consented to two pieces of legislation, one of which
looked backwards embodying the previous approach of religious discrimination, while the other looked forwards pointing to the beginning of a
new era of toleration. The first was the Bill of Rights 1688/89 which barred
Roman Catholics and their spouses from the Crown. The Bill of Rights pro-
claimed that it was 'inconsistent with the safety and welfare of this Protestant
Kingdome to be governed by a Popish Prince'. The second was the Act of
Toleration 1689, which allowed Trinitarian Protestants to have their own
places of worship provided their doors were unlocked when they met and
that notice was given to the local Church of England bishop.

The concurrence of these two instruments is telling. Whilst, over time,
toleration made alternative worship lawful and removed religious tests, it
did not remove the many constitutional and legal provisions which operated
on the presumption that England remained a 'Protestant Kingdome'.[65] This
section sketches the development of toleration and the effect that this had
upon the legal standing of the Church of England.

The recognition of difference

There were some important precursors to the Toleration Act[66] and there
are numerous examples of discriminatory and intolerant provisions being
enacted after 1689.[67] However, as a general trend it can be said that the
Age of Enlightenment saw the lifting of the disabilities previously placed on
those who did not conform to the Church of England.[68]

---

[63] See A. Lyons, *Constitutional History of the United Kingdom* (London: Cavendish Publishing,
2003), ch. 16.
[64] See H. Berman, *Law and Revolution II* (Cambridge: Harvard University Press, 2003). pp.
229–30.
[65] Indeed, the Bill of Rights remains on the statute books: see Chapter 4.
[66] E.g. 'Declarations of Indulgence' had been issued exempting Catholics from some of the legal
penalties.
[67] See, e.g. the Blasphemy Act 1698, the Occasional Conformity Act 1711 and the Schism Act
1714.
[68] For a useful summary see the Appendix in J. A. Robilliard, *Religion and the Law* (Manchester:
Manchester University Press, 1984).

Over time toleration was extended to worship by Protestants who did not believe in the Trinity[69] and also to Catholic worship, but this was subject to stricter conditions than for the Protestant dissenters.[70] Oaths and tests that had barred Catholics and non-conformists from certain public offices, school keeping and landowning were removed.[71] This included laws which prevented access to Parliament. The Roman Catholic Relief Act 1829 admitted Roman Catholics to Parliament[72] and to most offices under the Crown, while the Religious Disabilities Act 1846 removed many of the restrictions that had previously applied in relation to education, charities and property.[73] By the late nineteenth century, alternative religion was not only lawful, but was often facilitated by the law. Most notably, the Places of Worship Registration Act 1855 provided an optional system of registration for places of worship which did not belong to the Church of England. Registration resulted in certain fiscal and legal advantages.[74]

The effect upon the established Church

These changes had some effect upon the regulation of the Church of England, but the ad hoc recognition of alternative religion did not result in a situation where the established Church was simply one denomination among many.[75] Many of the laws affecting the Church of England were left untouched, whilst others simply modified aspects of establishment. For example, the Manchester Bishopric Act 1847 restricted the bishops to twenty-six seats in the House of Lords, removing the Church's right to increase its number of representatives by creating new bishoprics.

There was also some evidence of a distancing between Church and State.[76] For instance, the Local Government Act 1892 created 'civil' Parish Councils which divided the existing ecclesiastical parishes. However, the established Church remained in a privileged position. For example, while their jurisdiction was reduced,[77] the ecclesiastical courts remained part of the law of England.[78] In addition to being important in their own right, they also continued to have a bearing upon both the substantive laws and procedures

---

[69] Unitarians Relief Act 1813.   [70] Roman Catholic Relief Act 1791.

[71] Roman Catholic Relief Act 1778; Roman Catholic Charities Act 1832; Test Abolition Act 1867; Promissory Oaths Act 1868; Promissory Oaths Act 1871. See now the Oaths Act 1978.

[72] The Jews Relief Act 1858 extended this to Jews.

[73] There were a number of exceptions. For example, religious tests at the universities of Oxford, Cambridge and Durham universities were not removed until the passage of the University Tests Act 1871.

[74] This remains the current law: see Chapter 3.   [75] See further Chapter 4.

[76] A. Pearce, 'England's Law of Religion – The History of a Discipline' in N. Doe and R. Sandberg (eds.), *Law and Religion: New Horizons* (Leuven: Peeters, 2010), p. 13.

[77] For instance, the Court of Probate and Matrimonial Causes Act 1857 transferred jurisdiction over wills and marriage to the courts of the State. See R. B. Outhwaite, *The Rise and Fall of the Ecclesiastical Courts, 1500–1860* (Cambridge: Cambridge University Press, 2006).

[78] See Chapter 4.

of the common law courts. For example, although the Matrimonial Causes Act 1857 transferred jurisdiction over matrimonial causes from the ecclesiastical courts to the High Court, section 22 expressly provided that the proceedings and actions of the courts of the State should be 'conformable to the Principles and Rules on which the Ecclesiastical Courts have heretofore acted and given Relief'.[79]

There were also some moves towards greater autonomy on the part of the Church.[80] The Church of England Assembly (Powers) Act 1919 provided for a Church Assembly,[81] which would enjoy legislative powers.[82] The 1919 Act provided that the Assembly could draft laws in the form of Measures. Also, following the revision of the 1603 Canons in the 1960s,[83] the Synodical Government Measure 1969 renamed the Church Assembly as the General Synod and vested in it the power to create Canons which had previously been exercised by the Convocations of Canterbury and York. However, both Measures and Canons required Royal Assent and, in the case of Measures, Parliamentary approval. The legal position of the Established Church thus continued to differ from other religious groups. The difference now was that whilst alternative religion had become lawful, the Church of England alone was established. While Parliamentary involvement in the development of laws for alternative religious bodies remained exceptional, such involvement remained the norm for the Church of England. And this involvement became more controversial as the identification between Church and State became more of a historical anachronism than a sociological fact. For some, the establishment of the Church of England was more of a burden than a benefit.[84]

Positive religious freedom

For some commentators, the achievement of religious toleration marked the end of the story. For instance, Maitland boldly asserted that 'Religious liberty and religious equality are complete'.[85] And in some respects he

---

[79] This is still considered as good law: see N. Lowe and G. Douglas, *Bromley's Family Law*, 10th edn (Oxford: Oxford University Press, 2007), p. 71 fn. 213.

[80] This was part of a wider trend. The early years of the twentieth century also saw the Welsh Church Act 1914 and the Church of Scotland Act 1921, both of which are discussed in Chapter 4, as well as the development of the first Code of Canon Law for the Catholic Church in 1917.

[81] The National Assembly (commonly called 'Church Assembly') was renamed the 'General Synod of the Church of England' by the Synodical Government Measure 1969.

[82] See N. Doe, *The Legal Framework of the Church of England* (Oxford: Clarendon Press, 1996), ch. 3.

[83] An entirely new set of Canons came into force with the exception of Canon 113 from 1603 concerning the seal of the confessional, which remains in force. See M. Hill, *Ecclesiastical Law*, 3rd edn (Oxford: Oxford University Press, 2007), para. 1.18.

[84] See Chapter 4.

[85] F. W. Maitland, *Constitutional History of England* (Cambridge: Cambridge University Press, 1908), p. 520.

was correct. Alternative religion was no longer unlawful; instead it was recognised. Religious tests and oaths were largely a thing of the past.[86] However, this religious toleration stopped considerably short of recognising religious freedom – let alone religious equality. The concept of toleration is well explained by Jordan:

> Toleration was attained by the legal guarantee of free belief and the free public exercise of that belief. Legal toleration is limited in its scope, somewhat ignoble in some of its sources, but constitutes, none the less, one of the most significant advances that the human race has ever achieved.

> In its legal application, the word toleration signifies simply a refraining from persecution. It . . . refers to a somewhat limited and conditioned freedom. . . . In its very nature, however, it disapproves if it does not disallow, the point of view that is to be tolerated. Toleration, therefore, falls considerably short of religious liberty. It presumes an authority which has been and which again may become coercive; an authority which for subjective reasons is not brought to bear on the dissenting group. It implies, shall we say, voluntary inaction on the part of the dominant group'.[87]

Religious freedom was not seen as a legal right. The difference between religious toleration and the legal right to religious freedom can be shown by an analogy with a disruptive passenger on a train playing loud music. If I do nothing about this disturbance, I may be said to tolerate it. However, my toleration stops considerably short of recognising that the disruptive passenger has a legal right to play loud music. I may think that his or her actions are wrong and possibly unlawful; my voluntary inaction does not mean that I respect or approve of what is going on and I retain the right to change my current passive stance. Tolerance is often a pragmatic gesture. As Northcott puts it, 'the growth of toleration in England was often a tedious and inglorious procedure . . . with no excessive theorizing about religious liberty, but much determination to have it'.[88]

English law has now moved beyond toleration; but it is difficult to pinpoint a date when this occurred. Numerous pieces of religion law were enacted in the twentieth century which sought to facilitate and protect religion. Two views may be taken in relation to these developments. It may be said that these developments represented a move beyond toleration and were indicative of a new phase of religious freedom. Alternatively, these developments may have represented the swansong of religious toleration;

---

[86] See J. A. Robilliard, *Religion and the Law* (Manchester: Manchester University Press, 1984), pp. ix–x; and C. Northcott, *Religious Liberty* (London: SCM Press, 1948), ch. 1. For the notorious litigation concerning the atheist Bradlaugh, see *Clarke* v. *Bradlaugh* (1881) 7 QBD 38; (1884) 12 QBD 271.

[87] W. K. Jordan, *The Development of Religious Toleration in England* (London: Allen and Unwin, 1932), vol. 1, p. 17.

[88] C. Northcott, *Religious Liberty* (London: SCM Press, 1948).

and the new phase of religious freedom may be said to have only occurred at the very end of the twentieth century and the start of the twenty-first as a result of the Human Rights Act 1998 and new laws prohibiting discrimination on grounds of religion or belief.[89] According to this view, while religious freedom may have long been implicitly protected by the common law, the legislation of the twenty-first century marks a substantial shift in explicitly promoting religious freedom as a positive right. This section will look at legal developments which occurred in the twentieth century, asking whether these changes constituted a move beyond toleration.

Domestic developments

A number of pieces of religion law were enacted in the twentieth century. Many took the form of exceptions from the law provided on grounds of religion. Some of these exceptions were provided for those who professed a specific religious faith.[90] For instance, laws provided exemptions for Sikhs from laws obligating them to wear safety hats on a building site[91] and to wear protective headgear when riding motorcycles.[92] However, in most cases exceptions were provided on grounds of religion generally. Most of these were provided for religious groups, such as the exceptions from certain taxes enjoyed by registered places of worship[93] and the exceptions afforded in discrimination law.[94] However, sometimes the exceptions were addressed to individuals in the form of conscience clauses[95] or specific defences to criminal offences.[96] It is difficult to say that such provisions constituted a new phase of religious freedom. The exceptions were

---

[89] Employment Equality (Religion or Belief) Regulations 2003; Equality Act 2006 Part 2. The law is now to be found in the Equality Act 2010. See Chapter 6.

[90] See also the special rules on slaughter which apply exclusively for Jews and Muslims (Welfare of Animals (Slaughter or Killing) Regulations 1995 Reg. 2).

[91] Employment Act 1989 s.11.

[92] Motorcycle Crash Helmets Religious Exemption Act 1976; see now Road Traffic Act 1988 s.16.

[93] See Chapter 3.   [94] See Chapter 6.

[95] The best-known example is conscientious objection to military service (Military Service Act 1916 s.2), but note also s. 4 of the Abortion Act 1967, which provides a right of conscientious objection. This clause does not apply to 'any duty to participate in treatment which is necessary to save the life or to prevent grave permanent injury to the physical or mental health of a pregnant woman'. It also does not excuse a refusal by a medical secretary to type a letter about a case involving an abortion: *Janaway* v. *Salford Health Authority* [1989] 1 AC 537. Section 38 of the Human Fertilisation and Embryology Act 1990 provides a conscience clause for persons who may otherwise be under a duty to participate in any activity governed by the Act involving scientific experiments on human foetal tissue. It should be noted, however, that these are *conscientious* opt-outs, not religious ones. It is perfectly possible for a convinced atheist to have a conscientious objection to abortion or assisted conception.

[96] See, e.g. Criminal Justice Act 1988 s.139: it is a defence to charge for having a blade in a public place if the blade is carried 'for religious reasons'. The Carrying of Knives etc. (Scotland) Act 1993 s. 1(5) makes parallel provision.

rare, often hard fought for, specific and limited. They were not under-pinned by any notion of religious freedom being a human right. They were more in the tradition of religious toleration, removing specific legal disabilities.

Other laws went further–recognising religious belief as part of an individual's identity. This was typically the case in the context of children.[97] Adoption law, for example, required adoption agencies to 'give due consideration; to the child's religious persuasion, racial origin and linguistic background'.[98] However, this is subject to the general principle of the Children Act 1989 that the welfare of the child is paramount. While section 1 of the Act required a court to have regard to a child's background, including the child's religious and cultural heritage, this was simply one factor to be weighed in the balance.[99] The parent's religious beliefs are subservient against the welfare of the child.[100] Such provisions come close to the practice of balancing religious rights against other rights, a practice which was to become the norm in the twenty-first century as a result of the Human Rights Act 1998.

The Race Relations Act 1976 also foreshadowed later developments. This focused upon racial rather than religious discrimination. It forbade direct or indirect discrimination on the grounds of colour, race, nationality or ethnic origins in specified fields of activities, namely, employment, education and the provision of goods, facilities, services and premises. While Sikhs[101] and Jews[102] were protected as races under that Act, all other religious groups were left unprotected.[103] However, members of minority religions could often circumvent this by reliance on membership of a racial group rather than their religious group.[104] This meant that individuals could assert their rights. An example of this can be found in the decision of the Employment Appeal Tribunal in *J. H. Walker Ltd* v. *Hussain and others*.[105] This concerned an instruction not to take floating holidays in the busy months of May to July, which included the Muslim festival of Eid on 11 June. It was held that this constituted indirect unlawful discrimination on the ground of race due

---

[97] See also the educational law provisions discussed in Chapter 8 which recognised the religious freedom of parents and teachers.

[98] This law is now to be found in the Adoption and Children Act 2002 s. 1(5).

[99] See N. Lowe and G. Douglas, *Bromley's Family Law* 10th edn (Oxford: Oxford University Press, 2007), p. 390.

[100] *Re J (Specific Issue Orders: Child's religious Upbringing and Circumcision)* [2000] 1 FLR 571 at para. 12. See also the decision in *Re P (A Minor) (Residence Order: Child's Welfare)* [1999] 2 FLR 573, discussed by G. Douglas, *An Introduction to Family Law*, 2nd edn (Oxford: Oxford University Press, 2004), pp. 89, 171.

[101] *Mandla* v. *Dowell Lee* [1983] 2 AC 548.   [102] *Seide* v. *Gillette Industries Ltd* [1980] IRLR 427.

[103] *J. H. Walker Ltd* v. *Hussain and others* [1996] ICR 291.

[104] S. Poulter, 'Muslim Headscarves in School: Contrasting Legal Approaches in England and France' (1997) 17 *Oxford Journal of Legal Studies* 43, 64.

[105] [1996] ICR 291.

to reasons that the proportion of Asians who could comply was smaller than the number of Europeans, that it was not objectively justified irrespective of race and that they suffered detriment. Such cases were rare, and were argued on grounds of race rather than religion, but they pointed to future developments. Generally, however, the twentieth-century developments in domestic law seem to represent the final stages of toleration rather than the beginnings of a new era of religious freedom.

International developments

Religion law was also shaped by international pressures. From the 1950s onwards, English law began to be influenced by international human rights treaties and the ideals they embodied. At the global level, the United Nations (UN) developed a family of human rights instruments setting out freedom of religion, including Article 18 of the Universal Declaration on Human Rights (UDHR), Article 18 of the International Covenant on Civil and Political Rights (ICCPR) and Article 1 of the 1981 Declaration on the Elimination of All Forms of Intolerance and of Discrimination Based on Religion or Belief.[106] At the regional level, the Council of Europe produced the European Convention for the Protection of Human Rights and Fundamental Freedoms, generally known as the European Convention on Human Rights (ECHR). This is based on the UN model, but is policed by the European Court of Human Rights, located in Strasbourg.

The ECHR had the status of a treaty obligation under international law. Article 9 of the treaty dealt with freedom of religion, following closely the language of UN instruments.

The British Government was obliged to comply with the ECHR and since 1966 citizens had the right to appeal to individual petition to the European Court in Strasbourg. However, the ECHR was not part of domestic law:[107] English courts could not directly enforce it. Although courts sought to ensure that their decisions conformed to the ECHR, Articles of the Convention could only be regarded as an aid to interpretation. Courts were under no legal obligation to follow the ECHR, or the jurisprudence of the European Court of Human Rights, to the letter.

This meant that the ECHR had little effect upon English religion law. This is shown by the decision in *Ahmad* v. *Inner London Education Authority*,[108] a rare twentieth-century case concerning religious rights. The case concerned a Muslim schoolteacher who sought to take time off every Friday for prayer. When this was refused, he left his employment, claiming constructive unfair dismissal. The Court of Appeal dismissed his claim, holding that

---

[106] For interpretation, see the Human Rights Committee's General Comment 22.
[107] *Waddington* v. *Miah (Otherwise Ullah)* [1974] 2 All ER 377.   [108] [1978] QB 36.

the termination of employment was consistent with domestic education and employment law. However, the judgments showed differing views as to usefulness of the ECHR. Scarman LJ's dissenting judgment stressed that domestic law should be construed broadly using the ECHR. He held that both society and the law had changed and the need was 'not for a policy of the blind eye but for one of understanding. The system must be made sufficiently flexible to accommodate their beliefs and their observances'.[109] In contrast, the majority were less enthusiastic about the ECHR. Lord Denning, in particular, questioned whether Article 9 would help the claimant in particular and whether reference to the style and form of the Convention would be helpful generally if followed to the letter:

> The convention is not part of our English law, but, as I have often said, we will always have regard to it. . . . We will do our best to see that our decisions are in conformity with it. But it is drawn in such vague terms that it can be used for all sorts of unreasonable claims and provoke all sorts of litigation. As so often happens with high-sounding principles, they have to be brought down to earth'.[110]

The European Court of Human Rights agreed with the majority. In *Ahmad* v. *United Kingdom,*[111] the claim was dismissed as being 'inadmissible'. In general, such Article 9 challenges were rare both domestically and at the Court in Strasbourg. Religious matters rarely disturbed the Court. This only began to change after the judgment in *Kokkinakis* v. *Greece*[112] in 1994, in which it was held that:

> Freedom of thought, conscience and religion is one of the foundations of a 'democratic society' within the meaning of the Convention. It is, in its religious dimension, one of the most vital elements that go to make up the identity of believers and their conception of life, but it is also a precious asset for atheists, agnostics, sceptics and the unconcerned. The pluralism indissociable from a democratic society, which has been dearly won over the centuries, depends on it.[113]

The final years of the twentieth century saw an increase in the number of Strasbourg cases concerning religion. Many of these claims were unsuccessful. The European Court of Human Rights held that most matters concerning the regulation of religion fell within the 'margin of appreciation' of contracting states. This allowed states to differ from each other in relation to their laws and policies to some extent to allow for their different cultures.[114] However, at the turn of the century, this seemed to change. The European Court of Human Rights began to stress the State's role facilitating

---

[109] At 48.   [110] At 41.   [111] (1981) 4 EHRR 126.   [112] (1994) 17 EHRR 397.
[113] At para. 31.   [114] For examples of this in relation to blasphemy, see Chapter 7.

religious freedom. As the Grand Chamber in *Refah Partisi* v. *Turkey*[115] made it clear:

> The Court has frequently emphasised the State's role as the neutral and impartial organiser of the exercise of various religions, faiths and beliefs, and stated that this role is conducive to public order, religious harmony and tolerance in a democratic society. It also considers that the State's duty of neutrality and impartiality is incompatible with any power on the State's part to assess the legitimacy of religious beliefs and that it requires the State to ensure mutual tolerance between opposing groups.[116]

Strasbourg began to stress the need for states to be proactive in their dealing of religion. States were required to promote pluralism and religious equality and to foster a 'free market in religion',[117] whereby all citizens could exercise freely their religious freedom. The Court itself became more active. Cases concerning religion, argued under Article 9 and other Convention rights, are now commonplace. But this shift towards the active promotion of religious freedom only truly occurred in the twenty-first century.

This change in attitude can also be seen in relation to other supranational bodies, most notably the European Union.[118] Whereas the original traditional economic focus of the European Union (EU) meant that it paid little attention to religious matters, recent years have seen an increase in EU law on and affecting religion. Domestic religion law is shaped by EU law concerning religious discrimination,[119] data protection and the processing of personal data,[120] and the ritual slaughter provisions for Muslims and Jews.[121] Moreover, the Lisbon Reform Treaty recognises the importance of 'open, transparent and regular dialogue' with religious groups and recognises the rights, freedoms and principles set out in the Charter of Fundamental Rights 2000 as having 'the same legal value as the Treaties'. Article 10 of the Charter contains a freedom of religion clause which is clearly derived from Article 9(1) of the ECHR. Again, there has been a significant shift in emphasis over the last ten years.

The collective effect of these developments has meant that English religion law is now shaped more by international norms than it has been at any time since the medieval period. Moreover, these international norms require the State to facilitate religious freedom. It could therefore be said that in

---

[115] (2003) 37 EHRR 1.   [116] Para. 91.

[117] J. A. Beckford and J. T. Richardson, 'Religion and Regulation' in J. A. Beckford and N. J. Demerath (eds.), *The Sage Handbook of the Sociology of Religion* (London: Sage, 2007), pp. 396, 411.

[118] See N. Doe, 'Towards a "Common Law" on Religion in the European Union' (2009) *Religion, State and Society* 147; and J. Rivers, 'In Pursuit of Pluralism – The Ecclesiastical Policy of the European Union' (2004) 7 *Ecclesiastical Law Journal* 267.

[119] See Chapter 3.   [120] Directive 95/46/EC.   [121] Directive 93/119/EEC.

some respects English law has gone full circle since once again international pressures require a temporal-spiritual partnership.

A positive right to religious freedom?

Developments in the latter years of the twentieth century, especially the Race Relations Act 1976 and the creation of the ECHR, were simply signs of what was to come in the twenty-first century. They did not in themselves bring about a general positive right to religious freedom;[122] rather, the twentieth-century developments were piecemeal and, as such, represented the final stages of toleration. The law did not begin from the starting-point that people had a right to freedom of religion. The general position at common law was that, in the absence of a legal prohibition, people were permitted to do as they wished.[123] Religious freedom was protected negatively rather than positively.[124] The regulation of religion was characterised by a lightness of touch. The stance adopted by the legislature and judiciary was generally that of passive accommodation as opposed to prescriptive regulation.[125]

Although we can see the clear foreshadowing of future developments, the advent of religious freedom as a positive right did not really occur until the twenty-first century. Although numerous developments started to occur in the mid-twentieth century, the level of control and their complexity has increased substantially in the twenty-first century. The Human Rights Act 1998, in force from October 2000, has proved to be a watershed. The Act provided domestic courts with the jurisdiction directly to enforce ECHR rights, including freedom of religion under Article 9. Courts are now required to interpret UK legislation so far as is possible in a manner compatible with the rights outlined in the ECHR,[126] and in so doing they must take into account[127] – though not necessarily follow[128] – the decisions of

---

[122] M. Hill and R. Sandberg, 'Is Nothing Sacred? Clashing Symbols in a Secular World' [2007] *Public Law* 488, 489.

[123] *AG* v. *Guardian Newspapers Ltd (No. 2)* [1990] 1 AC 109 at 178: 'the starting point of our domestic law is that every citizen has a right to do what he likes, unless restrained by the common law . . . or by statute'. See also *Malone* v. *Metropolitan Police Commissioner* [1979] Ch. 344 at 355: England 'is not a country where everything is forbidden except what is expressly permitted; it is a country where everything is permitted except what is expressly forbidden'.

[124] See generally M. Hill, 'The Permissible Scope of Legal Limitations on the Freedom of Religion or Belief in the United Kingdom' (2005) 19(2) *Emory International Law Review* 1129, 1131–2.

[125] M. Hill and R. Sandberg, 'Is Nothing Sacred? Clashing Symbols in a Secular World' [2007] *Public Law* 488–506, 489; and S. Poulter, *Asian Traditions and English Law* (Staffordshire: Runnymede Trust, 1990), p. 1.

[126] Section 3(1). In the event of there being an irreconcilable inconsistency, the domestic legislation prevails subject to a 'fast-track' system of executive action to bring English law into line with the Convention. See s. 4 (declaration of incompatibility) and s. 10 (remedial action).

[127] Section 2(1).

[128] Lord Slynn in *R (Alconbury Developments Ltd)* v. *Secretary of State for the Environment, Transport and the Regions* [2001] UKHL 23 at para. 26 has suggested that courts should only

the European Court at Strasbourg. Moreover, it is now unlawful for public authorities to act in a way which is incompatible with a Convention right.[129]

The Human Rights Act 1998 has led to a number of high-profile cases concerning religious rights.[130] Moreover, subsequent laws outlawing religious discrimination have escalated this trend,[131] leading to a situation where litigation concerning religious rights has become the norm. The religion law of the twenty-first century represents a change from passive religious tolerance to the active promotion of religious liberty as a basic right. The content and effect of these laws will be explored in the chapters that follow.

Conclusions

This chapter has sought to provide the broad historical context for the chapters that follow, which will examine the current legal framework concerning religion. Many of the religion law provisions examined in this book are new. However, they do not exist in a historical or legal vacuum. The following chapters will examine the ways in which older and newer pieces of religion law interact and how the legal position of the Church of England continues to differ from other religious groups.

This chapter has shown how the regulation of religion in England has changed over time as a result of both revolution and evolution. The four phases described provide a generalised and selective picture, abridging complex and overlapping developments, contradictions and ambiguities. However, despite the limitations of this clarification, the four phases can help us to understand the current law. Many of the laws protecting the Church of England still derive from the Reformation settlement, while many laws protecting other religious groups and individuals often derive from the toleration legislation and later developments. However, in certain important respects, the religion law of the twenty-first century seems to mark a significant shift in the way in which law and religion interact.

In order to understand the future direction of religion law, it is important to know its historical journey. One way of understanding that journey is to focus upon how the definition of religion has changed. Prior to toleration the issue of defining religion did not arise. The Church of England was the only conceivable religion.[132] However, since toleration and the granting of many legal exceptions on grounds of religion, the question of definition has become important. As Edge points out, 'diffuse faiths can cause problems in determining who is an adherent, and who is not' and can 'cause problems in

---

feel under an obligation to follow Strasbourg case law where there is a 'clear and constant jurisprudence'.
[129] See s.6.   [130] See Chapter 5.   [131] See Chapter 6.
[132] J. A. Beckford, 'The Politics of Defining Religion in Secular Society' in J. G. Platvoet and A. L. Molendijk (eds.), *The Pragmatics of Defining Religion: Contexts, Concepts & Contests* (Leiden: Brill, 1999), p. 23.

determining what is religious devotion and what is not'.[133] The next chapter explores the question of how English law defines religion today. This requires reference to both older legislation concerning registration and charity law and to the newer laws concerning human rights and discrimination. The next chapter will explore how these newer and older laws interact and whether the definitions of religion in different areas of law argue against the existence of religion law as a distinct legal sub-discipline.

---

[133] P. W. Edge, 'The Legal Challenges of Paganisms and Other Diffuse Faiths' (1996) 1 *Journal of Civil Liberties* 216, 219.

3

Legal definitions of religion

Introduction

In the twenty-first century, English law interacts with religion in increasingly complicated ways. For instance, English charity law protects trusts, gifts and institutions as charitable (and thus entitled to legal and fiscal advantages) if they are for the advancement of religion,[1] whilst individuals have a human right to freedom of thought, conscience and religion,[2] and enjoy the right not to be discriminated against on grounds of religion or belief.[3] The focus of such legal provisions upon protecting 'religion' means that the question of the definition of religion is often a pivotal concern. It is important to determine to whom the legal benefit is addressed in order to work out who enjoys it. Definitions serve both as a means of inclusion and exclusion. Legal systems seek to define religion to determine which individuals and groups should be bestowed with legal advantages by virtue of the fact that they are 'religious' and which should not. These acts of inclusion and exclusion have legal, political, economic and social effects. This applies even where there is no explicit definition. Indeed, as Edge points out, the absence of a definition may harm minority religions and new religious movements as decision-makers are likely to 'work by analogy from what they regard as being "clearly religious"'.[4]

This chapter examines the definitions of religion currently found in key areas of English law – charity and registration law, human rights law and discrimination law – discussing the definitions currently used and their effects.[5]

Registration and charity law

Unlike the law of many European countries,[6] English law does not include detailed registration schemes for religious groups. However, although

---

[1] Charities Act 2006 s.2; Charities and Trustee Investment (Scotland) Act 2005 s.7.
[2] Article 9 ECHR. See Chapter 5.
[3] EU Directive 2000/78/EC; Employment Equality (Religion or Belief) Regulations 2003 SI 2003/1660; Part 2 of the Equality Act 2006; Equality Act 2010. See Chapter 6.
[4] P. W. Edge, *Legal Responses to Religious Difference* (The Hague: Kluwer Law, 2002), pp. 7, 9.
[5] The following develops arguments first made in R. Sandberg, 'Defining Religion: Towards An Interdisciplinary Approach' (2008) 17 *Revista General de Derecho Canonico y Derecho Ecclesiastico del Estado* 1.
[6] See L. Friedner (ed.), *Churches and Other Religious Organisations as Legal Persons* (Leuven: Peeters, 2007).

registration is not compulsory under English law, a multitude of over-lapping laws have been enacted to recognise religious groups and to enable them to benefit from legal and fiscal advantages, most notably in the form of exceptions from otherwise generally applicable obligations. A religious group may register as a place of public religious worship[7] and for the solem-nisation of marriage.[8] Moreover, such groups may seek to register as a charity for the advancement of religion.

Charity law provides the most well-known illustration of a trend con-cerning the question of the definition of religion in these areas of English law. Although originally charity law protected only gifts for the repair of churches but not for the advancement of religion itself,[9] it was soon accepted that trusts, gifts and institutions for the advancement of religion were char-itable and thus entitled to legal and fiscal advantages.[10] However, not all religious claims are recognised. It may be said that there are at least five different requirements which may be employed by the judiciary to exclude claims in relation to registration and charity laws. These may be understood as 'filtering devices', means by which a claim is excluded at the outset. A filtering device declares that the right or claim is outside or denied legal protection. This means that there is then no need to look at the merits of the claim since the claim has fallen at the first hurdle.[11]

The five filters

The first filter may be styled the 'Morality Filter': religious trusts are not recognised if they are immoral or encourage immorality. In *Thornton* v. *Howe*,[12] a trust for printing, publishing and propagating the sacred writings of Joanna Southcott (which were alleged to declare, maintain or reveal that the Holy Spirit impregnated her and a second Messiah was to be born) was held to be a valid charitable trust for the advancement of religion. However, it was held that the trust would have been declared void if it failed the

---

[7] Places of Worship Registration Act 1855. See also section 11 of Schedule 5 to the Local Government Finance Act 1988. Note also the 'Ecclesiastical Exemption': an ecclesiastical building used for the time being for ecclesiastical purposes is exempted from the need for listed building consent: Planning (Listed Buildings and Conservation Areas) Act 1990 s.60(1); Ecclesiastical Exemption (Listed Buildings and Conservation Areas) Order 1994; on which see M. Hill, *Ecclesiastical Law*, 3rd edn (Oxford: Oxford University Press, 2007), paras. 7.05–8.

[8] Marriage Act 1949 s.4.

[9] Preamble to the Statute of Charitable Uses 1601. Newark has pointed out that the omission is probably because religion did not sit well with the other purposes listed, which were concerned with financial and material matters: F. H. Newark, 'Public Benefit and Religious Trusts' (1942) 62 *Law Quarterly Review* 234, 234–5.

[10] *Pember* v. *Inhabitants of Kington* (1639) 1 Eq Cas Abr 95; Tot 34; *Special Commissioners of Income Tax* v. *Pemsel* [1891] AC 531. See, now, Charities Act 2006 s.2(2).

[11] If the court or tribunal do go on to examine the merits of the claim their discussion of this is mere *obiter*. It is not binding.

[12] (1862) 31 Beavan 14.

'morality test': if 'the tenets of a particular sect inculcate doctrines averse to the very foundations of all religion, and that are subversive of all religions', then a gift otherwise held charitable for the advancement of religion would be declared void as being contrary to public policy.[13]

The second filter is the 'Advancement Filter': religious trusts must advance religion in order to be recognised. In *United Grand Lodge of Ancient Free and Accepted Masons of England* v. *Holborn Borough Council*,[14] the High Court held that the United Grand Lodge was not entitled to a claim for rating relief as an organisation 'concerned with the advancement of religion'[15] because the objects of freemasonry did not 'add up to the advancement of religion':

> To advance religion means to promote it, to spread its message ever wider among mankind; to take some positive steps to sustain and increase religious belief; and these things are done in a variety of ways which may be comprehensively described as pastoral and missionary. There is nothing comparable to that in masonry.[16]

The third is the 'Exclusivity Filter': this excludes claims on the basis that they are not *solely* for the purpose of advancing religion[17] and therefore cannot be said to be exclusively charitable.[18] The question of where the line is to be drawn has proved contentious. In *Farley* v. *Westminster Bank*,[19] a trust for 'parish work' was not charitable since the term could encompass work not of a religious purpose. Yet in *Re Simson*,[20] a will leaving a gift to a vicar of a named church 'to be used for his work [as a vicar] in the parish' was a valid charitable gift since the words narrowed rather than extended the gift by excluding work done outside the parish and work done not in fulfilment of his functions as a vicar.[21]

The fourth requirement, which may be termed the 'Public Benefit Filter', has two different meanings depending upon the legal context. In the context of registration law, *Church of Jesus Christ of Latter-day Saints* v. *Henning*[22] establishes that the words 'place of public religious worship' cannot apply to a place from which the public is excluded.[23] In the context of charity law

---

[13] This was approved in *Re Watson* [1973] 1 WLR 1472 at 1483–4.   [14] [1957] 1 WLR 1080.

[15] Under the Rating and Valuation (Miscellaneous Provisions) Act 1955 s.8(2).

[16] Donovan J, 1090. See also the judgments of both the High Court and the Court of Appeal (but not the House of Lords) in *Keren Kayemeth le Jisroel Ltd* v. *Inland Revenue Commissioners* [1931] 2 KB 465.

[17] Moreover, as a general principle, trusts, gifts and institutions for political means are not charitable: *N.A.V.S.* v. *I.R.C.* [1948] AC 31, and *Re Shaw* [1957] 1 All ER 745 (compare: *RSPCA* v. *Attorney-General* [2002] 1 WLR 448, some limited political activity is permitted).

[18] See Charities Act 2006 s.1(1)(a).   [19] [1939] AC 430.   [20] [1946] Ch 299.

[21] See also the Charity Commission determination concerning Good News for Israel: www.charity-commission.gov.uk/library/start/gnfidecision.pdf.

[22] [1964] AC 420 (concerning the Rating and Valuation (Miscellaneous Provisions) Act 1955).

[23] [2008] UKHL 56 (concerning the Local Government Finance Act 1988). See R. Sandberg, 'Underrating Human Rights: *Gallagher* v. *Church of Jesus Christ of the Latter-day Saints*' (2009) 11 *Ecclesiastical Law Journal* 75.

it is commonly understood[24] that only 'religious service tending directly or indirectly towards the instruction or the edification of the public' is charitable.[25]

The fifth requirement, and the one which we are currently interested in, may be styled the 'Definition Filter'. Prior to toleration, a very restrictive definition of religion was used. Advancement of religion was seen as being synonymous with the promotion of the mission of the Church of England as the established church.[26] All other religious trusts failed as being 'against public policy as furthering the schisms of nonconformity, the errors of Rome or the infidelity of Judaism or heathenism'.[27] However, since the long march of toleration,[28] the concept of 'advancement of religion' widened considerably to include other faiths and denominations. 'Religion' is no longer interpreted narrowly as being synonymous with Christianity in general or the Church of England in particular. This has led the courts increasingly to rely upon the other filters in preference to the definition of religion.[29] Although this was sometimes criticised,[30] this reluctance was understandable given the considerable confusion as to where the boundary lay. It is significant that the most influential case in the first half of the twentieth century concerning the limits of what constituted a religion was concerned with company law and the crime of blasphemy: *obiter* comments by Lord Packer in *Bowman* v. *Secular Society Ltd* [31] were interpreted by many commentators to mean that the definition of religion for charity law purposes required belief in a god.

Towards a definition of religion

However, in the latter years of the twentieth century, domestic courts elucidated a (partial) definition of religion, based upon stated criteria, and used this definition to determine the case. This is often understood to have

---

[24] There is some debate as to whether there was a presumption of public benefit in the case of charities for the advancement of religion and whether this presumption has been removed by the Charities Act 2006. See J. Hackney, 'Charities and Public Benefit' (2008) 124 *Law Quarterly Review* 347; and P. Luxton, 'Public Benefit in the Advancement of Religion after the Charities Act 2006: Another Charity Muddle?' in N. Doe and R. Sandberg (eds.), *Law and Religion: New Horizons* (Leuven: Peeters, 2009), p. 117.

[25] *Cocks* v. *Manners* (1871) LR 12 Eq 574 at 585. This was approved in *Gilmour* v. *Coates* [1949] AC 426. Compare *Neville Estates* v. *Madden* [1962] Ch 832.

[26] *Bowman* v. *Secular Society Ltd* [1917] AC 406, 448, Lord Packer.

[27] F. H. Newark, 'Public Benefit and Religious Trusts' (1942) 62 *Law Quarterly Review* 234, 235.

[28] See Chapter 2.

[29] Indeed, many of the tests are (at least partially) reformulations of the definition test. For example, it is possible to say that the application of the 'morality test' is itself an application of the definition of religion as a filtering device since the courts are effectively saying that the gift will not be protected since the purpose of the gift is contrary to the court's view of what a 'religion' should be.

[30] See F. H. Newark, 'Public Benefit and Religious Trusts' (1942) 62 *Law Quarterly Review* 234.

[31] [1917] AC 406.

occurred in two cases, concerning registration and charitable status respectively. In the first, *R. v. Registrar General, ex parte Segerdal*, the Divisional Court[32] and the Court of Appeal[33] reviewed the decision by the Registrar General not to register a chapel of the Church of Scientology as a place of meeting for religious worship under section 3 of the Places of Worship Registration Act 1855. At first instance, Ashworth J upheld the decision. He noted that since it was conceded that the chapel is 'a place for meeting', the 'all-important words are "for religious worship"'.[34] Ashworth J noted that the reference to religious worship meant that there was a 'requirement that there must be some religion with which the worship is associated'.[35] Further, he found it difficult to reach the conclusion that Scientology was a religion on the basis that he was given an impression 'of an organisation serving as a meeting point or clearing house for persons of all religious beliefs, through which people may better appreciate their spiritual character'. However, he held that this was not definitive: 'even if Scientology were not a religion itself, the chapel could still be a place of meeting for religious worship, if persons met there to worship according to their own religious belief'.

The key question (or filter) was not therefore whether or not scientology was a religion, but whether or not there was worship. Ashworth J noted that although 'forms of worship vary enormously and that worship may take place without there being any set form of liturgy', there was 'nothing whatever to indicate' that the Scientology Church Service was 'a service of religious worship'.[36] Therefore, the chapel was not a place of meeting for religious worship. Although the Divisional Court paid attention to the question of defining religion, the case was actually determined on the definition of worship, rather than on the definition of religion.

The Court of Appeal upheld the decision of the Divisional Court.[37] However, although the decision was unanimous, the basis upon which their Lordships reached their conclusions differed. Buckley LJ and Winn LJ followed Ashworth J's approach by placing more emphasis upon the definition of worship. Winn LJ sought not to dwell on the definition of religion question, noting that the 'answer to that specific question must depend so directly upon the meaning that one gives, for the particular purpose and in the particular context, to the chameleon word "religion" or "religious"'.[38] He held that regardless of whether or not it is right to call this philosophy a religion, the appeal should be dismissed since 'the applicants have failed to show that the Divisional Court were in any sense wrong in declining to recognise that their building is a place of meeting to which persons come together as a congregation for the purpose of religious worship'.[39] Similarly, for Buckley LJ, the determinative factor was that there was no 'worship'. He noted that worship 'must have at least some of the

---

[32] [1970] 1 QB 430.   [33] [1970] 2 QB 679.   [34] At 443.   [35] At 444.
[36] At 445.   [37] [1970] 2 QB 679.   [38] At 708.   [39] At 709.

following characteristics: submission to the object worshipped, veneration of that object, praise, thanksgiving, prayer or intercession'.[40] He found that the evidence put forward, including the Church of Scientology's book of ceremonies, contained 'no element of worship at all'.[41]

By contrast, Lord Denning MR held that the correct approach would be to 'take the combined phrase, "place of meeting for religious worship" as used in the statute of 1855'.[42] For Denning, this connoted 'a place of which the principal use is as a place where people come together as a congregation or assembly to do reverence to God'; 'Religious worship means reverence or veneration of God or of a Supreme Being'. He noted that the Chapel of the Church of Scientology was not a 'place of religious worship' because the creed of the Church of Scientology was 'more a *philosophy* of the existence of man or of life, rather than a *religion*':[43] there was an absence of 'reverence or veneration' and 'considerable stress on the spirit of man'. However, despite these comments, the decision of the Court of Appeal, like that of the Divisional Court, centred on the definition of worship, not the definition of religion. Even Lord Denning's judgment was focused on defining 'religious worship', not religion per se.

However, while the judgments in *R. v. Registrar General, ex parte Segerdal* did not actually define religion, they were relied upon to put forward a definition of religion in the second leading case, *Re South Place Ethical Society*.[44] Although the case was heard only by the Chancery Division and concerned charity law, it is now understood to be authoritative and to constitute the common law definition of the term. Dillon J held that the South Place Ethical Society, a society for the 'study and dissemination of ethical principles and the cultivation of a rational religious sentiment',[45] was not charitable for the advancement of religion, but was otherwise charitable either for the advancement of education or under the fourth head of charity. For Dillon J, although it was 'natural that the court should desire not to discriminate between beliefs deeply and sincerely held', this did not warrant 'extending the meaning of the word "religion" so as to embrace all other beliefs and philosophies';[46] echoing Lord Denning in *Segerdal*, Dillon J curtly observed:

> Religion, as I see it, is concerned with man's relations with God, and ethics are concerned with man's relations with man. The two are not the same, and are not made the same by sincere inquiry into the question: what is God?[47]

---

[40]   He qualified this: 'I do not say that you would need to find every element in every act which could properly be described as worship, but when you find an act which contains none of those elements it cannot, in my judgment, answer to the description of an act of worship': at 709.

[41]   At 709.   [42]   At 707.

[43]   At 707 (original emphasis).   [44]   *Re South Place Ethical Society* [1980] 1 WLR 1565.

[45]   At 1569.   [46]   At 1571.

[47]   He continued: 'If reason leads people not to accept Christianity or any known religion, but they do believe in the excellence of qualities such as truth, beauty and love, or believe in the

Moreover, Dillon J noted that there was a 'further point': namely that for him, 'two of the essential attributes of religion are faith and worship; faith in a god and worship of that god'.[48] Quoting with approval Buckley LJ's definition of worship in *Segerdal*, Dillon J concluded that in the South Place Ethical Society, there was no 'worship in the sense which worship is an attribute of religion': 'indeed, it is not possible to worship in that way a mere ethical or philosophical ideal'.[49]

The current position

Dillon J's definition of 'religion' as requiring 'faith in a god and worship of that god' remains the common law definition. While the judiciary in *Segerdal* had stressed different parts of the phrase 'place of religious worship' to conclude that Scientology was to be excluded, Dillon J had not only used the definition of religion alone as the means to determine the case, but had also incorporated the differing requirements elucidated in *Segerdal* and had applied them to charity law. This is questionable. No explanation was given as to why worship ought to be a definitional aspect of the term 'advancement of religion'.

However, this fused minimalist definition of religion has been relied upon by the Charity Commissioners as a filtering device.[50] In 1999, the Commissioners held that the Church of Scientology would not be registered as a charity. It was not an organisation established for the charitable purpose of the advancement of religion because although 'it is accepted that Scientology believes in a supreme being', the 'core practices of Scientology, being auditing and training, do not constitute worship as they do not display the essential characteristic of reverence or veneration for a supreme being'.[51] The Charity Commission has also used this definition as a means of inclusion rather than exclusion.[52]

There have been a number of further legal developments affecting the definition of religion in charity law. In 2002 the Charity Commission recognised the 'promotion of religious harmony' as a new charitable purpose which is not restricted to 'religions' hitherto recognised under charity law,

platonic concept of the ideal, their beliefs may be to them the equivalent of a religion, but viewed objectively they are not religion': at 1571.

48 At 1572.   49 At 1573.

50 This, of course, only shed some light upon the effect of this definition. It is possible that it has even stopped cases (or applications to the Charity Commission) being brought which otherwise would have been brought.

51 www.charity-commission.gov.uk/library/start/cosfulldoc.pdf. See also *Re Gnostic Society* [2009] Charity Commission Determination (16 December 2009, confirmed 17 January 2010), available at: www.charity-commission.gov.uk/library/about_us/gnosticdec.pdf.

52 See their determination of an application by the Sacred Heads Spiritual Church in 2003: www.charity-commission.gov.uk/library/start/sacreddecision.pdf, para. 5.1.

but also includes 'beliefs' as recognised by the ECHR.[53] The Charities Act 2006 also provides a partial definition of religion:

'religion' includes –

(i) a religion which involves belief in more than one god, and
(ii) a religion which does not involve belief in a god.[54]

This supplements the common law definition. It removes theoretical uncertainty surrounding whether or not the *Segerdal-South Place Ethical Society* formula excluded those faiths which believe in more than one god, such as Hinduism, and those which do not (in principle at least), such as Buddhism. Despite being clearly outside the letter of the definition for many years, Buddhist charities and places of worship were nevertheless registered.[55] The *laissez-faire* attitude of the judiciary on this point, in sharp contrast to the treatment of Scientology,[56] shows how the legal definition of religion can be used for the very political act of exclusion.

The different positions of Buddhism and Scientology illustrate how the current legal approach may be criticised as being inherently unprincipled. There are a number of other flaws with the current legal definition. The emphasis upon 'faith and worship' reveals a rather narrow and conservative view of what a religion is, which seems to be outmoded.[57]

Human rights law

A second area where the definition of religion may be significant is in the interpretation of international human rights guarantees protecting religion.[58] As a general trend, although the question of definition has not been central in most legal disputes concerning religious freedom, when it *is* raised the definition question may become definitive. A textbook case of this approach is the American case of *Kuch,*[59] where the claimant contended that she had a constitutional right to take drugs because it was part of her religion, the Neo-American Church, of which she was an ordained minister. Presenting no evidence of her subjective beliefs, Kuch chose to rely on her office in the Church and evidence as to the requirements and attitudes of the Church. The sole 'duty' of the faithful was 'to partake of the

---

[53] www.charity-commission.gov.uk/library/harmony.pdf. See now Charities Act 2006 s. 2(2)(h).
[54] Section 2(3)(a).
[55] See Lord Denning in *Segerdal* [1970] 2 QB 679 at 707 and Dillon J in *Re South Place Ethical Society* [1980] 1 WLR 1565 at 1573.
[56] Of course, this criticism must be tempered by the fact that the courts have not addressed the actual question of whether Buddhism is included; but the very fact that they have not had to address this question is itself telling.
[57] Indeed, it could be argued that this is a breach of Article 9, which talks of the right to manifest religion or belief in 'worship, teaching, practice *or* observance'.
[58] See Chapter 2 for a discussion of the relevant global and regional instruments.
[59] *United States* v. *Kuch* 288 F Supp 439 (1968).

sacraments' consisting of marijuana and LSD which were described as the 'Host of the Church, not drugs'. The Church lacked a formal theology, but its catechism and handbook stated that members 'have the *right* to practice our religion, even if we are a bunch of filthy, drunken bums'.[60] The District Court determined that the Church was not a 'genuine' religion within the meaning of the First Amendment. Kuch had 'totally failed' in her effort to establish that the group was a religion since their desire to use and take drugs regardless of religious experience was the purpose. The court reached the 'inescapable conclusion' that the membership was 'mocking established institutions, playing with words and [was] totally irrelevant in any sense of the term'.

The actual decision in *Kuch* was unsurprising. However, that decision could have easily been reached on grounds other than the definition of religion. The District Court had held that even if the religion were 'genuine' then, nevertheless, Kuch's contentions were 'without merit' since the State's interference with her religious freedom would have been justified 'on grounds of public safety, health and order'. Yet, the decision was reached instead on the basis that the religion itself was not a 'genuine' religion. This reasoning seems unnecessary. The case could have been decided on other grounds. It is significant that recent cases on the use of drugs for a religious purpose indicate that English jurisprudence in this area has taken a different approach to the US district court in *Kuch*: rather than excluding claims on the grounds that the claimants' actions were not part of a legally protected 'religion', the Court of Appeal has rather simply held that any infringement of the right to religious freedom would be justified.[61] This seems to be a preferable approach.

The reluctance to define

The English cases on religious drug use are typical of the general approach to the definition of religion under human rights law. The definition of religion is rarely[62] used as a filtering device. There are four main reasons for this. Firstly, it will often not be in dispute that the religion being practised is a religion and that the claimant is an adherent of that

---

[60] The church had a nationwide membership of 20,000 and was headed by 'Chief Boo Hoo'. Each member carried a 'martyrdom record' to reflect their arrests; the church symbol is a three-eyed toad; the church key is the bottle opener; the official songs are 'Puff, the Magic Dragon' and 'Row, Row, Row Your Boat'; and the church motto is 'Victory over Horseshit'.

[61] *R. v. Taylor* [2001] EWCA Crim 2263; *R. v. Andrews* [2004] EWCA Crim 947. See P. W. Edge, 'Religious Drug Use in England, South Africa and the United States of America' (2006) 1(2) *Religion & Human Rights* 165–77.

[62] For an exception to this, see the deliberations of the Human Rights Committee of the United Nations, discussed by P. M. Taylor, *Freedom of Religion* (Cambridge: Cambridge University Press, 2005), p. 209.

religion.[63] Secondly, courts may be especially reluctant to assess whether a particular religious claim fits within a definition, since this may require courts to enter into questions with which they would prefer not to engage. In the House of Lords decision in *Williamson*, Lord Nicholls stressed that:

> It is not for the court to embark on an inquiry into the asserted belief and judge its 'validity' by some objective standard such as the source material upon which the claimant founds his belief or the orthodox teaching of the religion in question or the extent to which the claimant's belief conforms to or differs from the views of others professing the same religion. Freedom of religion protects the subjective belief of an individual.[64]

This links into the third reason: there are other means by which courts can exclude religious freedom cases as being outside the scope of the provision. Claims can be excluded by restrictively interpreting other parts of the right, creating other filtering devices or by reference to the prescribed limitations placed on the right. In *Williamson*, Lord Walker suggested an alternative filter was 'certainly required', but that this filter ought not to be the definition of religion.[65] Although, as we will see,[66] there seems to be a difference in relation to what other means are used; nevertheless the general trend is that other means are invariably used in preference to the definition of religion. Fourthly, it is commonly the case that the way in which the various religious freedom guarantees are worded indicates that a wide interpretation is to be taken.[67] The wording extends protection to cover more than just religion. Article 9 of the ECHR reads:

1. Everyone has the right to freedom of thought, conscience and religion; this right includes freedom to change his religion or belief, and freedom, either alone or in community with others and in public or private, to manifest his religion or belief, in worship, teaching, practice and observance.
2. Freedom to manifest one's religion or beliefs shall be subject only to such limitations as are prescribed by law and are necessary in a democratic society in the interests of public safety, for the protection of public order, health or morals, or the protection of the rights and freedoms of others.

The approach taken to the definition of religion in human rights law at both an international and domestic level is 'very broad' in that it has been left 'largely to individual nations and individual claimants to define the

---

[63] This was applied in *R. v. Secretary of State for Education and Employment and others, ex parte Williamson* [2005] UKHL 15 at para. 56, Lord Walker of Gestingthorpe.

[64] *Ibid.* at para. 22. See also the speech of Lady Hale at para. 75.

[65] At paras. 57, 58.   [66] See Chapter 5.

[67] See also the judgment of Lord Nicholls in *R. v. Secretary of State for Education and Employment and others, ex parte Williamson* [2005] UKHL 15 at para. 24.

boundaries'.[68] Strasbourg institutions have considered claims concerning scientology,[69] druidism,[70] pacifism,[71] communism,[72] atheism,[73] pro-life,[74] Divine Light Zentrum[75] and the Moon Sect,[76] and have invariably done so without questioning whether such claims fit the definition of religion or belief.[77] The general practice of the Convention institutions may be illustrated by their treatment of *X* v. *Austria*,[78] in which it was held that the conviction of a neo-Nazi did not breach Article 9. The question of whether Nazism was outside the scope of Article 9(1) was not addressed; the Commission simply relied on Article 9(2) to hold that the limitation was justified. Alternatively, the question of definition may be posed but left unanswered[79] or claimants may be required to prove the *existence* of the religion in question.[80] The general approach is characterised by liberalism.

The scope of religious freedom provisions

Although some further guidance and clarification has been given at the UN level,[81] there remains some confusion as to the true scope of human rights provisions on religion. The issue is clouded by the wording of such instruments. Like the text of Article 9, they all protect the absolute 'right to freedom of thought, conscience and religion' and the qualified right to manifest 'religion or belief' in 'worship, teaching, practice or observance'. Controversy surrounds the relationship between the four terms 'thought', 'conscience', 'religion' and 'belief'. The question is the extent to which the right to manifest 'belief' extends to the right to manifest one's thought and conscience. Three different perspectives on the relationship may be identified.

The first may be styled the 'Literal View', whose protagonists contend that the religious freedom Articles should be read literally – they protect freedom of thought, conscience and religion, but only the manifestation of

---

[68] J. Witte Jr, *God's Joust, God's Justice: Law and Religion in the Western Tradition* (Cambridge: William B Eerdman's Publishing Company, 2006), p. 99.

[69] *X and Church of Scientology* v. *Sweden* (1978) 16 DR 68.

[70] *Chappell* v. *United Kingdom* (1987) 53 DR 241.

[71] *Arrowsmtih* v. *United Kingdom* (1978) 19 D&R 5.

[72] *Hazar, Hazar and Acik* v. *Turkey* (1991) 72 D&R 200.

[73] *Angeleni* v. *Sweden* (1986) 51 D&R 41.

[74] *Plattform 'Ärtze für das Leben'* v. *Austria* (1985) 44 D&R 65.

[75] *Omkarananda and the Divine Light Zentrum* v. *Switzerland* (1981) 25 DR 105.

[76] *X* v. *Austria* (1981) 26 D&R 89.

[77] R. Ahdar and I. Leigh, *Religious Freedom in the Liberal State* (Oxford: Oxford University Press, 2005), p. 124; P. M. Taylor, *Freedom of Religion: UN and European Human Rights Law and Practice* (Cambridge: Cambridge University Press, 2005), p. 207.

[78] (1963) 13 CD 42.   [79] See *Chappell* v. *UK* (1987) 53 DR 241.

[80] *X* v. *UK* (1977) 11 DR 55.

[81] Namely the detailed elucidation provided by the Human Rights Committee in General Comment 22 and Article 6 of the 1981 Declaration on the Elimination of All Forms of Intolerance and of Discrimination Based on Religion or Belief.

religion or belief. Manifestations of thoughts and conscience are protected by virtue of the freedom of expression clause as opposed to the freedom of religion clause. Although the term 'belief' includes non-religious beliefs, it does not include manifestation of thought and conscience. In contrast, the second perspective, the 'Comprehensive View', contends that the religious freedom Articles should be read exhaustively – they protect the freedom to hold *and* the right to manifest thought, conscience and religion. The right to manifest 'belief' is seen as including manifestations of 'thought' and 'conscience'.

The third approach is a compromise between these two extremes. The 'Hybrid View' argues that the religious freedom Articles should be read as overlapping with those concerning freedom of expression. The right to manifest 'belief' is seen as including some manifestations of 'thought' and 'conscience', while the remainder are protected by the freedom of expression clauses. The absence of a clear distinction is justified by the idea that the Articles within an international treaty ought to be read together. It seems that the hybrid view is to be preferred. The literal view cannot be wholly persuasive since it seems to impose a requirement that, in order to be protected, beliefs must be similar to religious belief. That is not a part of UN or ECHR jurisprudence even if it might have been the intention of some of the drafters.[82] Similarly, the comprehensive view cannot be supported completely since it would transform the right to manifest religion or belief into to a general right to manifest conscience. The hybrid view thus seems the most logical.[83] The hybrid view is also supported by statements as to the definition of belief.

The definition of belief

The general position is that in order to be protected a belief must constitute a world-view rather than be merely an opinion. As the Office for Democratic Institutions and Human Rights has noted, the term belief 'typically pertains to deeply held conscientious beliefs that are fundamental about the human condition and the world. Thus, atheism and agnosticism, for example, are generally held to be entitled to the same protection as religious beliefs'.[84] These principles have been explained further in relation to the ECHR. In *Campbell and Cosans* v. *United Kingdom*,[85] it was noted that the term 'convictions' used in Article 2 of the first protocol to the ECHR[86] is not synonymous with the words 'opinions' and 'ideas', but was 'akin' to the

---

[82] P. M. Taylor, *Freedom of Religion: UN and European Human Rights Law and Practice* (Cambridge: Cambridge University Press, 2005), pp. 205–7.

[83] Lord Walker came close to accepting this view in *Williamson* [2005] UKHL 15 at para. 62.

[84] *Guidelines for Review to Legislation Pertaining to Religion or Belief* (2004) Section A, Paragraph 3. Available from www.osce.org/item/13600.html.

[85] *Campbell and Cosans* v. *United Kingdom* (1982) 4 EHRR 293.   [86] Discussed in Chapter 8.

term 'beliefs', which 'denotes views that attain a certain level of cogency, seriousness, cohesion and importance'.[87] The European Court of Human Rights added that the term 'philosophical convictions' also denotes that 'such convictions as are worthy of respect in a "democratic society" and are not incompatible with human dignity'. There is little doubt that these statements apply in relation to the definition of 'belief' in Article 9.[88] Strasbourg has held that to be protected by Article 9, there must be 'a coherent view on fundamental problems'.[89] In *Pretty* v. *the United Kingdom*,[90] the claimant's belief in and support for the notion of assisted suicide for herself did not 'constitute beliefs in the sense protected by Article 9(1) of the Convention' on the basis that 'not all opinions or convictions' are protected as beliefs under Article 9.[91]

This has been followed by the domestic judiciary. As Lord Nicholls noted in *Williamson*, in order to be protected as a manifestation of belief under Article 9:

> a belief must satisfy some modest, objective minimum requirements. . . . The belief must be consistent with basic standards of human dignity or integrity. . . . The belief must relate to matters more than merely trivial. It must possess an adequate degree of seriousness and importance. [It] must be a belief on a fundamental problem. . . . The belief must also be coherent in the sense of being intelligible and capable of being understood.[92]

Lord Nicholls held that these requirements applied to 'a non-religious belief, as much as a religious belief'; moreover, a non-religious belief 'must relate to an aspect of human life or behaviour of comparable importance to that normally found with religious beliefs'.[93] It is questionable, however, whether this 'comparable importance' test is narrower than the approach of Strasbourg in that it does not seem to protect the 'unconcerned'.[94]

However, Lord Nicholls stressed that 'too much should not be demanded in this regard':

> [Religion or belief] is not always susceptible to lucid exposition or, still less, rational justification. . . . Individuals cannot always be expected to express themselves with cogency or precision. Nor are an individual's beliefs fixed and static. The beliefs of every individual are prone to change over his lifetime. Overall, these threshold requirements should not be set at a level which would deprive minority beliefs of the protection they are intended to have under the Convention.[95]

---

[87] Para. 36.
[88] For a contrary view, see N. Addison, *Religious Discrimination and Hatred Law* (Oxford: Routledge, 2007), p. 9.
[89] *X* v. *Germany* (1981) 24 D&R 137.   [90] (2002) 35 EHRR 1.
[91] At para. 82.   [92] [2005] UKHL 15 at para. 23.
[93] At para. 24.   [94] Cf. *Kokkinakis* v. *Greece* (1994) 17 EHRR 397.
[95] [2005] UKHL 15 at para. 23.

Consequently the definition of belief has rarely been used as a filtering device in the English jurisprudence to date.[96] However, one exception to this trend is the House of Lords decision in *Whaley* v. *Lord Advocate*,[97] concerning the hunting ban. Lord Hope of Craighead noted that the appellant's contention that hunting with hounds constituted a non-religious belief would be outside the *Williamson* threshold, since looking at it 'objectively, hunting with hounds is carried on mainly for pleasure and relaxation for those who take part in it'. Lord Hope added:

> The current jurisprudence does not support the proposition that a person's belief in his right to engage in an activity which he carries on for pleasure or recreation, however fervent or passionate, can be equated with beliefs of the kind that are protected by Article 9. It would be surprising if it did so, as it would be hard in that event to set any limits on the range of beliefs that would be opened up for protection.[98]

However, although it would be difficult to limit the range of beliefs that *would* be protected, this does not mean that it would be difficult to limit the range of beliefs that *are* protected. A wide definition of belief would be permissible if there were other means by which superfluous claims could be dismissed. Moreover, the use of an objective standard in *Whaley* is contrary to *Williamson*[99] and should not be followed.

The reluctance to use the definition of religion or belief as a filtering device is therefore to be welcomed, even though the current legal stance is not unproblematic. The lack of attention given to the definition issue may mean that scope of protection is dictated by instinctive understandings of what 'freedom of religion' entails rather than by rigorous analysis. As Edge has argued, decision-makers have sought to define the application of Article 9 'by analogy with established beliefs entitled to protection, without understanding why an analogy may be drawn'.[100] The *Williamson* thresholds favour beliefs that are similar to a 'religion or belief' previously protected and could be said to favour religious beliefs over all other forms of belief.[101] This is problematic because, as Lord Walker so memorably put it in *Williamson*: 'In matters of human rights the court should not show liberal tolerance only to tolerant liberals.'[102]

---

[96] The cases of *R (on the Application of Playfoot (A Child)* v. *Millais School Governing Body* [2007] EWHC (Admin) 1698 and *R (on the Application of Ghai)* v. *Newcastle City Council* [2009] EWHC (Admin) 978, which have suggested that Article 9 only protects manifestations that are obligated by one's religion and extends only to manifestations of core dogmas and beliefs and not traditions, are discussed below in Chapter 5.

[97] *Whaley* v. *Lord Advocate* [2007] UKHL 53.   [98] At para. 18.

[99] See the statement in *Williamson* [2005] UKHL 15 that 'Freedom of religion protects the subjective belief of an individual' (Lord Nicholls at para. 22).

[100] P. W. Edge, *Legal Responses to Religious Difference* (The Hague: Kluwer Law, 2002), p. 47.

[101] M. D. Evans, *Religious Liberty and International Law in Europe* (Cambridge: Cambridge University Press, 1997), pp. 290–1.

[102] [2005] UKHL 15 at para. 23.

Discrimination law

Although domestic cases on Article 9 itself have tended not to use the definition of religion or belief as a filtering device, other areas of law claiming to follow Article 9 have actually used a narrower conception of these terms for this purpose. Most notably, this applies to the emergent jurisprudence under the new laws prohibiting discrimination on grounds of religion or belief. Discrimination on the grounds of religion or belief has been unlawful since 2003. The Employment Equality (Religion or Belief) Regulations 2003 prohibited direct and indirect discrimination, victimisation and harassment on the grounds of religion or belief in relation to employment, while Part 2 of the Equality Act 2006 prohibited direct and indirect discrimination and victimisation (but not harassment) on the grounds of religion or belief in relation to the provision of goods, facilities and services. The Equality Act 2010 has now consolidated the law in this area, repealing the older provisions.[103]

The original definition

While the original EU Framework Directive gave no further definition of the terms 'religion or belief',[104] Regulation 2(1) of the 2003 Regulations defined 'religion or belief' as meaning 'any religion, religious belief, or similar philosophical belief'. The precise scope of this definition was left to be determined by case law.[105] This prompted critics to remark that 'every employer is placed in the position of determining which belief systems are worthy of protection'.[106] Early Employment Tribunal decisions suggested, however, that Regulation 2(1) introduced a broad conception of 'religion', but a narrow conception of 'belief'.

In respect of religion, the case law followed Article 9 in being reluctant to define religion as being distinct from other belief systems. Moreover, the decision by the Employment Tribunal in *Hussain* v. *Bhuller Bros*[107] suggested that a liberal approach is to be adopted. The Tribunal found that 'attendance at home for bereavement purposes formed part of the Claimant's religion or religious belief'. The Tribunal recognised that 'religion, or religious belief, needs to be given a wide and liberal meaning'. It was also recognised that:

> If a person genuinely believes that his faith requires a certain course of action then that is sufficient to make it part of his religion. Attempting to differentiate between cultural manifestation, traditions and religious observance is likely to lead to unnecessary complications and endless debate. It would be wrong to

---

[103] For a fuller account of this body of law, see Chapter 6 below.
[104] Council Directive 2000/78/EC.
[105] See the comments of Lord Sainsbury, House of Lords Debate (17 June 2003) c 786.
[106] M. Javaid, 'Keeping the Faith' (2002) 99(48) *Law Society's Gazette* 14.
[107] *Hussain* v. *Bhuller Bros* ET, Case Number: 1806638/2004 (5 July 2005).

suggest that religion consists only of attending the Mosque or other place of worship. In our view religion must extend outwards to its interaction with the everyday life of the individual.

This view seems perfectly logical, especially given Lord Nicholls' assertion in *Williamson* that: 'Freedom of religion protects the subjective belief of an individual.'[108] However, as noted below, the case law on Article 9 of the ECHR has taken a much narrower approach and only protects acts that manifest one's religion or belief as opposed to acts that are motivated by it.[109] Given that it is only a first-instance employment tribunal decision, it is doubtful whether *Hussain* v. *Bhuller Bros* is persuasive.[110] However, a case could be made that it should be.

While the definition of religion adopted seems wider than under human rights jurisprudence, the definition of belief seems narrower. The Regulations stated that to be protected, non-religious beliefs had to be 'similar' to a 'religious' belief. This requirement concerned humanists and atheists. Although it remained highly probable that they were protected by the Regulations, they objected to the notion that their beliefs were being regarded as similar to religious beliefs.[111] The narrowness of the definition was underlined in early Employment Tribunal decisions. In *Williams* v. *South Central Ltd.*,[112] the Employment Tribunal excluded national beliefs, holding that discrimination on grounds of loyalty to a national flag or to one's native country was inconsistent with both the rules laid out in the Regulations. In *Baggs* v. *Fudge*,[113] the Tribunal excluded political beliefs from protection on the basis that they were not similar to religious beliefs. Even though it was not necessary for the Tribunal to make such a finding since the claimant had failed to make a prima facie case, the Tribunal found that membership of the British National Party (BNP) did not come under the definition of belief.

The revised definition

Section 77 of the Equality Act 2006 substituted a new definition of 'religion or belief' into the Regulations, ushering in two changes which commentators

---

[108] [2005] UKHL 15 at para. 22.

[109] This is the manifestation/motivation distinction: see *Arrowsmith* v. *United Kingdom* (1981) 3 EHRR 218, discussed in Chapter 5 below.

[110] The decision in *Eweida* v. *British Airways* [2010] EWCA Civ 8, discussed below in Chapter 6, suggests that this approach is not being followed.

[111] However, in the House of Lords, Lord Brennan pointed out that the word 'similar' related 'to the quality of the belief, not its nature': it 'addresses the state of mind in which someone holds that belief to the same thinking quality as a religious belief. It is not used to assimilate it in any way with a religion': House of Lords Debate (17 June 2003) c 788.

[112] *Williams* v. *South Central Ltd.* ET, Case Number: 2306989/2003 (16 June 2004).

[113] *Baggs* v. *Fudge* ET, Case Number: 1400114/2005 (23 March 2005).

have noted were 'made more in response to semantic concerns than to any legal problem with the previous definition'.[114] The first change is that lack of religion or belief is now explicitly included. This has been seen as simply clarifying what was previously assumed in the Parliamentary debate.[115] The second, and more controversial, change is the removal of the word 'similar': religion is now defined as 'any religion' and belief is defined as 'any religious or philosophical belief'.[116] The then government contended that there was no 'sinister motive' behind this change; the word 'similar' was removed because it 'added nothing and was, therefore, redundant'. As Baroness Scotland explained:

> The term 'philosophical belief' will take its meaning from the context in which it appears; that is, as part of the legislation relating to discrimination on the grounds of religion or belief. Given that context, philosophical beliefs must always be of a similar nature to religious beliefs.[117]

However, others have disputed this logic, contending that the effect must be to expand the protection provided. As Griffith points out, the term 'any philosophical belief' is 'very broad', extending, at least potentially, beyond critical thinking about the general nature of the world to cover ethical beliefs about the conduct of life.[118] This seems to question the decision in *Baggs* v. *Fudge*.

The definition of religion or belief is now to be found in section 10 of the Equality Act 2010, which reads:

(1) Religion means any religion and a reference to religion includes a reference to a lack of religion.
(2) Belief means any religious or philosophical belief and a reference to belief includes a reference to a lack of belief.

The adoption of the human rights jurisprudence

The revised statutory definition is not the end of the matter. Subsequent Employment Appeal Tribunal decisions indicate that an expansive definition of 'philosophical belief' is now being adopted. In *Grainger Plc* v. *Nicholson*,[119] the Employment Appeal Tribunal concluded that an asserted

---

[114] P. Griffith, 'Protecting the Absence of Religious Belief? The New Definition of Religion or Belief in Equality Legislation' (2007) (2) 3 *Religion & Human Rights* 149.

[115] On which see N. De Marco, *Blackstone's Guide to The Employment Equality Regulations 2003* (Oxford: Oxford University Press, 2004), pp. 12–13.

[116] The definition of religion or belief under s. 77 of the Equality Act 2006 now also states that 'a reference to religion includes a reference to lack of religion, and a reference to belief includes a reference to lack of belief'.

[117] House of Lords Debate (13 July 2005) c 1109–10.

[118] P. Griffith, 'Protecting the Absence of Religious Belief? The New Definition of Religion or Belief in Equality Legislation' (2007) (2) 3 *Religion & Human Rights* 149, 151–2.

[119] [2009] UKEAT 0219/09/ZT (3 November 2009).

belief in man-made climate change, together with the alleged resulting moral imperatives arising from it, was capable of constituting a 'philosophical belief' for the purpose of the 2003 Regulations because it met the criteria laid out by the Article 9 jurisprudence which was directly relevant. Burton J summarised the meaning of 'philosophical belief' as including five requirements:

(i) The belief must be genuinely held.
(ii) It must be a belief and not . . . an opinion or viewpoint based on the present state of information available.
(iii) It must be a belief as to a weighty and substantial aspect of human life and behaviour.
(iv) It must attain a certain level of cogency, seriousness, cohesion and importance.
(v) It must be worthy of respect in a democratic society, be not incompatible with human dignity and not conflict with the fundamental rights of others.[120]

In *Greater Manchester Police Authority* v. *Power*,[121] these five requirements were used to hold that a belief in spiritualism and life after death were capable of being a 'belief'.[122] *Grainger* and *Power* suggest that the removal of the word 'similar' has led to the wholesale adoption of the human rights jurisprudence on the definition of 'belief'. This is suspect, however, given that there are technical differences between discrimination law and human rights law in relation to definition. While for Article 9 purposes a belief needs to be a world-view and can therefore include political beliefs,[123] for discrimination law purposes, a belief must be 'religious or philosophical'[124] and, according to *Baggs* v. *Fudge*,[125] does not include political beliefs. More importantly, if Employment Tribunals are to make use of the human rights jurisprudence on the definition of belief, they should also take heed of Lord Nicholls' concern in *Williamson* that 'too much should not be demanded in this regard'.[126] Burton J's five requirements should not be interpreted too restrictively. If they are, the definition of belief will become increasingly used as a filter. For now, however, the emergent law on religious discrimination follows the practice of human rights law in not using the definition of religion as a filter and only sparingly using the definition of belief as a filtering device.

---

[120] At para. 24.   [121] [2009] EAT 0434/09/DA (12 November 2009).
[122] At the full Employment Tribunal hearing, Power lost on the merits of the case: ET Case No. 2404433/09 (23–4 November 2009).
[123] *X* v. *Austria* (1963) 13 CD 42.   [124] Equality Act ss. 44, 77(1).
[125] ET, Case Number: 1400114/2005 (23 March 2005). See also the decision in *Kelly* v. *Unison* [2009] ET Case No. 2203845/08 (22 December 2009).
[126] [2005] UKHL 15 at para. 23.

Conclusions

Generally, it may be observed that the underlying trend in English law – encompassing charity and registration law, human rights law and discrimination law[127] – is that the definition of religion is rarely used as a filtering device. This is to be welcomed. Deciding religious disputes solely by reference to the definition of religion is usually unnecessary. Rather than dismissing claims by saying that it was not 'religious', claims should be considered properly and fully. The fact that the definition of religion is sometimes used as a filtering device is therefore troubling. This is especially true in the charity and registration law cases where the definition filter has determined the success of the claim. In relation to human rights and discrimination law, in contrast, the trend to extend protection to religion or belief makes the use of definition as a filter more nuanced: it is the definition of 'religion or belief' which is used to exclude some non-religious beliefs rather than the definition of religion. It remains objectionable, however, that the definition filter is still used as a somewhat crude means of inclusion and exclusion.

Further, on the face of it, the existence of several different legal definitions of religion is one of the biggest challenges to the idea that religion law now exists as a separate legal sub-discipline.

In a debate on what was to become the Equality Act 2006, Baroness Scotland provided the rationale for the number of different definitions, arguing that they reflected 'the different purposes that the laws are intended to have'.[128] However, she pointed out that these definitions all had one thing in common:

> None seeks to define what actual faiths or beliefs are covered by the law. That is left to the courts to decide, which is proper. . . . The courts are best placed to make decisions on these difficult matters, taking into account all the information that they will have before them.

The statutory definitions are partial definitions. They seek to help the court by pointing out some key characteristics that a religion may have, but they do not provide a list of protected religions. The matter is left to case law. Reference to that case law suggests that although it remains true that there are numerous definitions of religion under English law, these definitions are

---

[127] In addition to the areas examined above, the definition of religion has also proved important in other areas such as asylum cases. See, in particular, the Court of Appeal decision in *Omoruyi* v. *Secretary of State for the Home Department* [2001] INLR 33, in which Simon Brown LJ held that the Ogboni were not to be considered to be a religion despite evidence that they worshipped idols and sacrificed animals: 'The notion that a "devil cult" practising pagan rituals of the sort here described is in any true sense a religion I find deeply offensive'. See further A. Good, 'Persecution for Reasons of Religion under the 1951 Refugee convention' in T. G. Kirsch and B. Turner (eds.), *Permutations of Order: Religion and Law as Contested Sovereignties* (Aldershot: Ashgate, 2009), p. 27.

[128] House of Lords debate (13 July 2005) c 1107–8.

increasingly homogeneous. As Lord Walker of Gestingthorpe commented in *Williamson*,[129] there is a trend towards a 'more expansive' definition of religion given that we live in 'an age of increasingly multicultural societies and increasing respect for human rights'.[130] The advent of a positive right of religious freedom in domestic law under the Human Rights Act 1998 has made uniformity more likely. The Charity Commission decisions are increasingly discussing and using the language of Article 9[131] and other human rights, while the decisions in *Grainger* and *Power* show that Employment Tribunals have adopted the human rights understanding of belief in the context of religious discrimination law. These trends suggest that English law is moving towards a common definition of 'religion or belief'.

This common definition may be seen as being part of something called religion law. Indeed, the fact that so many legal provisions protect 'religion' may be seen as further evidence of the existence of religion law as a separate legal sub-discipline. However, while the increasing importance of human rights and discrimination law provisions points towards the existence of religion law, it is important to remember that other legal provisions continue to be significant. The next chapter will explore collective rights to religious freedom. It will focus upon the legal status of religious groups, asking whether the differences between the legal status of the Church of England and all other non-established religious groups question the existence of religion law.

---

[129] [2005] UKHL 15.   [130] At para. 54.

[131] See, e.g. their 1999 decision on the Church of Scientology: www.charity-commission.gov.uk/library/start/cosfulldoc.pdf. See P. W. Edge and J. M. Loughrey, 'Religious Charities and the Juridification of the Charity Commission' (2001) 21 *Legal Studies* 36–64, 56–9. See further the 2010 decision of the Charity Commission in relation to the Druid Network (www.charitycommission.gov.uk/Library/about_us/druiddec.pdf). See especially para. 38.

4

The legal position of religious groups

Introduction

Many of the new pieces of religion law protect religious freedom mainly as an individual right. Chapters 5 and 6 will show how developments in human rights law and discrimination law are very much focused upon the religious individual.[1] However, this is not to say that religious groups are ignored. There are a number of laws which provide special treatment for religious groups and organisations. This chapter explores the main ways in which English law recognises and regulates religious groups.[2] A distinction is often made between the legal position of the Church of England on the one hand and all other religious groups on the other.[3] As we have seen,[4] following the Reformation the Church of England was the only lawful religion. Although over time other religious groups became tolerated, the Church of England was still seen as the norm. And that impression can still be found in the modern law in the way in which the Church of England remains established by law.

This chapter explores the extent to which the Church of England is in a different legal position from that of other religious groups and questions whether these differences should be regarded as being benefits or burdens. It falls into two sections. The first examines the legal position of the Church of England, while the second looks at the legal position of all other non-established groups. Although this chapter will focus on the English situation, brief mention will be made of the Church of Scotland, showing the milder

---

[1] However, as we will see there are exceptions to this trend as shown by the decision in *Eweida* v. *British Airways* [2010] EWCA Civ 80, discussed in Chapter 6.

[2] Other chapters in this book provide further examples of the law protecting religion as a collective affair. Chapter 6 elucidates the exceptions from discrimination law enjoyed by religious groups; Chapter 7 explains how many criminal offences concerning religion only protect religious individuals if they are members of a group; while Chapter 8 looks at faith schools.

[3] The constitutional position of religion differs in the four nations of the United Kingdom. While formerly there were established churches in all four nations, legislation disestablishing the national church has been enacted in respect of Ireland and Wales (Irish Church Disestablishment Act 1869; Welsh Church Act 1914). Two different established churches continue to exist in England and Scotland. This chapter will focus upon the English situation, but will also include discussion of the (established) Church of Scotland and the (disestablished) Church in Wales.

[4] See Chapter 2.

form of establishment that exists there. The conclusion will also make reference to the disestablished Church in Wales, suggesting that it is a hybrid – sharing some characteristics with the Church of England and others with non-established religious groups.

The Church of England

The Reformation resulted not only in the detachment from Rome, but also in the 'establishment' of the Church of England by legislation.[5] However, whilst it is fairly routine to call the Church of England an 'established church', there is less agreement as to what this actually means. As Lord Rodger of Earlsferry commented in *Aston Cantlow* v. *Wallbank*,[6] 'the juridical nature of the Church is, notoriously, somewhat amorphous'.[7] At its heart, the fact that the Church of England is 'established' simply refers to the existence of close links between the Church and the State. The fact that it is 'established by law' shows that these close links are articulated in law, meaning that the Church has a different and special legal position compared with non-established religious groups.

However, this is a simplification.[8] There are several different meanings of establishment and different forms of establishment exist in different countries.[9] Indeed, the Church of England has a rather different constitutional position from churches in other European countries which are variously styled as 'state', 'national', 'established' or 'folk' churches.[10] The meaning of establishment clearly varies depending upon the context. For convenience, it may be preferable to elucidate the legal features of English establishment (often referred to as the 'incidents of establishment'). These incidents of establishment can be understood as involving four interlocking constitutional relationships: between Church and Monarch, Church and Parliament, Church and the courts and Church and the public.[11]

---

[5] See Chapter 2. This is reflected in Canon A1: The Church of England is 'established according to the laws of this realm under the Queen's Majesty, belongs to the true and apostolic Church of Christ'.

[6] [2003] UKHL 37.   [7] At para. 154.

[8] For a fuller discussion, see N. Doe, *The Legal Framework of the Church of England* (Oxford: Oxford University Press, 1996), pp. 7–10; and M. Hill, 'Church and State in the United Kingdom: Anachronism or Microcosm' in S. Ferrari and R. Cristofori (eds.), *Law and Religion in the 21st Century* (Aldershot: Ashgate, 2010), p. 199.

[9] See the discussion by J. Oliva, 'Church, State and Establishment in the United Kingdom in the 21st Century: Anachronism or Idiosyncrasy?' [2010] *Public Law* 482, 484–6.

[10] See R. Sandberg and N. Doe, 'Church-State Relations in Europe' (2007) 1(5) *Religion Compass* 561; R. Sandberg, 'Church-State Relations in Europe: From Legal Models to an Interdisciplinary Approach' (2008) 1(3) *Journal of Religion in Europe* 329–52; and F. Cranmer 'Church/State Relations in Scandinavia' in R. M. Morris, *Church and State in 21st Century Britain: the Future of Establishment* (Basingstoke: Palgrave-Macmillan, 2009), p. 127.

[11] There is also some debate as to whether some of the incidents described below are characteristics of establishment, in that they predate the Reformation (J. Oliva, 'Church, State

The Church and the Monarch

The most well-known incidents of establishment concern the link between the Crown and the established Church. The Monarch is the Supreme Governor of the Church of England.[12] The Act of Settlement 1700/01 requires that the heir apparent must be a 'protestant' and that the monarch 'shall join in communion with the Church of England as by law established'. At succession, the monarch must make a declaration to uphold and maintain the established Church.[13] However, it is possible to over-emphasise these provisions. The references to royal supremacy in the law of the Church of England could be interpreted as a simple reiteration of Parliamentary supremacy. Moreover, it is not the case that the Monarch must be a member of the established Church: the requirement is that he or she be a Protestant in communion with it. George I (1714 to 1727) remained a Lutheran in belief and practice, but he became King because he was willing to receive communion from the Church of England. However, there is clearly a connection between the Crown and the established Church. The Monarch enjoys significant rights of patronage, including appointing all bishops and archbishops, twenty-six of whom sit in the House of Lords.[14]

The Church and Parliament

The presence of bishops in the House of Lords is just one of several connections between the Church of England and Parliament. The Lords Spiritual, as they are known, comprise the Archbishops of Canterbury and York and the bishops of London, Durham and Winchester *ex officiis* and the twenty-one most senior bishops by date of appointment.[15] Members of other religious traditions may be appointed to the Lords under the Life Peerages Act 1958, but do not sit as Lords Spiritual.[16] Unlike other life peers, the Lords Spiritual cease sitting in the House of Lords when they retire.[17] They owe no formal allegiance to any political party and it is often said that by convention they

---

and Establishment in the United Kingdom in the 21st Century: Anachronism or Idiosyncrasy?' [2010] *Public Law* 482, 492). This depends upon whether it is seen as referring specifically to the post-Reformation relationship between Church and State or whether establishment is understood to refer more generally to the state of affairs where any Church is favoured.

12 Canons of the Church of England, Canon A7.

13 Accession Declaration Act 1910; Coronation Oath Act 1689.

14 Appointment of Bishops Act 1533; Manchester Bishopric Act 1847; Ecclesiastical Commissioners Act 1847 s.2; Bishoprics Act 1878 s.5. Previously two names were passed to the Prime Minister. However, since 2007 only one name has been passed on.

15 Neither the Bishop of Sodor and Man (who sits and votes as of right in the Legislative Council and Tynnwald Court in the Isle of Man) nor the Bishop of Gibraltar in Europe (whose territorial jurisdiction is beyond the United Kingdom) may sit as lords spiritual.

16 Examples include Methodist peer Lord Soper and Rabbi Lord Sacks.

17 By convention, life peerages are conferred upon Archbishops on retirement and lately some bishops have been similarly honoured. In that case, the newly appointed peer sits as a lord temporal and is introduced to the House afresh.

do not speak or vote on party political issues. However, recent empirical work has suggested that they seem to have very similar concerns to those of the secular peers[18] and that there seems to be a trend of towards 'increased politicization'.[19]

The most overt 'religious' function of the Lords Spiritual is arguably the reading of prayers at the commencement of business in the Lords.[20] Prayers are also said at the beginning of sittings in the House of Commons, usually led by the Speaker's Chaplain. There is no religious representation as such in the House of Commons. Indeed, a bar on Church of England clerics becoming Members of Parliament was only removed in 2001.[21] However, there is an important connection with the established church through the Church Commissioners. A backbench Member of Parliament (traditionally from the party in government) is appointed by the Crown for the duration of the Parliament to serve as the Second Church Estates Commissioner. In this role he or she answers Parliamentary questions. The Member of Parliament is one of thirty-three Church Commissioners. The Commissioners' role is to manage the historic assets of the Church of England. Annual Reports are presented both to Parliament and the General Synod of the Church of England.[22]

In addition to these, one final connection between the Church and Parliament is, perhaps, both the most important and the one that is often overlooked: the requirement that the law of the Church of England requires Royal Assent. This requirement applies both to Measures and Canons.

Measures are pieces of legislation which are drafted by members of the Church of England in the General Synod.[23] They are dealt with in the Synod in a fashion analogous to a Bill in Parliament, but are then considered by the Ecclesiastical Committee of Parliament, comprising members of major parties in both Houses of Parliament.[24] The Ecclesiastical Committee then drafts a report on the nature and effect of the proposed Measure, which is communicated to the Legislative Committee of the General Synod. If the

---

[18] A. Harlow, F. Cranmer and N. Doe, 'Bishops in the House of Lords: A Critical Analysis' [2008] *Public Law* 490.

[19] A. Partington and P. Hickley, *Coming off the Bench: The Past, Present and Future of Religious representation in the House of Lords* (2007), available from the website of Theos: The Public Theology Think Tank www.theosthinktank.co.uk.

[20] Lambeth Palace arranges for a duty bishop to be assigned for every day the Lords sit. A list is circulated for bishops to sign up for two or three weeks' duty. In the absence of a Bishop, a member of the House who is a clergyman of the Church of England may read prayers; if no such person is present the Lord Speaker reads prayers. The five senior bishops do not take part in the rota for prayers.

[21] House of Commons (Removal of Clergy Disqualification) Act 2001, repealing the House of Commons (Clergy Disqualification) Act 1801. The bar previously also covered ministers of the Church of Scotland.

[22] See Church Commissioners Measures 1947, 1964 and 1970.

[23] Formerly the Church Assembly – see the Synodical Government Measure 1969.

[24] Church of England Assembly (Powers) Act 1919; Synodical Government Measure 1969.

report is unfavourable, the Synod may withdraw the proposed Measure; there is no provision for amending it. If approved by Resolution in both Houses, the draft Measure is sent for the Royal Assent and has the full force and effect of an Act of Parliament.[25] Measures enjoy the same 'invulnerability' from challenge by the State courts as an Act of Parliament.[26] A Measure is classified as primary legislation for the purposes of the Human Rights Act 1998.[27] A Measure may relate to any matter 'concerning the Church of England',[28] and may extend to the amendment or repeal in whole or in part of any Act of Parliament.[29]

Canons are legislation created by the General Synod.[30] Although they require no parliamentary approval, Canons require Royal Assent and Licence.[31] Canons must not be contrary to the Royal Prerogative, customs, statutes or laws of the realm,[32] and those dealing with liturgy and doctrine cannot be contrary to the doctrine of the Church of England as determined by the General Synod.[33] For the purposes of the Human Rights Act 1998, Canons are classified as a form of secondary legislation, inferior to Measures.[34] Unlike Measures, a canon may be challenged in the State courts on the basis that it is *ultra vires*.[35]

Measures and Canons are important incidents of establishment. The role of the State in their enactment is both a benefit to the established church and a burden on it. It is a benefit since it gives internal church laws the status of State law.[36] However, it is also a burden because of the limit that is placed on the autonomy of the Church to govern itself. Unlike other religious bodies, the internal law of the Church of England requires Royal Assent (and in the case of Measures, Parliamentary approval). This is underlined by provisions found in the Civil Partnership Act 2004 which provide that

[25] Church of England Assembly (Powers) Act 1919 s.4.
[26] *R. v. Archbishops of Canterbury and York, ex parte Williamson* (1994) *The Times* 9 March.
[27] Human Rights Act 1998 s.21. Remedial action under s. 10 does not apply to Measures. See M. Hill, *Ecclesiastical Law*, 3rd edn (Oxford: Oxford University Press, 2007), paras. 1.25–7, 2.04–9.
[28] Church of England Assembly (Powers) Act 1919, preamble. For interpretation, see *R. v. Ecclesiastical Committee of Both Houses of Parliament, ex parte Church Society* (1994) 6 Admin LR 670.
[29] Church of England Assembly (Powers) Act 1919 s.3(6).
[30] Synodical Government Measure 1969. Prior to 1970, the power to create canons had been exercised on a provincial basis by the respective convocations of Canterbury and York.
[31] Synodical Government Measure 1969 s.1(3)(a).   [32] Section 1(3)(b).
[33] Church of England (Worship and Doctrine) Measure 1974 s.4.
[34] For further elucidation of their legal status, especially in relation to the Human Rights Act 1998, see M. Hill, *Ecclesiastical Law*, 3rd edn (Oxford: Oxford University Press, 2007), paras. 1.28 et seq.
[35] *Brown* v. *Runcie* (1990) *The Times* 20 February; but see M. Hill, *Ecclesiastical Law*, 3rd edn (Oxford: Oxford University Press, 2007), para. 1.28.
[36] However, as we will see below, Parliament legislates for and about other religious organisations, albeit in an ad hoc manner.

Ministers may amend or repeal 'church legislation'.[37] It has been contended that this 'amounts to a curtailment of autonomy on the part of the Church of England, albeit partial, with a specificity of purpose, and reliant upon benign and consensual exercise by the Government' giving 'considerable power to the Executive, rather than to Parliament as a whole, in theory if not also in practice, to legislate for the Church of England'.[38] These provisions further suggest that the incidents of establishment can often be more of a burden than a benefit.

The interrelationship of Church and State in the enactment of Measures and Canons underlines the fact that the law of the Church of England is part of the general law of England.[39] To use the terminology adopted in Chapter 1, Measures and Canons can be seen as being both religion law and religious law. Indeed, their existence shows that no watertight distinction can be made between these two labels. The study of the law of the Church of England (and by implication the study of law and religion in the United Kingdom) requires both the study of both religion law and religious law.

The Church and the courts

There is an obvious connection between the Church and the court system because the law of the Church is part of the law of England. The ecclesiastical courts and their jurisprudence is part of the law of the land. It has been judicially recognised that although the enforcement of the law affecting the Church of England 'is divided between the ecclesiastical courts and the temporal courts', nevertheless the 'unity and coherence of the law is not affected by the division of jurisdiction as to its enforcement'.[40] Although much of their jurisdiction concerning the enforcement of the law of contract, trusts, defamation and wills has been moved to the ordinary courts,[41] there remain a growing number of courts and tribunals currently functioning within the Church of England.[42] These courts and tribunals now tend to focus upon two matters: the faculty jurisdiction in the case of courts established under the Ecclesiastical Jurisdiction Measure 1963,[43] and the

---

[37] See ss. 255 and 259.

[38] M. Hill, *Ecclesiastical Law*, 3rd edn (Oxford: Oxford University Press, 2007), para. 2.06. See by means of response S. Slack, 'Church autonomy and the Civil Partnership Act 2004' (2007) 9 *Ecclesiastical Law Journal* 206.

[39] *Mackonochie* v. *Lord Penzance* (1881) 6 App Cas 424.

[40] *AG* v. *Dean and Chapter of Ripon Cathedral* [1945] Ch 239, Uthwatt J.

[41] See generally R. H. Helmholz, *The Oxford History of the Laws of England. Volume 1, The Canon Law and Ecclesiastical Jurisdiction from 597 to the 1640s* (Oxford: Oxford University Press, 2004), and R. B. Outhwaite, *The Rise and Fall of the Ecclesiastical Courts, 1500–1860* (Cambridge: Cambridge University Press, 2006).

[42] Detailed discussion of these courts is outside the scope of this work. See M. Hill, *Ecclesiastical Law*, 3rd edn (Oxford: Oxford University Press, 2007), paras. 2.46 *et seq* and ch. 6 and 7.

[43] Its primary jurisdiction concerns the grant or refusal of faculties permitting alterations to the fabric or structure of church buildings and other matters concerning consecrated land,

discipline of clergy, now under the auspices of statutory tribunals pursuant to the Clergy Discipline Measure 2003.[44] Their decisions remain, however, part of English public law, which means that their decisions are subject to judicial review by the High Court.[45] While previous authorities seem to suggest that this applies only in relation to mandatory and prohibiting orders[46] and does not apply to quashing orders,[47] this rule has been the subject of criticism[48] and may be no longer sustainable, particularly in the light of general developments in judicial review.[49] Moreover, for the purposes of the Human Rights Act 1998, all courts and tribunals within the Church of England are public authorities and as such must act in a way which is compatible with Convention rights.[50]

The Church and public ministry

The final constitutional relationship is perhaps the one of most practical importance: the connection between the Church and the public at large.[51] Historically, at least, membership of the Church of England was synonymous with citizenship.[52] Accordingly, English law recognises various rights for all who are resident in parishes of the Church of England regardless of their religious belief or practice. People resident in Church of England parishes cannot be excluded from public worship.[53] It is also

particularly reservation of grave spaces and exhumation. See M. Hill, *Ecclesiastical Law*, 3rd edn (Oxford: Oxford University Press, 2007), ch. 7.

[44] Formerly, under the Ecclesiastical Jurisdiction Measure 1963, cases involving clergy discipline fell into two categories: conduct cases, involving the commission of ecclesiastical offences, such as neglect of duty or conduct unbecoming a cleric, and so-called reserved cases (involving doctrine, ritual or ceremonial). Different procedures applied to archbishops and bishops, and to priests and deacons. The Ecclesiastical Jurisdiction Measure 1963 continues to apply to reserved cases, but no longer applies to conduct cases. For a discussion of the practice and procedure of Clergy Discipline Tribunals, see M. Hill, *Ecclesiastical Law*, 3rd edn (Oxford: Oxford University Press, 2007), ch. 6.

[45] Ecclesiastical Jurisdiction Measure 1963 s.81. See M. Hill, 'Judicial Review of Ecclesiastical Courts' in N. Doe, M. Hill and R. Ombres (eds.), *English Canon Law* (Cardiff: University of Wales Press, 1998), pp. 104–14.

[46] See, e.g. *R. v. North, ex parte Oakey* [1927] 1 KB 491.

[47] *R. v. Chancellor of St Edmundsbury and Ipswich Diocese, ex parte White* [1948] 1 KB 195.

[48] *R. v. Chancellor of Chichester Consistory Court, ex parte News Group Newspapers Ltd* [1992] COD 48.

[49] See *R. v. Exeter Consistory Court, ex parte Cornish* (1998) 5 Ecc LJ 212.

[50] See M. Hill, *Ecclesiastical Law*, 3rd edn (Oxford: Oxford University Press, 2007), para. 2.62.

[51] Other 'incidents of establishment' reflecting this include the requirement that Standing Advisory Councils for Religious Education (SACREs) must include representatives of the Church of England (Education Act 1996 s.390; see Chapter 8) and the law on prison chaplaincy. Every prison must have a chaplain and, if large enough, may also have an assistant chaplain. Both must be clergy of the Church of England: Prison Act 1952 s.7. However, the Secretary of State may also appoint prison ministers representing denominations other than the Church of England: *ibid.*, s.10.

[52] *Town of Pawlet* v. *Clark* (1815) 13 US 292.   [53] *Cole* v. *PC* [1937] 1KB 316.

commonly understood that parishioners enjoy a legal right to be married in the parish church, deriving from the Marriage Act 1753.[54] Indeed, the categories of persons entitled to be married in the parish church have recently been extended beyond 'parishioner' to include others having certain 'qualifying connections'.[55] Parishioners also have the right to be buried in the parish church ground, provided that there is room.[56] Although there are other lawful means by which parishioners can be married and buried,[57] these important incidents of establishment provide legal rights which can be exercised by all residents regardless of religious practice or observance.

Challenges to establishment

For some, these 'incidents of establishment' are controversial. Much ink has been dedicated to debating the merits of establishment and, in particular, the political, theological and ecclesiological implications of establishment and disestablishment.[58] For current purposes, however, in focusing upon the legal dimension of establishment, it is necessary to examine a number of challenges to, and modifications of, establishment that have occurred in recent years. The following will briefly explore the question of whether the establishment of the Church of England is compatible with the standards of modern religion law, looking particularly at European Union (EU) obligations and the European Convention on Human Rights (ECHR). The discussion of establishment will then conclude with a brief comparison of the different and milder form of establishment found in Scotland.

---

[54] Commonly known as the Clandestine Marriage Act or Lord Hardwicke's Act, the 1753 Act required public religious ceremony in the parish church of the Church of England according to authorised rites at which a clergyman would officiate; and that the marriage be preceded by banns or licence. The Act made exceptions for Jews and Quakers and subsequently the Marriage Act 1836, some eighty years later, made provision for civil marriage. The case of *Argar v. Holdsworth* (1758) 2 Lee 515 is commonly taken as authority for the proposition that parishioners enjoy a legal right to be married in the parish church, but see N. Doe, *The Legal Framework of the Church of England* (Oxford: Clarendon Press, 1996), pp. 359–60 and M. Smith, 'An Interpretation of *Argar v. Holdsworth*' (1998) 5 *Ecclesiastical Law Journal* 39–41. Compare J. Humphreys, 'The Right to Marry in the Parish Church: A Rehabilitation of *Argar v. Holdsworth*' (2004) 7 *Ecclesiastical Law Journal* 405.

[55] Church of England Marriage Measure 2008. See S. Slack, 'The Right to Marry in Accordance with the Rites and Ceremonies of the Church of England' in N. Doe (ed.), *Marriage in Anglican and Roman Catholic Canon Law* (Cardiff: Centre for Law and Religion, 2009), p. 6. Note also the clerical conscience clause found in s.8(2) of the Matrimonial Causes Act 1965.

[56] Non-Christian burial services can be prohibited: *Kemp v. Wickes* (1809) 3 Phil Ecc 26; Burial Law Amendments Act 1880.

[57] Marriage and Registration Acts 1836; Burial Act 1852; Burial Laws Amendment Act 1880; Civil Partnership Act 2004.

[58] The most recent leading work is R. M. Morris (ed.), *Church and State in 21st Century Britain: The Future of Church Establishment* (London: Palgrave MacMillan, 2009). See also C. Buchanan, *Cut the Connection: Disestablishment and the Church of England* (London: Darton, Longman & Todd, 1994).

As discussed in Chapter 2, the EU and the ECHR are increasingly affecting the regulation of religion in the United Kingdom. However, both supranational bodies have shown a degree of deference towards their Member States as regards Church–State relations. The EU has been quick to insist that long-standing EU treaty provisions prohibiting discrimination on grounds of religion do not call into question preferential treatment given to State churches. A declaration appended to the Treaty of Amsterdam 1997[59] provided that:

> The Union respects and does not prejudice the status under national law of churches and religious associations or communities in the Member States.

Likewise, the European Court of Human Rights at Strasbourg has held that Article 9 permits religious autonomy and diversity in terms of the regulation of religious groups. Convention organs have accepted a variety of church–state relations as being part of a contracting state's margin of appreciation. Mild forms of state preference for one religion over another do not violate the ECHR. It was noted in *Darby* v. *Sweden*:[60]

> A State Church system cannot in itself be considered to violate Article 9 of the Convention. . . . However, a State Church system must, in order to satisfy Article 9, include specific safeguards for the individual's freedom of religion.

Mild forms of establishment are not incompatible with the ECHR; there is only incompatibility if that special treatment prevents the religious freedom of those who do not conform to the State Church. As Ahdar and Leigh point out, legal preference for a certain religion is compatible with freedom of religion 'provided that legal preference is not accompanied by distinct civil and legal disabilities for the non-adherents of the official religion'.[61]

This is not to say that the standards of EU and ECHR law have not affected the Church of England. Domestic decision-makers have changed rules that apply to the established Church on the basis that they are not compliant with EU law and ECHR standards. This can be illustrated by reference to the exception which organised religions enjoy from the law prohibiting discrimination on grounds of sex.[62] Previously this was buttressed in the case of the Church of England by section 6 of the Priests (Ordination of Women) Measure 1993. However, in face of new EU laws concerning sex discrimination, section 6 was repealed on grounds that it was not compatible with EU law since the Measure was not limited to reasons of religious

---

[59] Treaty of Amsterdam 1997, Appendix: Declaration on the Status of Churches and Non-Confessional Organisations.
[60] (1991) 13 EHRR 774.
[61] R. Ahdar and I. Leigh, *Religious Freedom in the Liberal State* (Oxford: Oxford University Press, 2005), pp. 129–30.
[62] Sex Discrimination Act 1975 s.19. Now found in Equality Act 2010 Sch. 19 para. 2. See Chapter 6.

conscience.[63] The problem was not the fact that a different law applied to the Church of England, but that the contents of those different laws were not considered to be EU compliant.

Many religious groups feared that the Human Rights Act 1998 would increase the amount of litigation against religious groups. In response to lobbying by a number of these religious groups,[64] section 13 was added to the Act as 'an attempt to reassure the Churches about the impact of the Act'.[65] The Labour Government contended that religious groups would not generally be 'public authorities' (and thus susceptible to claims under the Act), with the exception of where they stood in the place of the State providing a public service.[66] Section 13 reads:

> If a court's determination of any question arising under this Act might affect the exercise by a religious organisation (itself or its members collectively) of the Convention right to freedom of thought, conscience and religion, it must have particular regard to the importance of that right.

At first sight, section 13 seems to accord a special protection for the religious freedom of religious organisations. It is a provision which should be at the heart of British religion law. However, in practice it seems that the section is a dead letter. Commentators seem to agree that the section is 'rather mild',[67] largely symbolic[68] and 'at best an articulation and codification' of the pre-Human Rights Act position.[69] The emptiness of section 13 is shown by the fact that the question of whether and when religious groups could be public authorities needed to be determined by the House of Lords in *Aston Cantlow v. Wallbank*.[70] The case concerned a Parochial Parish Council (PCC) of the Church of England which sought to enforce the Wallbank's liability under the Chancel Repairs Act 1932 as lay rectors to pay for chancel repairs. The House of Lords focused squarely on the public authority point, holding that the PCC was not acting as a public authority for this purpose. A public authority could either be a 'core' public authority which exercised functions that were broadly governmental so they were all functions of a public nature, or a 'hybrid' public authority which exercised some functions of a public

---

[63] Employment Equality (Sex Discrimination) Regulation 2005 Reg. 20(2). See the Explanatory Memorandum at p. 26–8: www.uk-legislation.hmso.gov.uk/si/si2007/em/uksiem_20071263_en.pdf.

[64] P. Cumper, 'Religious Organisations and the Human Rights Act 1998' in P. W. Edge and G. Harvey, *Law and Religion in Contemporary Society* (Aldershot: Ashgate, 2000), p. 72.

[65] Jack Straw, then Home Secretary, Commons Hansard (20 May 1998) c 1021.

[66] Column 1017.

[67] R. Ahdar and I. Leigh, *Religious Freedom in the Liberal State* (Oxford: Oxford University Press, 2005), p. 359.

[68] P. Cumper, 'The Protection of Religious Rights under Section 13 of the Human Rights Act 1998' [2000] *Public Law* 265.

[69] M. Hill, 'Judicial Approaches to Religious Disputes' in R. O'Dair and A. Lewis (eds.), *Law and Religion* (Oxford: Oxford University Press, 2001), p. 419.

[70] [2003] UKHL 37.

nature. The PCC was not a 'core' public authority since, although the Church of England had special links with central government and performed certain public functions, the Church of England generally and PCCs in particular were essentially religious rather than governmental organisations. Even if the PCC was a 'hybrid' public authority, enforcement of chancel repair liability was not a function of a public nature; rather it was a private function.

Unlike section 13, *Aston Cantlow* provides some clarification about when human rights claims can be brought against religious groups. The position is basically in line with what the Government promised. Neither the Church of England nor its components are 'core' public authorities.[71] However, there is a possibility that human rights may be enforced against components of the Church of England if they are 'hybrid' public authorities fulfilling a public function; but this will only occur in certain situations where the group stands in the place of the State, such as in relation to marriage. For the most part, the established Church and its organs will not be a public authority and it is even more likely that the same will be true of other religious groups and their institutions. In short while religious groups must comply with other standards imposed by modern religion law, they will seldom have litigation brought against them under the Human Rights Act 1998.

However, the standards of modern religion law may well affect the establishment of the Church of England.[72] Many of the new laws concerning religion do not differentiate between the Church of England and other religious groups. More often than not, the protection is afforded on grounds of religion. Examples of this trend can be found in laws concerning the care of children,[73] criminal offences,[74] discrimination laws,[75] charity law and education provisions.[76] Pieces of religion law now tend to treat the Church

---

[71] Lord Nicholls held that to hold that PCCs are core public authorities would be 'an extraordinary conclusion': para. 15.

[72] This is shown by the decision in *R (Baiai and others)* v. *The Secretary of State for the Home Department and others* [2006] EWHC (Admin) 823. This concerned a scheme under the Asylum and Immigration (Treatment of Claimants, etc) Act 2004, which prescribed that any person who was subject to immigration control and wished to enter into a civil marriage in the United Kingdom had to apply to the Secretary of State for a certificate of approval to marry. The reference to 'civil marriage' meant that those who were married in a Church of England church were exempt from these requirements. Silber J in the High Court held that that this was discriminatory and violated Article 14 of the ECHR (in conjunction with the Article 12 right to marry). Silber J held that this could not be justified since there was no evidence that those who married in non-Church of England ceremonies were any more likely to engage in sham marriages than those who married in Church of England ceremonies. An appeal on this finding was not pursued by the Secretary of State in the Court of Appeal ([2007] EWCA Civ 478) and did not fall for consideration in the House of Lords ([2008] UKHL 53). However, a government circular, issued on 13 November 2009, conceded that the United Kingdom Borders Agency could not find a workable system which did not discriminate between civil and Anglican marriages: GRO Circular 9/2009.

[73] See Chapter 2.   [74] See Chapter 7.   [75] See Chapter 6.   [76] See Chapter 8.

of England like all other religious groups.[77] Moreover, the new religion law starts from the premise of religious equality; no special protection is afforded to any one religion as the State takes on the role of facilitating the religious marketplace.[78] Although establishment remains compatible with the letter of the new religion law, it is out of sync with some of the premises underpinning the new law. This does not mean that disestablishment is inevitable. The complex nature of establishment suggests that disestablishment is quite unlikely. But this does mean that it is likely that the establishment of the Church of England will evolve over time. Indeed, Ferrari has asserted that establishment in England has survived 'because the Church of England quickly understood the need to accept religious pluralism and chose to exercise its prerogatives and political power in favour of all religions'.[79] With this in mind, it is worth examining briefly the different kind of establishment found in Scotland. Can the Church of England learn anything from a system which is often described as being 'both established and free'?[80]

A milder form of establishment: the Church of Scotland

Like the Church of England, the Church of Scotland has been 'a creature of legislation' from the sixteenth century onwards.[81] However, it has been said to enjoy a 'lighter form of establishment' than the Church of England.[82] Scottish establishment can still be understood as involving the same four interlocking constitutional relationships as in England (between Church and Monarch, Church and Parliament, Church and the courts and Church and the public), but the legal framework of these relationships differs.

One of the major differences is that, although the Monarch swears an Oath on Accession to protect the Church and the Presbyterian form of Government, he or she is not Supreme Governor of the Church. The Monarch is simply a member of the Church and (unless she chooses to attend in person) is formally represented at the Annual General Assembly by the Lord High Commissioner.[83] The relationship between the Church of Scotland

---

[77] The abolition of blasphemy, described in Chapter 7, is further evidence of this.

[78] See, e.g. the judgment of the Grand Chamber in *Refah Partisi* v. *Turkey* (2003) 37 EHRR 1 at para. 91, discussed in Chapter 2.

[79] He gives the example that the Bishops in the House of Lords often claim to act as representatives of religion in the broader sense: S. Ferrari, 'Law and Religion in Europe' in L. Christoffersen *et al.* (eds.), *Religion in the 21st Century* (Aldershot: Ashgate, 2010), p. 153.

[80] T. M. Taylor, 'Church and State in Scotland' [1957] *Juridical Review* 121.

[81] Confession of Faith Ratification Act 1560 (Scotland). The Church of Scotland is Reformed in doctrine and Presbyterian in its government.

[82] C. R. Munro, 'Does Scotland Have An Established Church?' (1997) 4 *Ecclesiastical Law Journal* 639, 645.

[83] C. G. Brown, 'The Myth of the Established Church of Scotland' in J. Kirk (ed.), *The Scottish Churches and the Union Parliament 1707–1999* (Edinburgh: Scottish Church History Society, 2001), 48.

and Parliament also differs. The Church of Scotland Act 1921 recognised the Church's independence in 'matters spiritual' by recognising the Articles Declaratory passed by the Church General Assembly, which are appended to the Act.[84] It stated that no civil authority has 'any right of interference with the proceedings or judgments of the Church within the sphere of its spiritual government and jurisdiction'.[85] The Articles Declaratory also acknowledges the 'mutual duties' of Church and State to one another.[86] This explicit recognition of autonomy seems preferable to the English situation where there is 'no formal statement of how the Church of England and the State are to interact'.[87]

The recognition of autonomy in the 1921 Act also has ramifications for the relationship between the Church and the secular courts. A dividing line is drawn between 'matters spiritual', which are to be exclusively determined by the courts of the Church, and all other matters (which may be dubbed 'matters civil'), which are to be exclusively determined by the courts of the State. This protects the autonomy of the Church. Although the courts of the Church of Scotland are courts of the realm,[88] they are treated as a parallel jurisdiction and the secular courts have traditionally refused to review their decisions.[89] It also preserves the power of the State. Section 3 of the 1921 Act provides that nothing in that Act 'shall affect or prejudice the jurisdiction of the civil courts in relation to any matter of a civil nature'.

The application of these principles was tested in *Percy* v. *Church of Scotland Board of National Mission*,[90] a sex discrimination claim brought against the Church by a former minister. The House of Lords concluded that the claim did not fall into the category 'matters spiritual' under section 3 of the 1921 Act and was not, therefore, within the exclusive cognisance of the Church and its own courts. Lord Nicholls of Birkenhead opined that although the term 'matters spiritual' is not defined, the ordinary understanding of the expression did not extend to the exercise of statutory rights attached to a contract of employment.[91] So this was a matter for the courts of the State to determine.

The milder form of establishment in Scotland does not impede the public ministry of the Church. The Articles Declaratory state that as 'a national Church', the Church of Scotland 'acknowledges its distinctive call and duty . . . to the people in every parish of Scotland through a territorial

---

[84] All existing laws were said to be 'construed in conformity' with the Articles and be subordinate to them: Church of Scotland Act 1921 s. 1.

[85] Articles Declaratory, Art. IV.   [86] Article VI.

[87] P. W. Edge and G. Harvey, 'Introduction' in P. W. Edge and G. Harvey (eds.), *Law and Religion in Contemporary Society* (Aldershot: Ashgate, 2000), p. 2.

[88] *Presbytery of Lewis* v. *Fraser* (1874) IR 888; *Logan* v. *Presbytery of Dumbarton* (1995) SLT 1228.

[89] *Lockhart* v. *Presbytery of Deer* (1851) 13 D 1296; *Wight* v. *Presbytery of Dunkeld* (1870) 8 M 921; F. Cranmer, 'Judicial Review and Church Courts in the Law of Scotland' [1998] *Denning Law Journal* 49.

[90] [2005] UKHL 73.   [91] At para. 40. See also Lord Hope of Craighead at paras. 133–4.

ministry'.[92] Only Church of Scotland Ministers are automatically entitled to solemnise a marriage;[93] and the Marriage (Scotland) Act 1977 recognises as valid any form of ceremony recognised by the Church of Scotland 'as sufficient for the solemnisation of marriages'. The difference compared with English establishment in respect of marriage, therefore, is that the connections between Church and State in Scotland are to be found more explicitly in legislation and are clearer to understand. The Church of Scotland Act 1921 provides a significant level of protection for the religious freedom of that Church. Both advocates and critics of establishment in England might learn a great deal from the Scottish model.

Non-established religious groups

Another aspect of the establishment debate that is often overlooked is the way in which the legal position of other religious groups differs from that of the Church of England. This is necessary to shed further light upon what being 'established by law' means in practice and what the effect of disestablishment would be. The remainder of this chapter explores the legal status of the non-established religious groups.[94]

Since toleration, religious groups other than the Church of England have been lawful and allowed to practise their religion. As discussed in Chapter 3, there are several legal mechanisms which require religious groups to register to acquire a certain legal status, most notably in the form of registration as a place of religious worship,[95] for the solemnisation of marriage[96] or as a charity for the advancement of religion – and such registration brings with it considerable fiscal advantages. Regardless of registration status, however, all religious groups are usually treated as voluntary associations. The law relating to these may be summarised as comprising the doctrine of consensual compact, the principle of non-interference and the *Forbes* v. *Eden* exception, which will now be explored further.

The doctrine of consensual compact

Religion in the United Kingdom is organised on a private basis: in short, the legal status of religious groups is similar to that of a sports club.[97] Religious groups are treated as voluntary associations. These exist where two or more

---

[92] Church of Scotland Act 1921, Articles Declaratory, Art. III. This commitment to 'territorial ministry' is currently the subject of scrutiny by a commission appointed by the General Assembly of the Church.

[93] Marriage (Scotland) Act 1924 s. 18.

[94] For a fuller discussion, see J. Rivers, *The Law of Organized Religions* (Oxford: Oxford University Press, 2010), especially ch. 3.

[95] Places of Worship Registration Act 1855.   [96] Marriage Act 1949 s. 41.

[97] See M. James, *Sports Law* (Hampshire: Palgrave, 2010), ch. 2.

people voluntarily agree to be bound together for common purposes and to undertake mutual duties and obligations. The powers of the religious body derive from the agreement of its members. The relationship of the members as between themselves is governed by quasi-contract and, as a matter of law, the organisation is treated as a members' club or an unincorporated association. Unincorporated associations have no legal personality distinct from their members (unlike a corporation): they cannot sue or be sued and cannot hold property. Any property is held jointly by the members. However, institutions within the religious group may be legal owners of property if they have the status of corporations or trusts. Religious voluntary associations seeking legal personality can form a limited company.

The fact that religious groups are treated legally as voluntary associations means that the rules and structures of voluntary associations are binding on assenting members. This contractual bond may be referred to the doctrine of 'consensual compact'. As Lord Kingsdown acknowledged in *Long* v. *Bishop of Cape Town*,[98] members 'may adopt rules for enforcing discipline within their body which will be binding on those who, expressly or by implication, have assented to them'. Furthermore, it is often understood that these rules and structures are also binding on the association itself.[99] The doctrine is most fully elucidated in the Australian case of *Scandrett* v. *Dowling*,[100] where it was held that 'the binding effect of the "voluntary consensual compact" . . . must have come from the shared faith of the members of the Church, or . . . their baptism in Christ'. The binding effect of the rules of the Church arises from 'a willingness to be bound to it because of shared faith' rather than 'the availability of the secular sanctions of State courts of law'.

This means that unlike the Church of England, other religious groups are generally regulated by private rather than public law. Non-established groups are generally regulated by trusts and contract law.[101] However, religious groups are occasionally recognised by statute. Examples include the Sharing of Church Buildings Act 1969 as well as more specific pieces of legislation such as the Methodist Church Act 1976, Dawar-e-Hadiyah (England) Act 1993 and United Reformed Church Acts 1972, 1981 and 2000. Occasionally, an Act of Parliament gives some recognition to the law of religious groups. Notably, the Baptist and Congregational Trusts Act 1951 recognises the 'constitution' in the Baptist 'handbook', while the Methodist

---

[98] (1863) 1 Moore NS Cases 461.

[99] For example, in *Davies* v. *Presbyterian Church of Wales* [1986] 1 WLR 323, Lord Templemen held that: 'The law imposes on the church a duty not to deprive a pastor of his office which carries a stipend, save in accordance with the procedures set forth in [its] book of rules'.

[100] [1992] 27 NSWLR 483.

[101] The recognition of the canon law of the Roman Catholic Church may be typical. See N. Doe, *The Legal Framework of the Church of England* (Oxford: Clarendon Press, 1996), pp. 22–6. Of course, these private law instruments are also used in the Church of England, but alongside the public law instruments discussed above.

Church Act 1976 gave statutory recognition to and made further provision for the internal 'constitution' of the Methodist Church and its deed of union and model trust deeds. However, this public law recognition of non-established religious groups is exceptional.

The Principle of Non-Interference

The doctrine of consensual compact means that the religious groups are generally self-regulated, but that English law recognises the binding effect of their rules. This raises the question of when, if ever, English law will adjudicate on or enforce these internal rules. The general rule is that the courts of the State are normally reluctant to become involved in adjudicating internal disputes within religious groups. This discernible reticence on the part of the English courts to become involved in adjudicating disputes within churches can be described as the Non-Interference Principle.[102]

This principle is most fully elucidated in the High Court decision in *HH Sant Baba Jeet Singh Maharaj* v. *Eastern Media Group Ltd.*[103] A defamation claim was brought against the *Sikh Times* in respect of an article which alleged amongst other things that the claimant, His Holiness Sant Baba Jeet Singh Ji Maharaj, was the leader of a cult and an imposter. On the first day of the trial the defendant applied for the claim to be stayed as being non-justiciable. Eady J agreed that the action was to be stayed due to what he called 'the well-known principle of English law to the effect that the courts will not attempt to rule upon doctrinal issues or intervene in the regulation or governance of religious groups'.[104] He noted that there were two reasons for this rule. The first is that 'the courts are secular and stand back from religious issues while according respect to the rights of those who are adherents or worshippers in any such grouping'. The principle is therefore 'a matter of a self-denying ordinance, applied as a matter of public policy'. The second reason is that 'such disputes as arise between the followers of any given religious faith are often likely to involve doctrines or beliefs which do not readily lend themselves to the sort of resolution which is the normal function of a judicial tribunal'. He held that this was 'a question of simply recognising the natural and inevitable limitations upon the judicial function' in that 'questions of faith or doctrinal opinion . . . cannot be finally determined by the methodology regularly brought to bear on conflicts of factual and expert evidence'.

---

[102] This is also known as the 'doctrine of non-justiciability': see J. Rivers, *The Law of Organized Religions* (Oxford: Oxford University Press, 2010), p. 73. In *HH Sant Baba Jeet Singh*, it is only described as the 'doctrine of judicial abstention' (para. 6). Dingemans uses the term 'doctrine of non-interference' to describe the 'specific situation rule' discussed below in Chapter 5: see J. Dingemans, 'The Need for a Principled Approach for Religious Freedoms' (2010) 12(3) *Ecclesiastical Law Journal* 371.

[103] [2010] EWHC (QB) 1294.   [104] Para. 5.

Eady J was by no means the first judge to recognise this principle.[105] In *Gilmour* v. *Coats*,[106] Lord Reid held that: 'No temporal court of law can determine the truth of any religious belief: it is not competent to investigate any such matter and it ought not to attempt to do so.'[107] However, Eady J's judgment gives the fullest elucidation of the non-interference principle. Eady J held that, where this principle was to be invoked, it was desirable that the challenge should be made at an early stage in the litigation.[108] The role of the court would be 'to identify all the issues that the pleadings throw up for resolution and to decide whether they fall within the doctrine of judicial abstention'. This requires a specific inquiry to be made on the facts rather than a reaction based on general impressions. The question for the court is whether the facts can still be determined by the court once the primary doctrinal or other religious issues are excluded. Whilst it is possible for some questions to be resolved in purely factual terms, in other circumstances divorcing the facts from issues of religious doctrine 'may be disproportionate or distort the true extent of the parties' conflict'. Similarly, 'it may transpire that the residue or rump of purely factual questions [is] incidental or peripheral to the primary conflict. They may have become so isolated from their true context that there would be no point in the court going on to resolve them'. The question, put simply, is whether 'issues of a religious or doctrinal nature permeate the proceedings in this case'.[109] This is similar to the interpretation of the Church of Scotland Act 1921 following *Percy*:[110] the question is whether it is a civil or spiritual matter.

The non-interference principle means that, as a general rule, the variously styled courts and tribunals of all religious communities other than the Church of England are not subject to judicial review by the High Court.[111] In *R. v. Chief Rabbi, ex parte Wachmann*,[112] the claimant sought a judicial review of a decision by the Chief Rabbi, following a commission of enquiry, that Wachmann was no longer morally and religiously fit to hold rabbinical office on grounds of procedural unfairness. Simon Brown J refused leave on the grounds that there was no 'governmental interest in the decision-making power in question'. He held that the Chief Rabbi's 'functions are essentially

---

[105] See also the passages in *R* v. *Secretary of State for Education and Employment and others, ex parte Williamson* [2005] UKHL 15, cited in Chapter 3.

[106] [1949] AC 426.

[107] At 455. See also *Blake* v. *Associated Newspapers* [2003] EWHC 1960.

[108] Para. 6.   [109] Para. 28.   [110] [2005] UKHL 73.

[111] The position in Scotland is quite different. The Court of Session does not require a contested decision to contain any public law element in order for it to be reviewable (see *West* v. *Secretary of State for Scotland* [1992] SC 385). This means that it does not hesitate to review decisions by the tribunals of voluntary bodies where a patrimonial interest is involved. See, e.g. *Brentnall* v. *Free Presbyterian Church of Scotland*, [1986] SLT 470. For a recent example of Scottish judicial review proceedings of the decision of the Synod of the Free Presbyterian Church of Scotland see *Macdonald, Re Application for Judicial Review* [2010] ScotCS CSOH 55 (28 April 2010).

[112] [1992] 1 WLR 1036.

to initiate spiritual and religious functions which the government could not and would not seek to discharge in his place were he to abdicate his regulatory responsibility'. He held that courts are 'hardly in a position to regulate' religious functions: 'The court must inevitably be wary of entering so self-evidently sensitive an area, straying across the well-recognised divide between church and state.'[113]

The reasoning in *Wachmann* seems questionable on several counts. The 'incidents of establishment' discussed above undermine judicial rhetoric about a 'divide' between Church and State. Also, more technically, it may be observed that the test for judicial review is the presence of 'public' functions not 'governmental'.[114] However, the denial of judicial review in *Wachmann* has been followed in relation to decisions made, for instance, by an Imam,[115] a Jewish Beth Din[116] and the Provincial Court of the Church in Wales.[117] This does not mean, however, that there may not be a different outcome in a case where the necessary public element was present. Moreover, the absence of judicial review does not mean that these religious courts operate outside the legal system. As we will see in Chapter 9, some courts, including the Jewish Beth Din, operate under the Arbitration Act 1996. Moreover, whilst English law does not recognise the other religious courts as such, the doctrine of consensual compact means that English law does recognise the binding effect of their rules. This means that despite the general reluctance to intervene, secular courts will get involved in certain circumstances. The non-interference principle is subject to the *Forbes v. Eden* exception.

The *Forbes* v. *Eden* exception

Although the courts of the State are reluctant to become involved in adjudicating internal disputes within religious groups, they will exceptionally intervene to enforce the laws of a religious group where there is a financial interest and in relation to the disposal and administration of property. This exception to the rule may be described as the *Forbes v. Eden* exception, after the leading case.[118] The law was summarised by Lord Hope in the Supreme Court decision in *R (on the application of E) v. JFS Governing Body*.[119] Citing the cases mentioned above, Lord Hope held that: 'It has long been

---

[113] At 1043.   [114] *O'Reilly* v. *Mackman* [1983] 2 AC 237.

[115] *R.* v. *Imam of Bury Park, ex parte Sulaiman Ali* [1994] COD 142.

[116] *R.* v. *London Beth Din, ex parte Bloom* [1998] COD 131.

[117] *R.* v. *Provincial Court of the Church in Wales, ex parte Clifford Williams* (1999) 5 Ecc LJ 129.

[118] *Forbes* v. *Eden* (1867) LR 1 Sc & Div 568. See also *General Assembly of the Free Church of Scotland* v. *Lord Overtoun* [1904] AC 515. For a recent example see *Dean* v. *Burne* [2009] EWHC (Ch) 1250, discussed by J. Rivers, 'How Not to Change a Patriarch: A Discussion of *Dean* v. *Burne*' (2010) 12 *Ecclesiastical Law Journal* 71.

[119] [2009] UKSC 15. See Chapter 8.

understood that it is not the business of the courts to intervene in matters of religion.'[120] However, he went on to note that:

> It is just as well understood, however, that the divide is crossed when the parties to the dispute have deliberately left the sphere of matters spiritual over which the religious body has exclusive jurisdiction and engaged in matters that are regulated by the civil courts.[121]

The *Forbes* v. *Eden* exception can therefore be understood using the language of *Percy*:[122] State courts will get involved if the dispute relates to a civil rather than a spiritual matter. This balances the need to protect the autonomy of religious groups against the need to ensure that those religious groups still operate within the law of the State. The practice was expressed eloquently by Sir Robert Phillimore in *Brown* v. *Curé of Montréal*:[123]

> [If] this Church were to be regarded merely as a private and voluntary religious society resting only upon a consensual basis, Courts of Justice are still bound, when due complaint is made that a member of the society has been injured as to his rights, in any matter of a mixed spiritual and temporal character, to inquire into the laws or rules of the tribunal or authority which has inflicted the alleged injury.

Moreover, due to the doctrine of consensual compact, where the secular courts do intervene they will adjudicate the matter by reference to the rules and regulations of the religious group. As Lord Cranworth held in *Forbes* v. *Eden*, where courts intervene with regard to the disposal and administration of property, they 'must necessarily take cognizance of . . . the rules of a religious association [which] prescribe who shall be entitled to occupy a house, or to have the use of a chapel or other building'.[124] In other words, State courts will apply religious law, but only where they involve property – and not always even then.[125] However, even then the enquiry should be limited. The secular court may apply religious law to resolve the question of who owns property, but it should not seek to resolve questions concerning religious truths. As Patten J held in *Varsani* v. *Jesani*,[126] the State courts are not well equipped to resolve impasses caused by a division in belief between two groups. He held that in line with Article 9 of the ECHR, the role of the court is to make 'proper provision for both groups without adjudicating on the central issue that divides them'.[127]

Conclusions

The difference between the legal position of established and non-established religious groups is perhaps best illustrated by reference to the only church

---

[120] Para. 157.   [121] Para. 158.   [122] [2005] UKHL 73.   [123] (1874) LR 6 PC 157.
[124] (1867) LR 1 Sc & Div 568 at 584.   [125] See further Chapter 9.   [126] [1999] Ch 219.
[127] At paras. 11–12.

that has been disestablished during the twentieth century. The legal position of the Church in Wales is a hybrid of the established and non-established churches. The Welsh Church Act 1914 disestablished the Church of England in Wales and created the Church in Wales.[128] However, although the Act made the Church in Wales like all other non-established groups in several respects by removing many of the incidents of establishment, certain 'vestiges of establishment' continue to apply to it, meaning that the Church in Wales continues to enjoy some constitutional links with the State.[129]

On the one hand, the Welsh Church Act 1914 severed many of the relationships between Church and State. The Crown lost all powers of appointment and no bishops of the Church in Wales were to sit in the House of Lords.[130] From 31 March 1920, the Church of England, so far as it extended to and existed in Wales, ceased 'to be established by law'.[131] This meant that the 'ecclesiastical law of the Church in Wales' ceased to exist in Wales as the law of the land and the existing ecclesiastical courts in Wales ceased 'to exercise any jurisdiction'.[132] These provisions indicate what the vital characteristics of establishment are; ironically, it is the Welsh Church Act 1914 that provides the clearest statutory elucidation of how the Church of England is 'established by law' by defining what disestablishment required.

However, the 1914 Act did not simply disestablish the Church in Wales and leave it in the same legal position as all other religious groups.[133] There are two qualifications which need to be made. Firstly, the relationship between the Church and the people of Wales has not been severed. Despite disestablishment, many of the incidents of establishment concerning the public ministry of the church legal rights have remained as important 'vestiges of establishment', most notably the right to be married in the parish church[134] and burial rights.[135]

The second qualification is that the Act actually provided for the Church in Wales to become a voluntary association in a similar legal position as the non-established religious groups. As the judiciary has noted, the Act's

---

[128] See N. Doe, *The Law of the Church in Wales* (Cardiff: University of Wales Press, 2002), ch. 1.

[129] See T. G. Watkin, 'The Vestiges of Establishment: the Ecclesiastical and Canon Law of the Church in Wales' (1990) 2 *Ecclesiastical Law Journal* 110.

[130] Welsh Church Act 1914 s.2(2).　　[131] Section 1.　　[132] Section 3(1).

[133] *Representative Body of the Church in Wales* v. *Tithe Redemption Commission* [1944] 1 All ER 710.

[134] Welsh Church (Temporalities) Act 1919 s. 6; Marriage Act 1949 s. 78(2). Indeed, the Marriage (Wales) Act 2010 extends the categories of persons entitled to be married in the parish church beyond 'parishioner' to include others having certain 'qualifying connections'. This brings the Church in Wales in line with the Church of England, following the Church of England Marriage Measure 2008.

[135] Welsh Church (Burial Grounds) Act 1945. A further 'vestige of establishment' can be found in the law on prison chaplaincy. Welsh prison chaplains must be clerics of the Church in Wales: Prison Act 1952 s. 53(4). Interestingly, the 'incidents of 'establishment' in relation to education have not remained: see Chapter 8.

objective was 'to re-establish the Church in Wales on a contractual basis'[136] as a 'voluntary organisation'.[137] The Act provided that the existing law of the Church of England would continue to bind members of the Church in Wales 'in the same manner as if they had mutually agreed to be so bound', subject to modification or alteration, according to the constitution and regulations of the new institutional Church in Wales.[138] Further, the Church in Wales was permitted to establish courts; but such courts cannot exercise coercive jurisdiction and their decisions cannot be appealed against.[139] The Act stated that the law of the church was to 'be capable of being enforced in the temporal courts in relation to any property which by virtue of this Act is held on behalf of the said Church or any members thereof, in the same manner and to the same extent as if such property had been expressly assured upon trust to be held on behalf of persons who should be so bound'.[140] This provides the clearest statutory elucidation of the legal position of non-established religious groups – the difference being that in the case of the Church in Wales, the doctrine of consensual compact was imposed by statute.

As the diagram below shows, by examining the legal position of the Church in Wales it is possible to shed light upon the legal position of the Church of England and all religious groups as well as the differences between them:

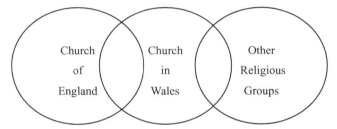

Figure 1: The legal position of the Church in Wales.

As Doe puts it, the 'Church in Wales is regulated by two broad categories of law: the law of the Church and the law of the State'.[141] However, a neat dividing line cannot be drawn between the two. The law of the Church is both 'received and enacted': 'the law of the Church is found in instruments that the Church has created for itself since disestablishment, and in a host of sources predating but inherited by the Church at disestablishment' as

---

136 *Powell* v. *Representative Body of the Church in Wales* [1957] 1 All ER 400 at 403.
137 *Re Clergy Orphan Corporation Trusts* [1933] 1 Ch 267.
138 Section 3(4) provided that: 'The power of making by such constitution and regulations alterations and modifications in ecclesiastical law shall include the power of altering and modifying such law so far as it is embodied in any Act of Parliament.'
139 Welsh Church Act 1914 s.3(3). See *R.* v. *Provincial Court of the Church in Wales, ex parte Clifford Williams* (1999) 5 Ecc LJ 217.
140 Welsh Church Act 1914 s.3(2).
141 N. Doe, *The Law of the Church in Wales* (Cardiff: University of Wales Press, 2002), p. 3.

well as by pieces of State law. The legal position of the Church in Wales thus gives further support to the overlapping nature of religion law and religious law discussed in Chapter 1. The law of the Church in Wales comprises both religion law and religious law.

Yet, on the other hand, the differences between the legal position of the Church of England and all other religious groups undermine the usefulness of 'religion law' as a label. It may be preferable to see the incidents of establishment as being part of 'ecclesiastical law' rather than of 'religion law'. The language of the Welsh Church Act 1914 underlines this conclusion. However, even if it is accepted that the term 'ecclesiastical law' ought to be used to describe the law that applies to the established Church, the law relating to other religious groups now seems so fully developed that it may be considered as part of religion law. The non-interference principle, in particular, may now be seen as a key proposition of religion law. Moreover, international developments and the plethora of new laws concerning religion mean that increasingly it is not possible to examine the law relating to the Church of England in isolation. The ecclesiastical law of the established Church interacts with wider religion law. As a result, even if one chooses to speak of the ecclesiastical law of the Church of England, that body of law can be understood as being a key part of religion law.

The next two chapters will explore in more detail the two major changes which have transformed twenty-first-century religion law: the jurisprudence under the Human Rights Act 1998, explored in Chapter 5, and the case law on religious discrimination, explored in Chapter 6. However, in exploring these new developments, it is important to understand that they do not exist in a legal or historical vacuum. The establishment of the Church of England provides part of the context in which these laws exist. Analysis of the interaction of law and religion in England and Wales is no longer an exclusive analysis of the law of the established Church – but the law pertaining to the Church of England remains an important part of that analysis.

5

Religious freedom as a human right

Introduction

It is often claimed that the Human Rights Act 1998 has brought about a legal revolution. As Chapter 2 contended, the human rights era marks a substantial shift in the way in which law and religion interact. Although a number of laws affecting religion were passed following toleration, no general explicit freedom of religion provision was to be found in English law. Religious liberty existed as a broad and largely negative freedom rather than a positive right. Laws protecting religion were ad hoc and exceptional. The Human Rights Act 1998 changed this, giving domestic force to Article 9 of the European Convention on Human Rights (ECHR). The passive tolerance of religious difference was superseded by the prescriptive regulation of religion and the active promotion of religious liberty as a right.

This chapter will examine the actual effect of the Human Rights Act 1998, exploring what effect the incorporation of the Article 9 right to freedom of thought, conscience and religion into domestic law has had so far.[1] In the context of religious freedom, the Act has already been argued in a plethora of cases concerning a range of issues such as corporal punishment, religious dress, purity rings, sacred bullocks and open air funeral pyres.[2] This chapter begins with a very brief description of the Article 9 case law of the European Court of Human Rights at Strasbourg before analysing the English case law chronologically to map the rise and fall of Article 9 in domestic jurisprudence.

---

[1] The following develops arguments first made in M. Hill and R. Sandberg, 'Is Nothing Sacred? Clashing Symbols in a Secular World' [2007] *Public Law* 488; and R. Sandberg, 'The Changing Position of Religious Minorities in English Law: The Legacy of *Begum*' in R. Grillo *et al.* (ed.), *Legal Practice and Cultural Diversity* (Aldershot: Ashgate, 2009), p. 267.

[2] The impact of other Articles upon religious individuals and groups are discussed elsewhere in this book. Although Article 9 is an individual right, Strasbourg has accepted that a religious group 'is capable of possessing and exercising the rights . . . in its own capacity as a representative of its members': *X and the Church of Scientology* v. *Sweden* (1979) 16 D&R 68. See also the discussion of s. 13 of the Human Rights Act 1998 which includes a special provision recognising the Convention rights of religious organisations and the House of Lords judgment in *Aston Cantlow* v. *Wallbank* [2003] UKHL 37, discussed in Chapter 4. On the human rights of religious groups, see J. Rivers, *The Law of Organized Religions* (Oxford: Oxford University Press, 2010), ch. 2.

Article 9 of the ECHR

The effect of the Human Rights Act 1998 is that Article 9 of the ECHR is now directly justiciable in domestic courts. It provides:

1. Everyone has the right to freedom of thought, conscience and religion; this right includes freedom to change his religion or belief, and freedom, either alone or in community with others and in public or private, to manifest his religion or belief, in worship, teaching, practice and observance.
2. Freedom to manifest one's religion or beliefs shall be subject only to such limitations as are prescribed by law and are necessary in a democratic society in the interests of public safety, for the protection of public order, health or morals, or the protection of the rights and freedoms of others.

In line with other international human rights instruments on religious liberty,[3] Article 9(1) provides a positive right to both the freedom of thought, conscience and religion (known as the *forum internum*) and the manifestation of one's religion or belief (the *forum externum*).

The right to freedom of thought, conscience and religion is unqualified. This includes the right to hold a religion or belief and to change it. In contrast, the right to manifest one's religion or belief is qualified by Article 9(1) in that the manifestation must be 'in worship, teaching, practice and observance' and, more importantly, by the possible qualifications in Article 9(2). These permit the State to interfere with the right if the three tests in Article 9(2) are met. The interference must be 'prescribed by law', have one of the legitimate aims listed in Article 9(2) and 'be necessary in a democratic society'.

An examination of the burgeoning Article 9 jurisprudence of the European Court of Human Rights at Strasbourg conveys that most decisions concern the right to manifest. Strasbourg decisions often follow a set formula. After stressing the importance of the right, quoting from its leading decision in *Kokkinakis* v. *Greece*,[4] the Court (and formerly the Commission)[5] begins by determining the question of interference; that is, whether there is an interference with the right to manifest under Article 9(1). If there is an interference, the focus then moves on to the question of justification, to determine whether the interference was justified under Article 9(2). The following examines how these two questions have been developed at Strasbourg.

---

[3] Universal Declaration on Human Rights 1948, Art. 18; International Covenant on Civil and Political Rights 1966, Art. 18; Declaration on the Elimination of All Forms of Intolerance and Discrimination based on Religion or Belief 1981, Art. 1 and 6.

[4] (1994) 17 EHRR 397.

[5] From November 1998, a Committee of three judges or a Chamber of seven judges considers the admissibility of an application. Prior to this, a Commission was charged with the task. Chambers of seven judges or a Grand Chamber of seventeen judges decide whether or not there has been a violation of the ECHR (Art. 27). See F. Cranmer, 'Religion, Human Rights and the Council of Europe' (2009) 162 *Law & Justice* 36.

Article 9(1): the question of interference

In most cases, the question of whether there is an interference (which is sometimes styled as asking whether Article 9 is engaged)[6] is a formality. This is to be welcomed. It is usually unnecessary to dismiss claims on the basis that the claimant's right to freedom of religion has not been interfered with. It is preferable for the Court to accept that there has been an interference and then to consider the factual merits of the claim properly and fully using the question of justification under Article 9(2).[7] Focusing solely on the question of interference leads to 'broad brush' judgments which may lack the nuance required not only to do justice in the instant case, but also to serve as useful precedents. Although the Strasbourg Court tends to examine the question of justification even when it has held that there was no interference, this analysis is invariably shorter and shallower as a result of this finding. Moreover, focusing on the question of interference may lead future courts to dispense entirely with the discussion of justification. After all, if there is no interference, the question of justification does not rise.

However, despite this tendency not to focus on the question of interference, three filtering devices have been developed by the Court to exclude superfluous claims at the interference stage: the definition of belief, the manifestation/motivation requirement and the specific situation rule. The following will discuss the Strasbourg application of these filtering devices in turn.

The definition of belief filter

As discussed in Chapter 3, Strasbourg institutions have adopted an expansive definition of religion or belief. Although exceptionally claimants have been required to prove the *existence* of the religion or belief in question,[8] it is the definition of 'belief', rather than the definition of 'religion' that is often employed as a filter. Strasbourg jurisprudence, relating to the use of the term in Article 2 of the first protocol to the ECHR,[9] requires that the belief for which protection is sought must be a world view held with 'a certain level of cogency, serious reflection and importance'.[10] However, Strasbourg has seldom held that a claim has not met this definition.[11]

---

[6] Sometimes these are seen as two separate tests, but most often they are seen as one test.

[7] See Chapter 3 for a similar argument in relation to the definition of religion.

[8] *X* v. *UK* (1977) 11 DR 55.

[9] Which provides, inter alia, that 'the State shall respect the right of parents to ensure such education and teaching in conformity with their own religious and philosophical convictions'.

[10] *Campbell and Cosans* v. *United Kingdom* (1982) 4 EHRR 293.

[11] For a rare example, see *Pretty* v. *United Kingdom* (2002) 35 EHRR 1.

The manifestation/motivation requirement

The second potential filter requires that the claimant's actions manifest their religion or belief as opposed to being merely motivated by it. The leading decision is *Arrowsmith* v. *United Kingdom*,[12] concerning Arrowsmith's conviction under the Incitement to Disaffection Act 1934 for distributing leaflets to soldiers discouraging them from accepting postings to Northern Ireland. The Commission held that the conviction did not breach the defendant's right to manifest her belief under Article 9 on the grounds that the term practice 'does not cover each act which is motivated or influenced by a religion or a belief'. Although the applicant was 'motivated or influenced' by her belief, she did not 'actually express the belief concerned'. The leaflets did not reflect her pacifist beliefs, but were simply opposed to the UK Government's policy in Northern Ireland. This distinction between 'manifestation' and 'motivation' has proved controversial. As Edge has suggested, as a matter of logic, it is the motivation of the claimant which is important:

> Consider an individual with their hands clasped, reciting the Lord's Prayer aloud – This would seem to constitute an act religious in nature. Add the individual's atheism, a camera crew, and a line in a film script 'Actor Prays' and it is no longer religious in nature. The distinctive feature is the presence or absence of religious motivation.[13]

The more recent tendency of the Court not to apply the manifestation/motivation requirement is therefore to be welcomed.[14] The test now tends to be articulated in broader terms: it has often been rephrased as requiring, for example,[15] that the action is 'intimately linked' to the claimant's religion or belief.[16] This requirement is less strict. It simply requires a form of causation between the claimant's actions and his or her religion or belief.

The specific situation rule

The third filtering device recognises that a person's Article 9 rights may be influenced by the particular situation of the individual claiming that freedom. This principle is not of universal application: it only applies where someone has voluntarily submitted themselves to a system of norms, usually

---

[12] (1981) 3 EHRR 218.

[13] See P. W. Edge, 'Current Problems in Article 9 of the European Convention on Human Rights' (1996) *Juridical Review* 42, 45–6.

[14] S. Knights, *Freedom of Religion, Minorities and the Law* (Oxford: Oxford University Press, 2007), p. 44.

[15] In *Knudsen* v. *Norway* (1985) 42 DR 247, the question asked was whether the actions 'give expression' to their religion or belief.

[16] *C* v. *UK* (1983) 37 DR 142, 144; *Hasan and Chaush* v. *Bulgaria* (2002) 34 EHRR 55.

by means of a contract. This voluntary submission creates a 'specific situation' which limits the claimant's right to manifest. Strasbourg has applied this rule in relation to a detained person,[17] a person who voluntarily submits to military service,[18] a person who voluntarily enters into a contract of employment[19] and those who voluntarily enrol at a university.[20] Strasbourg has held that once the claimant is in such a situation, then they cannot subsequently claim a breach of Article 9.[21] This has been criticised as being very limited and impracticable.[22] It means that Article 9 has a very limited application in the employment sphere.[23]

In *Jewish Liturgical Association Cha'are Shalom Ve Tsedek* v. *France*,[24] Strasbourg seemed to go further by imposing an 'impossibility test': the Court commented that an 'alternative means of accommodating religious beliefs had . . . to be "impossible" before a claim of interference under article 9 could succeed'. This gave general applicability to the specific situation rule. However, more recent cases have seen a change in approach. As Knights points out, Strasbourg now takes 'a broader view of what amounts to an interference'.[25] A slacker approach is clearly visible in *Şahin* v. *Turkey*,[26] concerning a university regulation banning a student from wearing a headscarf at enrolment, lectures and examinations. Although the specific situation rule was referred to by the Court,[27] the Court proceeded 'on the assumption that the regulations in issue, which placed restrictions of place and manner on the right to wear the Islamic headscarf in universities, constituted an interference with the applicant's right to manifest her religion'.[28] The same was true in *Dogru* v. *France*,[29] concerning the wearing of the Islamic headscarf at school. The argument of the French Government and the focus of the Court was upon the question of justification under Article 9(2) and not the question of interference under Article 9(1).[30] Such cases

---

[17] *X* v. *United Kingdom* (1974) 1 D&R 41 (on the basis that the prisoner had broken his contract with society).

[18] *Kalaç* v. *Turkey* (1997) 27 EHRR 552.

[19] *Stedman* v. *United Kingdom* (1997) 5 EHRR 544; *Ahmad* v. *United Kingdom* (1981) 4 EHRR 126.

[20] *Karaduman* v. *Turkey* (1993) 74 DR 93.

[21] Dingemans has referred to the 'specific situation rule' as the 'doctrine of non-interference'. For a critique of the doctrine, see J. Dingemans, 'The Need for a Principled Approach for Religious Freedoms' (2010) 12(3) *Ecclesiastical Law Journal* 371–8.

[22] See, e.g. L. Vickers, *Religious Freedom, Religious Discrimination and the Workplace* (Oxford: Hart, 2008), p. 116.

[23] As well as in other public institutions such as prisons and Higher Education.

[24] (2000) 9 BHRC 27.

[25] S. Knights, *Freedom of Religion, Minorities and the Law* (Oxford: Oxford University Press, 2007), p. 44.

[26] (2005) 41 EHRR 8.

[27] 'Article 9 does not protect every act motivated or inspired by a religion or belief and does not in all cases guarantee the right to behave in the public sphere in a way which is dictated by a belief': para. 66.

[28] Para. 71.   [29] [2008] ECHR 1579.   [30] See para. 34.

convey a preference on the part of Strasbourg institutions whereby the use of filtering devices is minimised.

Article 9(2): the question of justification

The question of whether the interference with the claimant's right to manifest is justified is answered by reference to the three tests laid out in Article 9(2). The tests are applied one by one. Firstly, the interference must be 'prescribed by law'. This means that the limitation must have some basis in domestic law, should be accessible and its effects foreseeable.[31] This requirement ensures that 'rights and freedoms are not restricted except by due process of law'.[32] Secondly, the interference must have a 'legitimate aim'. These aims are outlined in Article 9(2): 'public safety, for the protection of public order, health or morals, or for the protection of the rights and freedoms of others'. These legitimate aims overlap substantially. Taylor has noted that Strasbourg institutions 'tend to accept rather than challenge the aim claimed by the State, and accordingly pass over this precondition with little detailed analysis'.[33] Thirdly, and most importantly, the interference must be 'necessary in a democratic society'. Strasbourg has held that there are two requirements: the interference must correspond to a 'pressing social need' and be 'proportionate to the legitimate aim pursued'.[34] These tests, though elastic, require courts to examine the merits of the claims weighed against societal concerns and pressures. At Strasbourg the application of the tests is buttressed further by the concept of the 'margin of appreciation', which permits a level of discretion to states in recognition of local circumstances. This allows nuanced determinations to be made.

Strasbourg jurisprudence on Article 9 as a whole shows an increasing focus upon the question of justification under Article 9(2) rather than the question of interference under Article 9(1).

The role of filtering devices is minimal and is decreasing. This is surely desirable. The devices are unnecessary since if it was simply accepted that Article 9 was engaged, the claim could nevertheless be dealt with by the use of the Article 9(2) justifications. The three filtering devices used by Strasbourg interpretation are underpinned by a rather narrow view of religion which seems to be somewhat conventional and traditional. The definition of belief excludes belief systems that fall short of a world view and which lack a degree of cogency, thus limiting protection to beliefs similar to those previously protected. The manifestation requirement seems to be underpinned by an

[31] *Kokkinakis* v. *Greece* (1994) 17 EHRR at para. 52.

[32] C. Evans, *Freedom of Religion under the European Convention on Human Rights* (Oxford: Oxford University Press, 2000), p. 138.

[33] P. M. Taylor, *Freedom of Religion: UN and European Human Rights Law and Practice* (Cambridge, Cambridge University Press, 2005), pp. 301–2.

[34] *Serif* v. *Greece* (2001) 31 EHRR 20.

assumption that religious freedom affects only a limited aspect of a person's life and that it is possible to identify activities and times where one's religion comes to the fore. Everyday activities that might have a religious motivation are excluded. Similarly, the specific situation rule is underscored by the view that there are dimensions of a person's life (most notably the employment sphere) where religion takes a back seat. In short, these filters seem to rest upon an assumption that religion belongs in the private sphere. The move beyond these filters at Strasbourg is therefore to be welcomed. Strasbourg's new focus upon the question of justification under Article 9(2), rather than the question of interference under Article 9(1), is a welcome acceptance of the multi-faced nature of religious life.

The rise of article 9 in domestic jurisprudence

The Human Rights Act 1998 has led to a number of domestic judgments concerning Article 9. The earliest decisions following the enactment of the Act were commendable in that they followed the Strasbourg approach in their interpretation of Article 9, focusing upon the question of justification rather than the question of interference. Moreover, domestic courts were not afraid to question and finesse some aspects of the Strasbourg jurisprudence. This is true of the House of Lords decision in *R. v. Secretary of State for Education and Employment and others, ex parte Williamson*[35] and the lower court judgments which followed it.

The House of Lords decision in *Williamson*

The case was brought by head teachers, teachers and parents of children at four independent Christian schools where discipline was enforced by the use of mild corporal punishment. The appellants, claiming to speak on behalf of a large body of the Christian community, contended that the ban on corporal punishment in schools[36] was incompatible with their belief that it was part of the duty of education in a Christian context. They claimed that it infringed their right to freedom of religion (under Article 9) and the right for the State to respect the rights of the parent to ensure their children's education conforms to their religious and philosophical convictions (under Article 2 of first protocol).

While lower courts sought to exclude the claim largely by reference to the Article 9(1) question of interference,[37] the House of Lords dealt with Article 9 'overly and comprehensively, paying careful attention to freedom

---

[35] [2005] UKHL 15.   [36] Education Act 1998 s. 548 (as amended in 1998).
[37] [2002] EWCA Civ 1926, see especially para. 262.

of religion and belief'.[38] The House held that although there had been interference with the appellants' Article 9 rights, this was justified under Article 9(2) as being prescribed by law,[39] necessary in a democratic society for the protection of the rights and freedoms of others, and as having a legitimate aim to protect children as a vulnerable group and promote their well-being.[40]

In reaching that decision, the law lords made a number of valuable comments about the application of Article 9. For instance, Lord Nicholls stressed that '(f)reedom of religion protects the subjective belief of an individual' and sought to clarify that while Courts may be concerned with whether the claim was made *in* good faith, they are not concerned whether it is *a* good faith in terms of judging the validity of that faith.[41] Their lordships also considered the use of filters. Lord Walker doubted whether it was right for courts, except in extreme cases, 'to impose an evaluative filter' at the stage of identifying whether there was a belief, 'especially when religious beliefs are involved'.[42] And although both Lord Nicholls[43] and Lord Walker[44] defended the use of the manifestation/motivation requirement, they seemed to support a re-formulated version of this rule. Lord Nicholls noted that:

> If, as here, the belief takes the form of a perceived obligation to act in a specific way, then, in principle, doing that act pursuant to that belief is itself a manifestation of that belief in practice. In such cases the act is 'intimately linked' to the belief, in the Strasbourg phraseology. . . . This is not to say that a perceived obligation is a prerequisite to manifestation of a belief in practice. It is not. . . . I am concerned only to identify what, in principle, is sufficient to constitute manifestation in a case where the belief is one of perceived obligation.[45]

Lord Nicholls also rejected the application of the 'specific situation' rule: although he recognised the existence of the rule, he held that this rule did not apply on the facts since there was 'no comparable special feature affecting the position of the claimant parents'.[46] He rejected the submission of the Secretary of State that there had been no interference (since the parents had 'several adequate, alternative courses of action') as being unrealistic.[47] More generally, Lord Walker contended that a holistic approach to the Article should be taken.[48]

---

[38] S. Langlaude, 'Flogging Children with Religion: A Comment on the House of Lords' Decision in *Williamson*' (2006) 8 *Ecclesiastical Law Journal* 335, 345.

[39] Since the ban was 'prescribed by primary legislation in clear terms', Lord Nicholls at para. 48.

[40] Lord Nicholls at para. 49. The means chosen to achieve that aim were appropriate and proportionate: Lord Nicholls at para. 50

[41] At para. 22–3. See further Chapter 3.   [42] At para. 57.   [43] At para. 31.

[44] At para. 62.   [45] At paras. 32–3.   [46] At paras. 38–9.

[47] At para. 40–1.   [48] At para. 57.

Lower court decisions following *Williamson*

Subsequent decisions by lower courts followed a similar approach to that adopted by the House of Lords in *Williamson*. For instance, cases on the use of drugs for a religious purpose avoided using a restrictive definition of religion as a filtering device,[49] and instead used the limitations under Article 9(2) as the means by which to determine the matter.[50] The same was true of the notable Court of Appeal judgment in *Copsey* v. *WBB Devon Clays Ltd*.[51]

The appeal brought by a claimant was dismissed after he had refused to agree to a contractual variation in his working hours which included some Sunday working. Although he was prepared to help on Sundays in an emergency, he refused to accept regular Sunday working on grounds of his Christian belief and claimed that this constituted unfair dismissal contrary to the Employment Rights Act 1996 and was in breach of Article 9.

The Court of Appeal dismissed the appeal, applying the Strasbourg specific situation rule, but singled it out for stringent criticism, stressing the importance of considering Article 9(2). Mummery LJ, in particular, was very critical of the specific situation rule, commenting that the Strasbourg rulings were 'repeated assertions unsupported by the evidence or reasoning that would normally accompany a judicial ruling', which were 'difficult to square with the supposed fundamental character of the rights'.[52] Rix LJ argued that the Strasbourg jurisprudence did not represent a body of consistent decisions where an *employer* rather than the employee sought to vary the employee's working hours.[53] The early case law therefore indicated that domestic courts were as willing as, if not more willing than, Strasbourg to focus on Article 9(2) questions of justification rather than Article 9(1) questions of interference.

The fall of article 9 in domestic jurisprudence

However, a subsequent House of Lords decision concerning Article 9 has ushered in a different, more restrictive approach. *R (on the application of Begum)* v. *Headteacher and Governors of Denbigh High School*[54] concerned Shabina Begum, a Muslim born in the United Kingdom to parents of Bangladeshi origin, who attended Denbigh High School, a mixed-sex secondary community school for pupils aged eleven to sixteen. The school

---

[49] Compare the approach in *United States* v. *Kuch* (1968) 288 F. Supp 439, as discussed in Chapter 3.

[50] *R.* v. *Taylor* [2001] EWCA Crim 2263; *R.* v. *Andrews* [2004] EWCA Crim 947. See P. W. Edge, 'Religious Drug Use in England, South Africa and the United States of America' (2006) 1(2) *Religion & Human Rights* 165–77; and R. Sandberg, 'Judging Religious Drug Use: The Misuse of the Definition of "Religion"' in H. Jungaberle, B. C. and Labate R. Verres (ed.), *The Globalization of the Use of Ayahuasca* (forthcoming).

[51] [2005] EWCA Civ 932.   [52] See paras. 30–9.

[53] See paras. 65–6.   [54] [2006] UKHL 15.

offered girls three uniform options: navy-blue trousers, knee-length skirt or *shalwar kameez* (a sleeveless smock-like dress worn to between knee and mid-calf length). On the first day of term in September 2002 Ms Begum went to the school wearing a *jilbab* (which has been judicially described as 'a long shapeless dress ending at the ankle and designed to conceal the shape of the wearer's arms and legs') and was told to go home, change and return wearing school uniform. She did not return to the school; and a solicitor's letter later contended that she had been 'excluded/suspended' from the school in breach, inter alia, of Article 9 and Article 2 of the First Protocol of the European Convention of Human Rights.[55]

While Begum was unsuccessful at first instance,[56] on the basis that her refusal to respect the school uniform policy was merely 'motivated by religious beliefs' and not a manifestation of them, that decision was reversed by the Court of Appeal.[57] Brooke, Mummery and Scott Baker LJJ held that there had been interference with Article 9(1) and that it was not justified under Article 9(2) because the school had not used a Convention-compliant decision-making structure.[58] This rests on a basic mistake.[59] While courts apply such a proportionality test when reviewing decisions of public authorities after they have been made, there is nothing in the Human Rights Act 1998, the ECHR or Convention jurisprudence that requires public authorities themselves to adopt a proportionality approach to the structuring of their own decision-making. The requirement is solely that the outcome of the decision-making is Convention compliant. The school therefore sought leave to appeal to the House of Lords.

The House of Lords decision in *Begum*

It was not surprising that the confused analysis of Article 9(2) in the Court of Appeal was reversed in the House of Lords. However, in so doing the majority of their Lordships repeated and compounded the error originally made at first instance in respect of Article 9(1). Lords Bingham of Cornhill, Hoffmann and Scott of Foscote held that there had been no interference with the applicant's rights under Article 9(1) because Article 9 does not protect all acts motivated or inspired by belief.[60] Lord Bingham summed up the specific situation rule as follows:

> The Strasbourg institutions have not been at all ready to find an interference with the right to manifest religious belief in practice or observance where a person has

---

[55] For a fuller discussion and critique of the decision, see M. Hill and R. Sandberg, 'Is Nothing Sacred? Clashing Symbols in a Secular World' [2007] *Public Law* 488.

[56] [2004] EWHC 1389.   [57] [2005] EWCA Civ 199.   [58] Paras. 75–6, 78.

[59] T. Poole, 'Of Headscarves and Heresies: The *Denbigh High School* Case and Public Authority Decision Making under the Human Rights Act' [2005] *Public Law* 685, 689–90.

[60] Para. 22.

voluntarily accepted an employment or role which does not accommodate that practice or observance and there are other means open to the person to practise or observe his or her religion without undue hardship or inconvenience.[61]

Then quoting selectively from numerous Strasbourg and domestic cases on the 'specific situation' rule, and omitting to mention references to the caveats to the rule,[62] his Lordship applied the rule to the facts of the case without explanation. Although he recognised the view of the Court of Appeal in *Copsey* v. *WBB Devon Clays Ltd*,[63] Lord Bingham effectively gave the specific situation rule general application, concluding that:

> Even if it be accepted that the Strasbourg institutions have erred on the side of strictness in rejecting complaints of interference, there remains a coherent and remarkably consistent body of authority which our domestic courts must take into account and which shows that interference is not easily established.[64]

This seems to overstate the law. Although Strasbourg has applied this rule beyond the employment sphere to include other contractual submissions to rules such as joining the military or enrolling at a university, outside these situations there is no support for the very broad proposition that 'interference is not easily established'. Lord Bingham's questionable elucidation of the specific situation rule is at odds with Strasbourg jurisprudence, taking a much more restrictive interpretation of Article 9(1). This does not adequately protect religious freedom.

Moreover, although Lord Bingham's elucidation of the specific situation rule required both voluntary acceptance of a rule *and* an alternative means to manifest religion or belief, Lord Bingham seemed to place great emphasis upon this second limb: he held that there was no interference with Begum's right to manifest her belief in practice or observance since Begum's family chose the school from outside their own catchment area and that there was 'no evidence to show that there was any real difficulty in her attending'

---

[61] Para. 23.

[62] For example, although Lord Bingham was correct to quote *Williamson* for the proposition that 'What constitutes interference depends on all the circumstances of the case' (para. 22), Lord Bingham did not point out that Lord Nicholls had stated that the rule did not apply in *Williamson* since there was 'no comparable special feature' on the facts of the case ([2005] UKHL 15 at paras. 38–9). Similarly, although Lord Bingham correctly quoted the Strasbourg case of *Ahmad* v. *United Kingdom* as stating that freedom of religion may 'be influenced by the situation of the person claiming that freedom' (para. 22), he did not mention that the Commission went on to qualify this last statement by saying that '[t]he Commission has recognised this in the case of a detained person, and in the case of a person with special contractual obligations': (1981) 4 EHRR 126 at para. 11. In his quotation of *Kalaç* v. *Turkey* (1999) 27 EHRR 552, he again failed to mention how specific Kalac's 'specific situation' was: the rule only applied due to his membership of the armed forces, which he had accepted voluntarily.

[63] [2005] EWCA Civ 932.   [64] At para. 24.

another school.[65] This conclusion was supported by Lords Hoffmann and Scott, Lord Hoffmann deciding that it was irrelevant that her choice was not contractual since 'it was a choice which she could have made'.[66] This, coupled with Lord Scott of Foscote's 'principle' concerning what he erroneously called the 'Article 9(2) right to manifest religion',[67] suggests that provided there is a choice then an applicant's Article 9 right to manifest is not even engaged. This brings domestic law in line with the Strasbourg case of *Jewish Liturgical Association Cha'are Shalom Ve Tsedek* v. *France*,[68] ironically a judgment that both Lord Hoffmann and Lord Bingham questioned.[69]

The preferable approach in *Begum* is that of Lord Nicholls and Lady Hale, who, although concurring with the ultimate disposal of the appeal, differed from the other three Law Lords in that they dealt with the appeal on the question of justification rather than the question of interference. They recognised that Article 9 had been engaged, but that the interference was justified under Article 9(2). Although their speeches did not explain why their approach was the consistent interpretation of the Strasbourg jurisprudence, their treatment of Article 9(2), together with the *obiter* treatment of Article 9(2) made by the majority, showed how the same decision could have been reached in a more satisfactory way by focusing on the question of justification rather than that of interference. The House unanimously held that if there had been interference, it would have been justified under Article 9(2) as being prescribed by law because the school authorities had the statutory authority to make rules on uniform and those rules had been very clearly communicated to those affected by them,[70] having the legitimate aim of protecting the rights and freedoms of others,[71] and being necessary in a democratic society;[72] as Lady Hale concluded, the school's uniform policy was 'a thoughtful and proportionate response to reconciling the complexities of the situation'.[73]

Lower court decisions following *Begum*

Article 9 cases since *Begum* have dwelt upon Lord Bingham's questionable assertion that 'interference is not easily established' to reject Article 9 arguments on the question of interference rather than the question of justification. In *R (on the application of X)* v. *Y School*,[74] Silber J considered the *Begum* decision as an 'an insuperable barrier'[75] to a claim for judicial

---

[65] At para. 25. This ignores the fact that it is not the family's right to manifest that is in issue; it is Begum's right.
[66] Paras. 56–7.   [67] Para. 87.   [68] (2000) 9 BHRC 27.
[69] For Hoffmann, for example, ' "impossible" may be setting the test rather high': para. 52.
[70] Lord Bingham at para. 26.
[71] Lord Bingham at para. 26, Lord Hoffmann at para. 58 and Lady Hale at para. 94.
[72] Lord Bingham para. 26, Lady Hale at para. 94.   [73] Para. 98.
[74] [2006] EWHC (Admin) 298.   [75] Para. 100.

review by a twelve-year-old schoolgirl who wished to wear a *niqab* veil while she was at school and being taught by male teachers or was likely to be seen by men. Drawing on Lord Bingham's elucidation of the 'specific situation' rule in *Begum*, Silber J interpreted this as meaning that there would be no interference *either* where a person has voluntarily accepted an employment or role that does not accommodate that practice or observance *or* where there are other means open to practise or observe that religion without undue hardship or inconvenience.[76] Ironically, Silber J's *obiter* comments on Article 9(2) underlined the weakness of this *Begum*-inspired approach: although Silber J commended the school on having in place a well-thought-out policy, the approach now taken by English law makes the quality of the policy irrelevant, since provided that the right to manifest can be exercised elsewhere, there is no interference.

Although the decision in *R (on the Application of Playfoot (A Child)* v. *Millais School Governing Body*[77] did not go quite as far as *X* v. *Y School*, the judgment nevertheless shows a stricter approach to Article 9(1) than that which existed prior to *Begum*.[78] An application for judicial review on behalf of a schoolgirl who had wanted to wear a 'purity' ring at school as a symbol of her religiously motivated commitment to celibacy before marriage was refused because the wearing of the ring was not a manifestation of that belief. Michael Supperstone QC, sitting as a Deputy High Court Judge, held that there was no interference with Article 9 since the claimant had voluntarily accepted the school's uniform policy and there were other means open to her to practise her belief without undue hardship or inconvenience.[79] He also held that the wearing of the ring was not 'intimately linked' to the belief in chastity before marriage because the claimant was under no obligation, by reason of her faith, to wear the ring. This seems to misunderstand Lord Nicholls' statement in *Williamson*. Although Lord Nicholls recognised that doing an act in pursuance of a perceived religious obligation would be a manifestation of that religion, he stressed that this did not mean that the reverse is also true: if there was no such obligation, that does not mean that the act *cannot* be a manifestation of that belief.[80]

Other post-*Begum* decisions not concerning religious dress and symbols have also displayed a restrictive and sometimes confused approach to Article 9. The High Court decision in *R (on the Application of Ghai)* v. *Newcastle City Council*[81] again stressed that interference with Article 9 is not easily established and that protection is only afforded to a narrow

[76] At para. 26.   [77] [2007] EWHC (Admin) 1698.

[78] For a fuller discussion and critique of the decision, see R. Sandberg, 'Controversial Recent Claims to Religious Liberty' (2008) 124 *Law Quarterly Review* 213.

[79] Para. 32.

[80] *R.* v. *Secretary of State for Education and Employment and others, ex parte Williamson* [2005] UKHL 15 at para. 33.

[81] [2009] EWHC (Admin) 978.

range of activities that are at the core of religious life. The case was brought by Hindus and Sikhs who sought to have cremations on open-air funeral pyres. Noting the Secretary of State's contention 'that the weight to be given to religious rights depends on how close the subject matter is to the core of the religion's values', and rejecting the submission 'that the determination of the core content of the Hindu religion is not a matter for the court', Cranston J held that Hindus' belief about an open air funeral pyre satisfied what he styled 'the *Williamson* thresholds': they had 'the requisite degree of seriousness and importance' and were 'concerned with central rather than peripheral matters'.[82] In relation to Hindu claims the High Court held that there had been an interference with Article 9(1), but that this interference was justified under Article 9(2). In contrast, Cranston J held that 'Article 9 accords no protection to the Sikh tradition of using open air funeral pyres'; because it was conceded that their use was 'simply a matter of tradition' and 'not a matter of dogma and belief'.[83] Although the High Court's decision was later reversed on appeal,[84] the Court of Appeal judgment did not focus upon the Article 9 claim.[85] Rather it was held that the accommodation of the claimant's wishes would not in fact necessarily infringe the legislation relating to cremation.[86] This does not affect the High Court's decision regarding Article 9. Although the High Court judgment in *Ghai* does not go as far as *Playfoot*, Cranston J's judgment is actually at odds with the principles found in Strasbourg jurisprudence as elucidated clearly in *Williamson*. According to *Ghai*, Article 9 protects only 'central' beliefs.

Exceptions to the rule

As a result of these judgments, significant weight is now given to the Article 9(1) filtering devices. *Begum* gave general application to the specific situation rule, while the High Court decisions in *Playfoot* and *Ghai* have narrowed the manifestation/motivation requirement so that the requirement that the action be 'intimately linked' to the claimant's belief is now interpreted as requiring that the action must be obliged by the belief or central to it. This has required courts to determine questions of theology and doctrine, which they have been traditionally reluctant to deal with.[87] However, the

---

[82] Para. 101.   [83] Para. 102.   [84] [2010] EWCA Civ 59.

[85] See P. Cumper and T. Lewis, 'Last Rites and Human Rights: Funeral Pyres and Religious Freedom in the United Kingdom' (2010) 12(2) *Ecclesiastical Law Journal* 131.

[86] Examination of the evidence suggested that Ghai's religious belief did not in fact require him to be cremated, after his death, on a pyre in the open air. His religious belief would be satisfied if the cremation process took place within a structure, provided that the cremation was by traditional fire, rather than by using electricity, and sunlight could shine directly on his body while it was being cremated. The Court of Appeal held that the legislation relating to cremation stated that cremation can only lawfully take place in a structure which is a 'building'. There was no reason why the structure acceptable to Ghai could not be a 'building'.

[87] See the 'non-interference principle' discussed in Chapter 4.

judgments of *Playfoot* and *Ghai* can be contrasted with that of *New Testament Church of God* v. *Stewart*,[88] which concerned the long-running question of whether ministers of religion should be seen as employees.[89] The church appealed against the finding of the Employment Tribunal that a minister of religion whose position as a pastor had been terminated was an employee, arguing inter alia that this decision infringed their Article 9 rights. The Court of Appeal dismissed the appeal, but expressed some enthusiasm for the Article 9 claim. Pill LJ held that the law should not readily impose a legal relationship on members of a religious community which would be contrary to their religious beliefs, while Arden LJ held that Article 9 was engaged since one aspect of freedom of religion is the freedom of a religious organisation to be allowed to function peacefully and free from arbitrary state intervention.[90] Arden LJ held that:

> A religious organisation may, as one of its beliefs, consider that ministers should not have contracts of employment or that the state should not interfere in the way they conduct their organisation. If the state interferes with that belief, there may be an interference with the group's article 9 right (though the interference will not constitute a violation of article 9 if the conditions in article 9(2) are satisfied).[91]

In contrast to other decisions post-*Begum*, this seems to recognise that the focus ought to be on the question of justification under Article 9(2) rather than that of interference under Article 9(1). Moreover, Arden LJ rejected the contrary argument that 'for article 9 to be engaged it had to be an express tenet of the religion that no contract is formed between the minister and the religious body or some part of it'. He held that rather:

> In my judgment . . . article 9 is engaged if one of the beliefs of a religious organisation is that, for instance, all adherents are equal and participate in the church's affairs as such, provided that this belief is in the context of all the factual background inconsistent with the implication of an employment relationship. . . . It is sufficient that the beliefs are found to be inconsistent with the implication of any contract or alternatively any contract of employment. . . . There must be religious beliefs that are contrary to or inconsistent with the implication of the contract or a contract of employment.[92]

The approach of Arden LJ in *Stewart* is wider than the High Court in *Playfoot* and *Ghai* and is preferable to it. Article 9 protects manifestations of religious

---

[88] [2007] EWCA Civ 1004.
[89] See also the judgments in *Percy* v. *Church of Scotland Board of Mission* [2005] UKHL 73 and *MacDonald* v. *Free Presbyterian Church of Scotland* [2010] UKEAT S/0034/09/B1 (10 February 2010). See J. Duddington, 'God, Caesar and the Employment Rights of Ministers of Religion' (2007) 159 *Law and Justice* 129–35; F. Cranmer, 'Clergy Employment, Judicial Review and the Free Presbyterian Church of Scotland' (2010) 12(3) *Ecclesiastical Law Journal* 355–60; and J. Rivers, *The Law of Organized Religions* (Oxford: Oxford University Press, 2010), ch. 4.
[90] Paras. 57, 60.   [91] Para. 61.   [92] Para. 62.

belief; it is not constrained merely to manifestations of 'central' religious beliefs as *Ghai* suggests or manifestations of 'obligatory' religious beliefs as *Playfoot* suggests.

Stewart is not the only exception to the rule. Notably the High Court in *R (on the Application of Swami Suryananda) v. Welsh Minister*[93] focused on the question of justification rather than interference, but followed the erroneous approach of the Court of Appeal in *Begum*.[94] A decision by the Welsh Assembly Government to order the slaughter of Shambo, a sacred bullock at the Hindu temple, who had tested positive for the bacterium that causes bovine tuberculosis (TB), was quashed on the basis that the Welsh Assembly Government had failed to follow an ECHR-compliant procedure. The Court of Appeal[95] unanimously allowed the appeal. Lloyd LJ held that the High Court had erroneously focused upon 'whether the decision maker proceeded in the right way', when the focus should have simply been on 'whether the decision taken does or does not infringe the relevant rights'.[96] The interference under Article 9(2) was justified: the Welsh Ministers had a public health objective, the eradication or at least control of bovine tuberculosis, and so the Minister was entitled to make the decision she did.

The significance of *Watkins-Singh*

However, other cases show that a restrictive approach to Article 9 is now the norm.[97] This impression is underscored by the decision in *R (on the application of Watkins-Singh) v. The Governing Body of Aberdare Girls' High School*.[98] The case concerned a fourteen-year-old girl of Punjabi-Welsh heritage, who was told to remove her *kara* bangle at school. She was successful because, while the school saw the issue as one concerning Article 9, the claimant's legal team relied instead on race and religious discrimination laws. This difference, stressed by Silber J at the start of his judgment,[99] allowed the court to distinguish the claim from the Article 9 case law. The question of whether the wearing of the *kara* was obligatory to the claimant, fatal to the claim in *Playfoot*, was sidestepped. Although the expert evidence

---

[93] [2007] EWHC (Admin) 1736.
[94] For a fuller discussion and critique of the decision, see R. Sandberg, 'Controversial Recent Claims to Religious Liberty' (2008) 124 *Law Quarterly Review* 213.
[95] [2007] EWCA Civ 893.   [96] Para. 103.
[97] See also the House of Lords decision in *Gallagher (Valuation Officer) v. Church of Jesus Christ of Latter-day Saints* [2008] UKHL 56, in which an argument based on Art. 9 in conjunction with Art. 14 was quickly rejected. See R. Sandberg, 'Underrating Human Rights: *Gallagher* v. *Church of Jesus Christ of the Latter-Day Saints*' (2009) 11 *Ecclesiastical Law Journal* 75–80.
[98] [2008] EWHC (Admin) 1865.
[99] The previous cases did not have this option. Part 2 of the Equality Act 2006 which extended religious discrimination to cover goods and services and the exercise of public functions was not in force: para. 3.

suggested that it was only initiated Sikhs who were required to observe all five K's, of which the *kara* was one, and Watkins-Singh was an observant but non-initiated Sikh, Silber J held that the defendant's contention that there would *only* be a disadvantage where a member of the group is prevented from wearing something that they are *required* to wear was too high a threshold.[100] Instead, he held that the needed disadvantage would occur – but would not *only* occur – where a pupil is forbidden from wearing an item where 'that person genuinely believed for reasonable grounds that wearing this item was a matter of exceptional importance to his or her racial identity or his or her religious belief' and where 'the wearing of the item can be shown objectively to be of exceptional importance to his or her religion or race, even if the wearing of the article is not an actual requirement of that person's religion or race'.[101] This objective test is seemingly contrary to *Williamson*,[102] but it is clearly more lenient than the approach in *Playfoot* or *Ghai*.

Having decided that there was a particular disadvantage, Silber J turned to the question of justification, again seeking to distinguish the instant case from the Article 9 case law: for Silber J 'decisions on justification which were successfully used by schools in the *Begum, X v. Y School* and *Playfoot* cases' did not apply since 'many of the aspects of justification relied on in those cases are related to the extremely clearly visible and very ostentatious nature of the religious dress ought to be worn'.[103] Silber J distinguished the Article 9 case law on the basis that it could not be said that allowing pupils to wear a Kara caused substantial difficulties because they may stand out or that it undermines the uniform policy's aim of fostering a community spirit because the Kara is small and is usually hidden by a long-sleeved sweater. However, while such reasoning is sustainable in relation to Muslim dress, this is hardly true of the ring in *Playfoot*. The argument that the Kara unlike a ring could be covered up is erroneous on two grounds: firstly, the Kara must have been seen by the teacher on the day on which Watkins-Singh was asked to remove it; secondly, as Silber J's language conceded, it was simply the case that it was 'usually' covered by a long sleeve as opposed to *always* being covered. In any case, it is questionable whether visibility should be a criterion.[104]

On the basis of justification, it is difficult to see why the decision in *Watkins-Singh* was the opposite of that in *Playfoot* (and, indeed, the Sikh claimant in *Ghai*).

The only conclusion that can be reached from *Watkins-Singh* is that, in relation to religious dress and symbols at least, those seeking to protect their individual religious freedom will seek to argue anything *but* Article 9. While

---

[100] Paras. 51–5.   [101] Para. 56.
[102] 'Freedom of religion protects the subjective belief of an individual': Lord Nicholls at para. 22.
[103] [2008] EWHC (Admin) 1865 at para. 78.
[104] Compare the position of the Sikh turban: see *Mandla* v. *Dowell Lee* [1983] 2 AC 548.

the threshold drawn concerning the issue of interference remains high in *Watkins-Singh*, the threshold drawn in *Begum*, *X* v. *Y School*, *Playfoot* and *Ghai* is excessively high. The result of the House of Lords decision in *Begum* is that Article 9 is of little use in religious rights claims.

Conclusions

All of the high profile cases discussed in this chapter have one thing in common: the Article 9 argument failed.[105] However, more recently the reason for the failure seems to have changed. Originally claims failed because, although there had been an interference with the claimant's Article 9(1) right, that interference had been justified under Article 9(2). The House of Lords decision in *Williamson* epitomises that approach. Now, however, it is most frequently the case that claims fail because there is no interference. The House of Lords decision in *Begum* embodies this new approach. And, although it is true that not all Article 9 cases post-*Begum* have failed on Article 9(1) grounds,[106] it is true to say that *Begum* has ushered in a more restrictive and confused approach.

The new interpretation of Article 9 post-*Begum* is inconsistent with Strasbourg jurisprudence. It rests upon a mistaken interpretation of the specific situation rule. Post-*Begum* the specific situation rule has been given general application. The new mantra of the domestic courts is that interference with Article 9 'is not easily established'. This means that little attention is now paid to the now *obiter* question of whether the interference would have been justified under Article 9(2). Instead the focus upon Article 9(1) requires courts to get into vexed questions concerning doctrine, which traditionally courts have been reluctant to entertain.[107] Requiring courts to address such questions is not only inappropriate, but also unnecessary. In most cases the same decisions could have been reached more easily by reference to Article 9(2). Lower court decisions following *Begum* have taken an increasingly restrictive line. While Strasbourg has said that there will be no breach when an employee can resign from their job, domestic courts have held that there will be no breach per se when a believer can simply go elsewhere. This seems to stem from a view that religion ought to be confined to the private sphere. This is buttressed by the stricter interpretation of the manifestation/motivation requirement in *Playfoot* and *Ghai*. The result is that Article 9 only protects a very restrictive and conservative form of religious life.

---

[105] Interestingly, the decisions of the ecclesiastical courts concerning exhumation provide an exception to this trend: see, e.g. *Re Crawley Green Road Cemetery, Luton* [2001] Fam 308 and *Re Durrington Cemetery* [2001] Fam 33, as discussed by R. Sandberg, 'Human Rights and Human Remains: The Impact of *Dödsbo* v. *Sweden*' (2006) 8 *Ecclesiastical Law Journal* 453.

[106] Notably, *R. (on the Application of Swami Suryananda)* v. *Welsh Minister* [2007] EWCA Civ 893.

[107] See Chapter 4.

Given the traditional reluctance of the judiciary in religious matters, the largely negative approach to religious freedom found at common law and the different approaches to interpretation required by the Human Rights Act, it is unsurprising that domestic courts have struggled with the interpretation of Article 9. The judgment in *Watkins-Singh* suggests that litigants are now best advised to argue cases under religious discrimination laws instead. The next chapter will assess whether this really is the case. It will address the effectiveness of the new laws specifically prohibiting discrimination on grounds of religion or belief.

6

Discrimination on grounds of religion

Introduction

The opening years of the twenty-first century have seen a great deal of litigation concerning religious rights, with many of these cases enjoying a high profile in the media. Most of these cases have been argued under the new law on religious discrimination. Indeed, one of the most significant changes to the way in which English law regulates religion has been the extension of discrimination law specifically to cover religion or belief. Whereas, previously, racial discrimination laws only protected some religious groups, discrimination on grounds of religion or belief is now specifically prohibited both in relation to employment and the provision of goods and services. However, this is not the only way in which discrimination law interacts with religion. Religious groups also benefit from a number of specific exceptions from laws prohibiting discrimination on grounds of sex, religion and sexual orientation.

This chapter explores the extent to which English law both prohibits and permits discrimination on grounds of religion. It falls into four sections. The first outlines the legal framework concerning religion or belief discrimination. The second and third sections examine the law on direct and indirect religious discrimination respectively as well as analysing the interaction between discrimination law provisions and Article 9 of the ECHR.[1] The final section examines the law on religious exceptions. It examines the extent to which religious groups enjoy exceptions from the law on sex, sexual orientation and religious discrimination. This chapter questions the effect of the new laws and examines the impact of the Equality Act 2010 which now consolidates the law in this area: in short, it asks whether recent developments have increased religious freedom or merely stimulated more litigation.

The legal framework

Laws prohibiting discrimination specifically on grounds of religion or belief are a recent development. As noted in Chapter 2, the Race Relations Act 1976

---

[1] For an earlier review of the case law, see R. Sandberg, 'Flags, Beards and Pilgrimages: A Review of the Early Case Law on Religious Discrimination' (2007) 9 *Ecclesiastical Law Journal* 87. See also see L. Vickers, 'Religious Discrimination in the Workplace: An Emerging Hierarchy?' (2010) 12(3) *Ecclesiastical Law Journal* 280.

forbade direct or indirect discrimination on the grounds of colour, race, nationality or ethnic origins and this was interpreted to include members of certain religious groups, such as Sikhs[2] and Jews.[3] However, adherents to all other religious groups remained outside that protection and could only bring claims by stressing the disadvantage suffered by their racial group – not on grounds of religion.

This changed as a result of EU law. In 2000, an EU Directive[4] stated that, in addition to existing prohibitions against discrimination on grounds of sex, race and disability, discrimination on grounds of sexual orientation, age and religion or belief 'should be prohibited throughout the Community' in relation to employment. In respect of religion or belief, this led to the Employment Equality (Religion or Belief) Regulations 2003, which prohibited direct discrimination, indirect discrimination, victimisation and harassment on grounds of religion or belief in relation to employment and vocational training. Part 2 of the Equality Act 2006 subsequently extended this to prohibit direct and indirect discrimination and victimisation (but not harassment) on grounds of religion or belief in relation to the provision of goods and services.[5] The law is now to be found, however, in the Equality Act 2010.

The Equality Act 2010

The Equality Act 2010 consolidates and repeals most of the existing non-discrimination legislation, including the laws on religion or belief discrimination.[6] The Act protects 'religion and belief' alongside seven other 'protected characteristics': age; disability; gender reassignment; marriage and civil partnership; race; sex; and sexual orientation.[7] It outlaws the 'prohibited conduct' of direct discrimination, indirect discrimination, harassment and victimisation in relation to particular areas such as goods and

---

[2] *Mandla* v. *Dowell Lee* [1983] 2 AC 548; compare this with the decision in the Court of Appeal which had considered Sikhs a religious group and thus outside the scope of the legislation: *Mandla* v. *Dowell Lee* [1983] QB 1.

[3] *Seide* v. *Gillette Industries Ltd* [1980] IRLR 427.   [4] 2000/78/EC.

[5] A further Council Directive to cover this is currently being considered in Brussels. The Directive would prohibit discrimination on grounds of disability, religion or belief, sexual orientation and age in relation to goods and services, housing, education, social protection, social security and social advantage. Although English law currently goes beyond existing European obligations, the Directive may well extend protection to the areas now covered by English law in different ways and to differing extents. Sections 203–4 of the Equality Act 2010 provide for harmonisation between domestic and EU law.

[6] Despite the change of government, the vast majority of the provisions of the Act came into force in October 2010 (including those relating to religion or belief discrimination). At the time of writing, the Government is consulting on provisions concerning the public sector Equality Duty and is considering a range of provisions, including those which permit civil partnerships on religious premises. See www.equalities.gov.uk/equality_act_2010.aspx.

[7] See ss. 4–12.

services, premises, employment and education.[8] In respect of religion or belief discrimination, it remains the case that harassment is not prohibited in relation to goods and services.

The Act also includes a number of religious exceptions, which were previously found within various different pieces of discrimination law.[9] They can now be found in the Schedules to the Act.[10] The Act also extends the public sector duty to religion for the first time.[11] This would place a duty on public authorities to pay 'due regard' to the need to 'remove or minimise disadvantages suffered by persons' on grounds of religion or belief, to take steps to meet their needs and to encourage them to participate in public life.[12]

The Equality Act 2010 shows how discrimination law is underpinned by the premise that religion or belief can be protected in the same way and largely to the same extent as the other 'protected characteristics'. However, this premise may be questioned.[13] As Sedley LJ held in *Eweida* v. *British Airways*,[14] whilst all of the other protected characteristics apart from religion or belief 'are objective characteristics of individuals; religion and belief alone are matters of choice'. Although this is, of course, somewhat of a simplification,[15] it serves to highlight concerns that religion or belief is different from the other 'protected characteristics' and ought to be protected differently. As Lord Nicholls stressed in *Williamson*.[16] 'Freedom of religion protects the subjective belief of an individual.' This is not true of the other protected grounds. Throughout this chapter we will see whether this tension between religion or belief and the other protected characteristics has affected the ways in which the law has been interpreted.

Defining religion or belief

The different nature of religion or belief as opposed to the other protected characteristics explains why considerable attention has been paid to the definition of religion or belief in discrimination law, as discussed in Chapter 3. In line with human rights provisions, the term 'religion' is undefined and has been interpreted broadly. In contrast, discrimination law

---

[8] See ss. 13, 19, 26, 27 and Pts 3–7 of the Act.

[9] See R. Sandberg and N. Doe, 'Religious Exemptions in Discrimination Law' (2007) 66(2) *Cambridge Law Journal* 302.

[10] See also Pt. 14.   [11] See Pt. 11.   [12] Section 149.

[13] See, for instance, in relation to harassment, L. Vickers, 'Is All Harassment Equal? The Case of Religious Harassment' (2006) 65(3) *Cambridge Law Journal* 579.

[14] [2010] EWCA Civ 80 at para. 40.

[15] Vickers gives the example that given the availability of gender reassignment procedures, it is arguable that gender can be chosen: see L. Vickers, 'Religious Discrimination in the Workplace: An Emerging Hierarchy?' (2010) 12(3) *Ecclesiastical Law Journal* 280.

[16] *R.* v. *Secretary of State for Education and Employment and others, ex parte Williamson* at [2005] UKHL 15 para. 22.

originally protected a rather narrow conception of 'belief'. At first the regulations only protected religious beliefs, and 'similar' philosophical beliefs[17] and Employment Tribunals asserted that national and political beliefs were outside the scope of the regulations.[18] The Equality Act 2006, however, removed the word 'similar' with the effect that now 'religious or philosophical' beliefs are protected.

A more expansive approach seems to be taken with the Employment Appeal Tribunal in *Grainger PLC* v. *Nicholson*[19] following the understanding of 'belief' developed in the human rights jurisprudence.[20] The test is whether the belief is genuinely held, is more than an opinion or viewpoint, relates to a weighty and substantial aspect of human life and behaviour and has a certain level of cogency, seriousness, cohesion and importance.[21] An asserted belief in man-made climate change and a belief in spiritualism and psychic powers both met this definition. Lack of religion and lack of belief are both expressly included for protection.[22] Although the increased tendency not to use the definition of religion or belief as a filter may be welcomed,[23] the new approach followed in *Grainger* is problematic in that, unlike the Equality Act 2010, Article 9 does not differentiate between philosophical and non-philosophical beliefs. The *Grainger* approach is also difficult to reconcile with earlier Employment Tribunal decisions holding that political and national beliefs are not protected since these are protected under Article 9.[24]

Victimisation and harassment

The next two sections will explore the law prohibiting direct and indirect discrimination on grounds of religion or belief. In line with the other protected characteristics, religious discrimination laws also outlaw victimisation and harassment. However, in practice these tend to be argued alongside direct and indirect discrimination claims.

Victimisation occurs where A subjects B to a detriment because B is bringing proceedings, giving evidence, providing information or making an allegation under the Equality Act.[25]

---

[17] Employment Equality (Religion or Belief) Regulations 2003 reg. 2(1).

[18] *Williams* v. *South Central Ltd* ET, Case Number: 2306989/2003 (16 June 2004); *Baggs* v. *Fudge* ET, Case Number: 1400114/2005 (23 March 2005).

[19] [2009] UKEAT 0219/09/ZT (3 November 2009).

[20] See also *Greater Manchester Police Authority* v. *Power* [2009] EAT 0434/09/DA (12 November 2009), discussed in Chapter 3.

[21] *Grainger Plc* v. *Nicholson* [2009] UKEAT 0219/09/ZT at para. 24. These tests are also elucidated in the Explanatory Notes to the Equality Act 2010: see para. 52.

[22] Equality Act 2010 s. 10.   [23] See Chapter 3.   [24] *X* v. *Austria* (1963) 13 CD 42.

[25] Equality Act 2010 s.27. It covers the situation where B has done a 'protected act' or A believes that B has done or may do a 'protected act'. It is not victimisation where B gives false evidence or information or makes a false application if B is acting in bad faith. The Equality Act 2010 removed any need for a comparator.

For example, it is victimisation if B is denied promotion by A because A regards B to be a 'troublemaker' after B gave evidence in support of a claim of religious discrimination by C.

Harassment occurs where A engages in unwanted conduct related to religion or belief which has the purpose or effect of violating B's dignity or creating an intimidating, hostile, degrading, humiliating or offensive environment.[26] For example, it is harassment if A constantly teases B about his partner's religious convictions. Conduct should be regarded as constituting harassment only if, having regard to all the circumstances-including in particular the perception of B, it should reasonably be considered as having that effect.[27]

Harassment on grounds of religion or belief is only outlawed in relation to employment.[28] A clause in what was to become the Equality Act 2006 outlawing religious harassment in relation to goods and services discrimination was removed by the House of Lords. Their Lordships considered that the clause could have been used by religious groups to obtain an injunction to stop other religions staging events that they considered offensive.[29] Under the Equality Act 2010 harassment does not apply to religion or belief or sexual orientation discrimination in the provision of goods and services.[30]

Direct discrimination

Direct discrimination occurs where A treats B less favourably than A treats or would treat others.[31] The less favourable treatment must be 'because of a protected characteristic'; in this case, because of religion or belief. So, it is direct discrimination if A refuses to offer a job to B because B is a Sikh. It is also direct discrimination if the less-favourable treatment is because the claimant is associated with someone who has a protected characteristic (for instance, A sacks B because B's wife is an atheist).[32]

Prior to the Equality Act 2010, the requirement was that direct discrimination needed to be 'on grounds of religion or belief'.[33] The 2010 Act

---

[26] Section 26(1). In *Saini* v. *All Saints Haque Centre and others* [2008] UKEAT/00227/08 (24 October 2008), the Employment Appeal Tribunal confirmed that this applies not only where an employee is harassed on the grounds of his or her own religious beliefs, but also where he or she suffers harassment because of the religious beliefs of another person.

[27] Equality Act 2010 s. 26(4).   [28] For criminal offences concerning harassment, see Chapter 7.

[29] Harassment was originally included in the Northern Ireland equivalent (Equality Act (Sexual Orientation) Regulations (Northern Ireland) 2006), but in *Christian Institute and others, Re Application for Judicial Review* [2007] NIQB 66, the harassment provisions were quashed. See R. Sandberg, 'Gods and Services: Religious Groups and Sexual Orientation Discrimination' (2008) 10 *Ecclesiastical Law Journal* 205.

[30] Section 29(8). However, a proposed EC directive does outlaw such harassment, which suggests that the law may be extended at some point in the future. See fn. 5 above.

[31] Equality Act 2010 s. 13.   [32] Equality Act 2010 Explanatory Notes para. 59.

[33] Employment Equality (Religion or Belief) Regulations 2003 reg. 3(1)(a); Equality Act 2006 s. 45(1).

replaces the words 'on grounds of' with 'because of', and according to the Explanatory Notes,[34] this had the intention not of changing the meaning, but making the legislation more accessible.[35] However, the change in wording may have the effect of broadening the definition. For instance, previously it was thought necessary to state explicitly that it is direct discrimination if the discriminator treats the victim less favourably because he wrongly thinks that the victim has a protected characteristic (for instance, A refuses to employ B because he thinks B is a Muslim).[36] This is no longer explicitly stated in the Equality Act 2010, the Explanatory Notes suggesting that the broadness of the new definition means that this situation would still constitute direct discrimination.[37] It is less clear, however, whether the revised definition covers the situation where A discriminates on grounds of his own religion or belief. Previously, this was explicitly excluded in the legislation.[38] Even if A and B were of the same religion, it would only be direct discrimination if the less favourable treatment was on the grounds of B's religion or belief, not A's. This was an implicit recognition of A's religious freedom. Presumably this remains the case; but it is regrettable that this is no longer spelt out on the face of the Act.

Making a prima facie case

In direct discrimination claims the claimant must prove facts from which the tribunal could conclude that unlawful discrimination has occurred. If the claimant makes such a prima facie case, then the burden of the proof passes to the respondent.[39] Direct discrimination cannot be justified: there is no defence of reasonableness. The only defence open to the respondent is to prove that the discrimination did not occur. *Bodi* v. *Teletext*[40] provides a rare example of a successful direct discrimination claim. Bodi claimed that

---

[34] Like all Explanatory Notes, the Notes on the Equality Act are to be treated with caution. Their sole purpose is to assist the reader in understanding the Act. They do not form part of the Act and have not been endorsed by Parliament. If the matter comes before a court, the judge will look at the Act and not the Notes. However, in the absence of a judicial decision or clear Hansard evidence, the Explanatory Notes are the best guide to the intended meaning of the Act.

[35] Equality Act 2010 Explanatory Notes para. 61.

[36] At least in relation to goods and services discrimination: see Equality Act 2006 s.45(2).

[37] Equality Act 2010 Explanatory Notes para. 59.

[38] Originally in Employment Equality (Religion or Belief) Regulations 2003 reg. 3(2). This was repealed by s. 77 of the Equality Act 2006 and replaced by a revised reg. 3(1)(a). For goods and services, see Equality Act 2006 s. 45(1).

[39] *Wong* v. *Igen Ltd (formerly Leeds Careers Guidance)* [2005] EWCA Civ 142. In *Ladele* v. *London Borough of Islington* [2008] UKEAT/0453/08/RN (10 December 2008), the Employment Appeal Tribunal noted that it was not necessary for a Tribunal to follow this two-stage procedure in every case. In some cases it may be appropriate for the Tribunal simply to focus on the reason given by the respondent if they are satisfied that this discloses no discrimination, effectively acting on the assumption that even if a prima facie case had been made, the claim would nevertheless fail because there was no discrimination.

[40] [2005] ET Case Number: 3300497/2005 (13–14 October 2005).

he had not been short-listed for a job on grounds of his Asian race or Muslim religion; he compared his treatment with that of the short-listed candidates with equivalent or lesser experience. The Employment Tribunal found that Bodi had been directly discriminated against on grounds of race and/or religion. The respondent could not show that its actions were because of anything other than the claimant's race or religion.

Bodi, however, is the exception to the rule. Most direct discrimination claims have failed because a prima facie case has not been made. For instance,[41] in *Mohamed* v. *Virgin Trains*,[42] the claimant was repeatedly asked at work to trim his beard. He was later dismissed by Virgin Trains on grounds of his lack of enthusiasm and poor performance. He claimed that he had been discriminated against on grounds of religion since he wore his beard for religious reasons. Both the Employment Tribunal and the Employment Appeal Tribunal both held that he had not made his case: there was no evidence that he was at actual risk of dismissal because he had a beard for religious reasons. He was sacked for his poor performance.

The case law demonstrates the requirement that claimants will be expected to articulate their beliefs clearly. For instance, in *Devine* v. *Home Office*,[43] Devine claimed that he had been rejected for a job at the Home Office due to his sympathy for underprivileged asylum seekers. He claimed that he had been discriminated against on grounds of religion or belief since his care for disadvantaged people was a demonstration of the Christian virtue of charity. The Tribunal found his claim to be 'far too vague and ill defined to amount to a case to answer'. Moreover, where a claimant cites other arguments in support of his or her belief, this may actually hinder the case. In *McClintock* v. *Department of Constitutional Affairs*,[44] a Justice of the Peace resigned since he could not in conscience agree to place children with same-sex couples, contending in part that further research was needed on the effect this would have upon the children. Both the Employment Tribunal and the Employment Appeal Tribunal held that there had not been any direct discrimination, since McClintock had not made it plain that his objection was underscored by conscientious or religious objection. Although the requirement to couch one's claim as religious discrimination may not appear taxing, it poses special difficulties in relation to religion or belief discrimination. It is commonly accepted that there are many reasons why believers may decide not to say explicitly that their actions are prompted by their religious belief.[45] The nature of religion or belief may

---

[41] See also *Ferri* v. *Key Languages Ltd* [2004] ET, Case Number: 2302172/2004 (12 July 2004).

[42] [2005] ET Case Number: 2201814/2004 (12–14 October 2004; 20 May 2005); EAT, (2006) WL 25224803 (30 August 2006).

[43] [2004] ET Case Number: 2302061/2004 (9 August 2004).

[44] [2007] UKEAT/0223/07/CEA (31 October 2007).

[45] This is the rationale for the reasonableness requirement in some of the religious exceptions permitted in discrimination law, discussed below.

require a different approach here than in relation to the other prohibited grounds.

The focus upon the respondent

In direct discrimination claims the focus is on the respondent, not on the claimant. This was highlighted in the leading Court of Appeal decision of *Ladele* v. *London Borough of Islington.*[46] The case concerned a registrar who refused on grounds of conscience to perform civil partnership ceremonies. When Islington Council insisted that she should undertake at least some of these duties and disciplined her, threatening her with dismissal, she alleged that she had suffered discrimination on the grounds of religion or belief. The Council denied this, claiming that she had been treated in this way because of her refusal to officiate at civil partnerships, not because of her religious beliefs. The Council would have treated any registrars who refused to perform civil partnerships in the same way. Agreeing with the Council, the Court of Appeal stated that the focus of the enquiry was why the direct discrimination occurred.[47] For the claim to succeed, the 'explanation given by the employer for the less favourable treatment' must be Ms Ladele's religious beliefs.[48] The Court of Appeal upheld the Employment Appeal Tribunal's decision, which stressed that it was important not to confuse the claimant's reasons for acting as she did with the respondent's reasons for treating the claimant as it did.[49] Even though the claimant's actions were on grounds of religion or belief, the actions of the respondent were not. The claim for direct discrimination therefore failed.

On one level, this is surely correct. The Council's actions were not on grounds of Ladele's religion. However, on another level, the reasoning seems rather artificial. It allows respondents to dodge direct discrimination claims provided that they can show their actions were because of anything but religion. It is misleading to say that religion did not play a part in their decision. Religion or belief was at least part of the context. Using the new language it seems perfectly natural to say that Ladele was dismissed *because of* religion or belief. The Council's actions were caused by Ladele's refusal to officiate at civil partnerships and that refusal was caused by her religion or belief. This was recognised by one of Ladele's line managers, who commented that it was wrong to 'be accommodating people's religious beliefs in the Registry Services'. The Employment Appeal Tribunal in *Ladele* held that in order to establish that there has been discrimination on grounds of religion or belief, the tribunal must be satisfied that religion or belief was one of the significant reasons for the treatment; 'significant' was defined as being more than trivial. Applying this test, a case could be made that religion

[46] [2009] EWCA (Civ) 1357.   [47] Para. 30.   [48] Paras. 30, 33.
[49] [2008] EAT Case Number: UKEAT/0453/08/RN (10 December 2008).

or belief was a significant cause of Ladele's treatment. The law is currently unclear.

A restrictive approach

It seems clear that the courts and tribunals to date have taken a restrictive view of direct discrimination. This is merited by the fact that direct discrimination is a blunt instrument because it does not allow for a defence of justification. This restrictive approach is unproblematic provided that other courses of action are available to claimants. Indeed, many of the cases discussed above fit more clearly with the language of indirect discrimination. This is true, for example, of *Ladele*. As the Court of Appeal explained, a failure to accommodate religious difference rather than a complaint that the claimant had been discriminated against because of that difference will not amount to direct discrimination, but should be dealt with as indirect discrimination.[50] It is unsurprising, therefore, that direct discrimination claims have seldom been successful. *Bodi* shows that making a successful direct discrimination claim is not impossible – but it might be more accurate to say that the claimant needs to provide a convincing case rather than merely a prima facie one.

Indirect discrimination

Indirect discrimination occurs where A applies a provision, criterion or practice (PCP) against B which is discriminatory in relation to B's religion or belief. A PCP is discriminatory where: (i) it is applied equally to persons who do not share B's religion or belief; (ii) it puts persons of B's religion or belief at a particular disadvantage compared with others; (iii) it actually puts B at that disadvantage; and (iv) A cannot show it to be a proportionate means of achieving a legitimate aim.[51] For example, A applies a 'no headwear' policy to all staff. B, an employee, is a Sikh. This rule disadvantages Sikhs in general and B in particular. The 'no headwear' PCP is therefore discriminatory unless A can show that it is justified. Indirect discrimination also occurs where a PCP would create discrimination if it were applied. Indirect discrimination would therefore protect a claimant who did not apply for a job, knowing that a discriminatory PCP was to be applied.

The key point about indirect discrimination is that it can be justified, for example, by security or health and safety concerns. Its operation is therefore similar to the analysis of the right to manifest under Article 9, where the focus is on interference followed by justification.[52] In both cases,

---

[50] [2009] EWCA (Civ) 1357 at para. 29.
[51] Equality Act 2010 s. 19(2). This mirrors the previous law: Employment Equality (Religion or Belief) Regulations 2003 reg. 3(1)(b); Equality Act 2006 s. 45(2).
[52] See Chapter 5.

the analysis by the court or tribunal is often twofold. Firstly, the court determines whether there is interference with the right. In discrimination law, this is often expressed as asking whether there is a 'disadvantage', but it is effectively the same question. Secondly, if there has been interference (or 'disadvantage'), attention is then given to the question of justification: can the interference be justified? There have been a number of successful indirect discrimination claims, especially in relation to working hours and religious dress. However, there have also been a number of unsuccessful claims. Many of these have failed on grounds of justification, but, more problematically, some claims have failed on grounds of interference. This raises the question of whether the same difficulties which inhibit the success of Article 9 claims now also exist in discrimination law.

Successful claims concerning working hours

Indirect discrimination is more common than direct discrimination and there have been some successful cases, especially where employees have been required to work on holy days. In *Williams-Drabble* v. *Pathway Care Solutions*,[53] the claimant was a Christian who was employed at a children's home. The employer brought in a new work rota which meant that she would be unable to attend church. The Employment Tribunal found that there had been indirect discrimination: the rota was applied equally, but put Christians at a disadvantage and actually disadvantaged Williams-Drabble. The employer had failed to provide 'an adequate explanation' and had not shown that the disadvantage was 'a proportionate means of achieving a legitimate aim'. Similarly, in *Fugler* v. *MacMillan – London Hairstudios Ltd*,[54] a new 'no Saturdays off work' rule at the hairdressers was held to constitute indirect discrimination. Although the rule was applied equally, this put Jews at a disadvantage and actually put the Jewish claimant at a disadvantage on a particular Saturday. Although serving clients on a Saturday was a legitimate aim, the employers should have considered how or if they could rearrange Fugler's duties and customers for that Saturday. In this area the new law on religious discrimination has gone further than the Human Rights Act 1998, where such cases have been unsuccessful due to the specific situation rule.[55]

Successful claims concerning religious dress

A further example of a successful claim of indirect discrimination in relation to religious dress is the Employment Tribunal's decision in *Noah* v. *Sarah*

[53] [2004] ET Case Number: 2601718/2004 (2 December 2004).
[54] [2005] ET Case Number: 2205090/2004 (21–3 June 2005).
[55] *Copsey* v. *WBB Devon Clays Ltd* [2005] EWCA Civ 932. See Chapter 5 above and L. Vickers, *Religious Freedom, Religious Discrimination and the Workplace* (Oxford: Hart, 2008), Ch. 4.

Desrosiers (t/a Wedge).[56] The claimant, Mrs Noah, applied for a job as an assistant stylist at the respondent's hairdressing salon. When Noah attended the interview wearing a headscarf, the interview was terminated on the basis that the hair salon was known for 'ultra modern' hair styles which staff were supposed to display to clients. No other person was ultimately appointed to the job. The Tribunal held the provision, criterion or practice (PCP), that an employee would be required to display her hair at work for at least some of the time, put persons of the same religion as the claimant at a particular disadvantage and disadvantaged the claimant notwithstanding the fact that she would not in fact have been offered a job (given that no assistant stylist was ever appointed). The law on religious discrimination sought to make unlawful discrimination in relation to job applicants and did not merely make reference to whether or not they were offered a job, but also covered discrimination in relation to other arrangements made as part of the recruitment process. This indirect discrimination was not justified. Although it was reasonable for the respondent to take the view that the issue posed a significant risk to her business, too much weight was accorded to that concern.

As noted in Chapter 5, *R (on the application of Watkins-Singh)* v. *The Governing Body of Aberdare Girls' High School*[57] provides a further example of a successful indirect discrimination claim. It was the first reported case to be argued under the goods and services provisions originally found in the Equality Act 2006. The success of the claims in *Noah* and *Watkins-Singh* suggests that litigants are now best advised to argue discrimination law claims in preference to Article 9 claims, at least in relation to the wearing of religious dress and symbols.[58] This is underscored by the contrast between Silber J's judgment and the much more restrictive approach taken in the Article 9 case law.[59] In contrast to the Article 9 case law, including Silber J's own judgment in *R (on the application of X)* v. *Y School*,[60] *Watkins-Singh* recognises that religious beliefs can be exercised in the public sphere and that a religious practice does not have to be obligatory before it is protected.

Unsuccessful claims which failed on grounds of justification

However, a number of indirect discrimination claims are unsuccessful and, unlike the Article 9 case law, many claims have failed on grounds of justification, not interference. The claimant loses because the respondent can justify the discrimination. For instance, in *Azmi* v. *Kirklees Metropolitan*

---

[56] [2008] ET Case Number: 2201867/07 (29 May 2008).   [57] [2008] EWHC (Admin) 1865.

[58] R. Sandberg, 'The Changing Position of Religious Minorities in English Law: The Legacy of *Begum*' in R. Grillo *et al.* (eds.), *Legal Practice and Cultural Diversity* (Aldershot: Ashgate, 2009), p. 267.

[59] See Chapter 5.   [60] [2006] EWHC (Admin) 298.

Council,[61] concerning a teaching assistant who was suspended for insisting on wearing a full-face veil when male members of staff were present contrary to a school instruction not to wear the full face-veil when teaching children, both the Employment Tribunal and the Employment Appeal Tribunal held that the indirect discrimination was justified. Although the 'no face-veil when teaching rule' put Muslims at a disadvantage and actually put Azmi at a disadvantage, it could be justified as a proportionate means of achieving the legitimate aim of children being taught properly.

The indirect discrimination claim was also unsuccessful in *Ladele* v. *London Borough of Islington*.[62] The Court of Appeal held that the Council's policy decision to designate all registrars as civil partnership registrars had a legitimate aim: fulfilling the Council's policy to combat discrimination on grounds of sexual orientation. For Dyson LJ, the aim of the Council's Dignity for All policy 'was of general, indeed overarching, policy significance [having] fundamental human rights, equality and diversity implications, whereas the effect on Ladele of implementing the policy did not impinge on her religious beliefs: she remained free to hold those beliefs, and free to worship as she wished'.[63] Further, Ladele was employed in a public job and was being 'required to perform a purely secular task, which was being treated as part of her job'.[64]

Aspects of the reasoning in *Ladele* are questionable.[65] The argument seems one-sided. Preventing discrimination on grounds of sexual orientation is described as being of 'overarching, policy significance', while freedom of religion is defined very narrowly. Surely the equality policy protects discrimination on grounds of religion as well as sexual orientation. Taken literally, the Court of Appeal in *Ladele* seemed to suggest that freedom of religion only included the right to hold beliefs and worship. This is not the case as the text of Article 9 makes clear. It appears that the laudable aim of preventing discrimination on grounds of sexual orientation was used to annihilate the claim of religious discrimination. *Ladele* was followed in the factually similar case of *McFarlane* v. *Relate Avon Ltd*.[66] The case concerned a Christian counsellor who was dismissed because he refused to counsel same-sex couples on sexual matters. Both the Employment Tribunal and Employment Appeal Tribunal rejected McFarlane's claims of

---

[61] [2006] ET Case Number: 1801450/06 (6 October 2006); [2007] UKEAT 0009 07 30003 (30 March 2007).

[62] [2009] EWCA (Civ) 1357, discussed above under 'Direct discrimination'.

[63] At para. 51. Dyson LJ held that this conclusion was reinforced by Art. 9 of the ECHR: see paras. 54–61.

[64] Para. 52.

[65] See further R. Sandberg, 'The Implications of the Court of Appeal Decision in *Ladele*', paper presented to the Interfaith Legal Advisers Network (Lambeth Palace, 1 March 2010), available as part of the Working Paper Series coordinated by the Centre for Law and Religion at Cardiff University. See: www.law.cf.ac.uk/clr/research/WorkingPapers.html.

[66] [2010] EWCA Civ 880.

unfair dismissal and religious discrimination.[67] It was held that although McFarlane had been disadvantaged, Relate's actions had had a legitimate aim (the provision of counselling services to all sections of the community regardless of their sexual orientation) and was proportionate. Both the Employment Appeal Tribunal[68] and the Court of Appeal found *Ladele* to be definitive on this point. As Laws LJ noted, the two cases 'cannot sensibly be distinguished'.[69]

Unsuccessful claims which failed on grounds of interference

Other indirect discrimination claims, however, have failed on the question of interference rather than justification. In some cases, tribunals have held that the claimant had not proved that they had suffered a disadvantage. In *Harris* v. *NKL Automotive Ltd and another*,[70] a Rastafarian driver was not allocated work or transferred to full-time employment on the basis of his untidy hair (which the respondent considered did not represent the company well). The claimant contended that this was indirect discrimination since it disadvantaged Rastafarians who wore dreadlocks. Both the Employment Tribunal and the Employment Appeal Tribunal concluded that there was no disadvantage. Although Rastafarianism was protected as a belief, the 'no untidy hair' rule did not disadvantage Rastafarians. Having dreadlocks could be compatible with tidy hair since they could be kept in a tidy manner. The Employment Tribunal further stated that if it did constitute discrimination, it would have been justified: a requirement of tidy hair would also be a proportionate means to achieving the aim of a presentable appearance to customers and clients.

Indirect discrimination claims have also failed on the basis that the claimant has been unable to show that the PCP has put persons who share their religion or belief at a particular disadvantage compared with others. In *Eweida* v. *British Airways*.[71] a member of check-in staff wore a silver cross in breach of BA's uniform policy, which prohibited visible religious symbols, unless their wearing was mandatory. The Court of Appeal held that there was no indirect discrimination: the uniform policy did not put Christians at a particular disadvantage. There was no evidence that practising Christians

---

[67] See further R. Sandberg, 'Laws and Religion: Unravelling *McFarlane* v. *Relate Avon Ltd*' (2010) 12(3) *Ecclesiastical Law Journal* 361.

[68] [2009] UKEAT 0106/09/3011 (30 November 2009).

[69] [2010] EWCA Civ 880 at para. 27. The application was noteworthy because the case was supported by a witness statement by the former Archbishop of Canterbury, Lord Carey of Clifton, in which he argued for 'a specially constituted Court of Appeal of five Lords Justices who have a proven sensibility to religious issues'. This is discussed further in Chapter 10.

[70] [2007] UKEAT/0134/07/DM; 2007 WL 2817981 (3 October 2007).   [71] [2010] EWCA Civ 80.

considered the visible display of the cross to be a requirement of the Christian faith and no evidence that the provision created a barrier to Christians employed by BA. The Employment Appeal Tribunal held that the whole purpose of indirect discrimination is to deal with the problem of group discrimination.[72]

Although Sedley LJ in the Court of Appeal said that he did not share this view that on the basis that its overall purpose is rather 'to deal with the discriminatory impact of facially neutral requirements', he rejected the argument that the reference to 'persons' includes a single individual. There was no indication that the original Directive intended that solitary disadvantage should be sufficient. It was noted that Eweida herself described it as a personal choice rather than a religious requirement. Sedley LJ doubted that the provisions in the Equality Act 2010 would now include solitary disadvantage. He further held that if it had been held that there was indirect discrimination, the claim would nevertheless be defeated by BA's case on justification.

Eweida was followed by the Employment Tribunal decision in *Chaplin* v. *Royal Devon & Exeter NHS Foundation Trust*,[73] which concerned a nurse who wished to wear a crucifix around her neck. Despite evidence that another nurse had been asked to remove her cross and chain,[74] the Employment Tribunal held that this other nurse had not been put at a particular disadvantage since her religious views were not so strong as to lead her to refuse to comply with the policy.[75] This meant that the uniform policy did not 'place "persons" at a particular advantage'.[76] This was the decision of the majority. Mr Parkhouse, by contrast, held that both nurses had been placed at a disadvantage, but that this was justified. This seems to be a preferable conclusion. On the face of it, the claimant was disadvantaged and, unlike Eweida, there was clear evidence that she was not alone. It seems wrong to ignore the other nurse on the basis that her religious objection was not strong enough.

As with recent domestic Article 9 cases, this tendency to focus on questions of interference (or disadvantage) rather than justification may be criticised as being unnecessary. *Harris*, *Eweida* and *Chaplin* could all easily have been decided on grounds of justification. The latter two cases are particularly troubling. Even if it is accepted that the courts are entitled to conclude that a ban on wearing a cross would not disadvantage Christians as a whole, these cases suggest that beliefs held by a few individuals (including beliefs held by a minority of believers within a larger religious group) will

---

[72] [2008] UKEAT/0123/08LA (20 November 2008).
[73] [2010] ET Case Number: 17288862009 (6 April 2010).   [74] See para. 15.
[75] It was held that in order for there to be a 'particular disadvantage', the disadvantage needed to be 'noteworthy, peculiar or singular': para. 27.
[76] Paras. 27–8.

not be protected. This contradicts the general position of religion law – as shown by the text of Article 9 – which protects both religious individuals and religious groups.[77]

This is not to say, however, that Eweida's claim should have succeeded. The argument is simply that it should have been decided on grounds of justification. The approach of *Azmi*, which focused on justification rather than disadvantage, is to be applauded. Courts and Employment Tribunals should distinguish successful and non-successful claims largely by addressing the question of whether the employer's actions were a proportionate means of achieving a legitimate aim. In other cases too much weight has been given to the question of whether there was disadvantage. The unsuccessful claimants in *Harris*, *Eweida* and *Chaplin* arguably suffered more than the successful claimant in *Noah*. It seems ludicrous to say that not being offered a job that never actually existed does constitute a disadvantage, but being made to comply with a uniform policy which prohibited visible religious symbols unless their wearing was mandatory or a tidy hair rule does not constitute a disadvantage. Harris', Eweida's and Chaplin's detriments were real. That is not to say that the claims should have been successful. They should simply have been decided on the question of justification. *Azmi* and *Noah* show that focusing upon this question provides a nuanced situation-specific conclusion, leading to different results in the differing contexts of the education and retail sectors.

The interaction with Article 9

It is clear that the laws prohibiting discrimination on grounds of religion or belief have resulted in a great deal of litigation as a greater emphasis has been placed upon the notion of religious rights. Together with the Human Rights Act 1998, the laws prohibiting religious discrimination epitomise a clear shift in the way in which religion is regulated.[78] It is not only the case that these are the two sets of laws which have provoked the most litigation. It is also the case that other disputes concerning other areas of religion law commonly refer to these two areas. For instance, in her discussion of the law on prison chaplains, Knights notes that in addition to the specific law

---

[77] The position taken in charity law is preferable where even the smallest religions are protected. See, *Thornton* v. *Howe* (1862) 31 Beavan 14 (discussed in Chapter 3), in which a trust for printing, publishing and propagating the sacred writings of Joanna Southcote was held to be a valid charitable trust for the advancement of religion. The Master of the Rolls, Sir John Romilly, held that although the claimant was, in his opinion, 'a foolish, ignorant woman, of an enthusiastic turn of mind', the Court should not 'make any distinction between one sect and another'. The stance in *Thornton* v. *Howe* seems preferable to the judgmental approach of *Eweida* and *Chaplin*.

[78] See further Chapter 2.

relating to prison chaplaincy,[79] the Human Rights Act 1998 and the Equality Act 2006 would 'impact directly on this area'.[80] It may be expected that in litigation concerning any of the older pieces of religion law it would now be argued that the old law needed to be considered in the light of these two areas of law. For instance, before blasphemy was abolished, it was often discussed in relation to Article 9.[81]

Article 9 and the law on religious discrimination can be seen as the 'two pillars' of religion law in the United Kingdom in the twenty-first century. They are concerned with different things. Article 9 may be said to be concerned with *positive* religious freedom – the liberty actively *to* believe and manifest one's belief; while the law on religious discrimination may be said to be concerned with *negative* religious freedom – the liberty *from* coercion or discrimination on the grounds of belief.[82] However, there are similarities between the two, especially in relation to indirect discrimination. As we have seen, in both cases, the analysis by the court or tribunal is often twofold, focusing upon interference and then justification. Moreover, in *McClintock* v. *Department of Constitutional Affairs*,[83] the Employment Appeal Tribunal suggested that evidence that a disadvantage is justified under the Regulations would satisfy the question of whether the interference was justified under Article 9. The Employment Appeal Tribunal held that there would be 'considerable difficulties' in making a claim under Article 9 since, given the tribunal's finding on justification, 'it would almost inevitably have concluded that there was a defence under Article 9(2)'.

Although tribunals were initially reluctant to refer to Article 9, in more recent decisions discussion of human rights is commonplace. The earlier attitude was perhaps epitomised in the original Employment Tribunal decision in *Eweida* v. *British Airways*,[84] which disregarded counsel's references to comparative material, including reference to jurisprudence of the European Court of Human Rights, on the basis that their inquiry had to proceed within much more limited confines. Noting that it had no power to consider any separate free-standing convention claim, but had to interpret the Regulations so far as possible taking account of Article 9 of the European Convention on Human Rights (ECHR), the tribunal held that the sufficient compatibility between the terms of the Regulations and the

---

[79] Prison Act 1952 and by secondary legislation, the Prison Rules 1999.
[80] S. Knights, *Freedom of Religion, Minorities and the Law* (Oxford: Oxford University Press, 2007), para. 7.38.
[81] See Chapter 7.
[82] This distinction was drawn between Art. 9 and Art. 14 ECHR by R. Ahdar and I. Leigh, *Religious Freedom in the Liberal State* (Oxford: Oxford University Press, 2005), p. 100.
[83] EAT, Appeal No. UKEAT/0223/07CEA (22 October 2007) at paras. 60–1.
[84] (2007) ET Case Number: 2702689/06 (19 December 2007).

Convention required no further interpretative assistance from the Convention or the Strasbourg case law.[85] This was supported by cases such as *Hussain* v. *Bhuller Bros*[86] and *Watkins-Singh*,[87] which suggested that the new law on religious discrimination was to be interpreted more broadly than Article 9, suggesting that no benefit would be derived from the Article 9 case law.

However, tribunal decisions concerning religious discrimination law now routinely make reference to the Article 9 case law. As we have seen, this is especially the case in relation to the definition of belief.[88] More generally, the Employment Tribunal in *Azmi*[89] deemed it 'appropriate to examine the treatment of the manifestation of a religion or a belief under the ECHR' given that the EU Directive to which the Regulations gave effect referred to the 'fundamental rights' guaranteed by the ECHR. In *Eweida*,[90] the Employment Appeal Tribunal stated that since under section 3 '[i]t is incumbent on domestic courts to construe domestic laws compatibly with Convention rights', it followed that 'the same (or at least no less favourable) approach must be adopted to the concept of religion and belief in the 2003 Regulations'.[91]

However, in all cases to date, the tribunals have noted that Article 9 would make no difference. As Sedley LJ put it in the Court of Appeal judgment *Eweida*,[92] 'the jurisprudence on Art. 9 does nothing to advance the claimant's case'.[93] The reason for this is the increasingly restrictive interpretation of Article 9 by domestic courts. As Chapter 5 explained, since the House of Lords decision in *Begum*,[94] domestic courts have tended to interpret the Article 9 rights in a narrow and conservative fashion, uncritically following Lord Bingham's questionable assertion that 'interference [with Article 9] is not easily established'[95] and making repeated use of the specific situation rule. The result of this is that Article 9 is rendered of little use. This is underscored by the decisions in *Ladele*[96] and *McFarlane*,[97] in which the laudable aim of preventing discrimination on grounds of sexual orientation was used to annihilate the equally laudable aim of preventing religious discrimination.[98]

---

[85] See para. 5.9.

[86] ET, Case Number: 1806638/2004 (5 July 2005), discussed in Chapter 3.

[87] [2008] EWHC (Admin) 1865, discussed in Chapter 5.

[88] *Grainger Plc* v. *Nicholson.* 2009] UKEAT 0219/09/ZT (3 November 2009), discussed above and in Chapter 3.

[89] ET, Case Number: 1801450/06 (6 October 2006); [2007] UKEAT 0009 07 30003 (30 March 2007).

[90] Employment Appeal Tribunal Case Number: UKEAT/0123/08LA (20 November 2008).

[91] Para. 27.   [92] [2010] EWCA Civ 80.   [93] Para. 22.

[94] *R. (on the application of Begum)* v. *Headteacher and Governors of Denbigh High School* [2006] UKHL 15.

[95] See para. 24.   [96] [2009] EWCA (Civ) 1357.   [97] [2010] EWCA Civ 880.

[98] See further R. Sandberg, 'Laws and Religion: Unravelling *McFarlane* v. *Relate Avon Ltd*' (2010) 12(3) *Ecclesiastical Law Journal* 361.

This does not, however, undermine the conclusion that Article 9 of the ECHR and the laws prohibiting discrimination on grounds of religion or belief may be seen as being the 'two pillars' of religion law. The jurisprudence in these two areas is no longer separated. Propositions of religion law are being formed not only in relation to the definition of belief, but also in the way in which it has been suggested that evidence that a disadvantage is justified under indirect discrimination would satisfy the question of whether the interference was justified under Article 9. This is proof of the emergence of religion law as a legal sub-discipline. An argument can now be made that these laws and their respective case laws are best seen as part of something called religion law rather than being best understood as part of human rights law or discrimination law respectively. Common points between the two are best understood to be seen as being propositions of religion law (rather than propositions of human rights or discrimination law). The remainder of this chapter will explore the way in which discrimination law permits, rather than prohibits, discrimination on grounds of religion: the religious exceptions which permit discrimination on grounds of religion.

Religious exceptions

While discrimination law focuses upon the outlawing of the practice of discrimination, the law exceptionally permits discrimination in certain limited and specified circumstances. Most of the time, these exceptions are uncontroversial. The Equality Act 2010 contains a plethora of exceptions, and exceptions are routinely made to accommodate recognised activities such as sport.[99] However, religious exceptions[100] have proved controversial. A number of religious exceptions have existed for some time in discrimination law, which allow religious employers and groups to act in ways which would otherwise be prohibited. However, in recent years the granting of such exceptions and the scope of the exceptions has led to some of the greatest controversies surrounding law and religion in the United Kingdom in the twenty-first century.

These religious exceptions exist in addition to other exceptions such as those that apply where there is a general occupational requirement. The beneficiary and terms of the exception vary significantly, but a broad distinction can be made between exceptions that apply in relation to employment and those which apply in relation to goods and services. In all cases, the exceptions are narrowly drawn. The religious exceptions were previously

---

[99] See M. James, *Sports Law* (London: Palgrave Macmillan, 2010), pp. 234–40.
[100] The provisions are also sometimes referred to as 'exemptions' or 'statutory defences'. The Equality Act 2010, however, uses the term 'exception' and so this chapter adopts this term.

dispersed in a number of discrimination law statutes which outlawed discrimination on grounds of sex, sexual orientation and religion in relation to both employment and the provision of goods and services.

However, the exceptions can now be found in the Equality Act 2010. Although originally there were plans to alter the scope of some of the exceptions in the new Act, during the parliamentary passage of the Act a number of these changes were rejected as the Government sought to get the Act onto the statute books before the dissolution of the 2005–10 Parliament.[101] The overall effect of this is that the exceptions found in the 2010 Act are generally similar to those found in the old law. The following table shows where the exceptions were found in the old law and where they can now be found in the Equality Act 2010:

Exception	Old Law	New Law
Exception from laws forbidding discrimination on grounds of sex in relation to employment.	Sex Discrimination Act 1975 s. 19.	Equality Act 2010 Sch. 9 para. 2.
Exception from laws forbidding discrimination on grounds of sexual orientation in relation to employment.	Employment Equality (Sexual Orientation) Regulations 2003 reg. 7(3).	Equality Act 2010 Sch. 9 para. 2.
Exception from laws forbidding discrimination on grounds of religion in relation to employment.	Employment Equality (Religion or Belief) Regulations 2003 reg. 7(3).	Equality Act 2010 Sch. 9 para. 3.
Exception from laws forbidding discrimination on grounds of sex in relation to the provision of goods and services.	Sex Discrimination Act 1975 s. 35.	Equality Act 2010 Sch. 3 para. 29.
Exception from laws forbidding discrimination on grounds of sexual orientation in relation to the provision of goods and services.	Employment Equality (Sexual Orientation) Regulations 2007 reg. 14.	Equality Act 2010 Sch. 23 para. 2.
Exception from laws forbidding discrimination on grounds of religion in relation to the provision of goods and services.	Equality Act 2006 s. 57.	Equality Act 2010 Sch. 23 para. 2.

There are two other important influences to note. The first is the European Commission. In November 2009 the Commission sent a reasoned opinion to

---

[101] See F. Cranmer, 'Parliamentary Report' (2010) 12(2) *Ecclesiastical Law Journal* 229, 235.

the UK Government asserting that exceptions for religious employers under UK law were broader than those permitted under the EC Directive. Although the Government responded by saying that it was studying this reasoned opinion,[102] the defeat of the reconfigured exceptions in the Equality Act 2010 raises the question of whether the exceptions could now be subject to challenge under EU law.[103] Secondly, it is important to note that there have been a number of cases which have considered these exceptions. In many of these cases the discussion was *obiter*, the court dealing with claims by individuals who were clearly unable to enjoy exceptions which are afforded to religious groups. However, it is of note that in all of them the narrowness of these religious exceptions was stressed.

The following discussion begins by examining the exceptions in relation to employment before examining these in relation to goods and services. The focus will be on the terms of the exception found in the Equality Act 2010, but mention will also be made of the old law and the cases which interpreted those exceptions.[104]

Employment exceptions

The exceptions for employment[105] are now to be found in Schedule 9 to the Equality Act 2010. Paragraph 2 provides a separate exception from laws prohibiting discrimination on grounds of sex, marriage and sexual orientation, while paragraph 3 provides a further exception allowing employers with an ethos based on religion or belief to discriminate on grounds of religion or belief. Paragraph 2 applies where three criteria are met.

Firstly, the employment must be for the purposes of an organised religion. In *R (Amicus MSF Section)* v. *Secretary of State for Trade and Industry*,[106] Richards J held that the term 'organised religion' was narrower than 'religious organisation': he gave the example that 'employment as a teacher in a faith school is likely to be "for purposes of a religious organisation" but not "for purposes of an organised religion"'.[107] The use of the phrase 'organised religion' seems intended to limit the ambit of the exception. The Explanatory Notes state that this is 'intended to cover a very narrow range of employment: ministers of religion and a small number of lay posts, including those

---

[102] See F. Cranmer, 'Parliamentary Report' 233–4.

[103] A previous challenge in *R. (Amicus MSF Section)* v. *Secretary of State for Trade and Industry* [2004] EWHC 860 was unsuccessful on the basis that it was clear from the parliamentary material that the exceptions were intended to be of very narrow scope, tightly drawn and were to be construed strictly. See para. 103.

[104] For a detailed analysis of the old law, see R. Sandberg and N. Doe, 'Religious Exemptions in Discrimination Law' (2007) 66(2) *Cambridge Law Journal* 302.

[105] Discrimination in the employment sphere is regulated by Pt 5 of the Equality Act 2010.

[106] [2004] EWHC 860.   [107] Para. 116.

that exist to promote and represent religion'.[108] This is undoubtedly the meaning which would have been given to employment for the purposes of an organised religion had the revised exceptions found in earlier drafts of the Equality Bill become law.[109] However, given the text of the actual exception, it is not obvious that the phrase has this restricted meaning. The precise scope of the phrase remains unclear. Moreover, given that Parliament in enacting section 13 of the Human Rights Act 1998 has made it clear that particular regard is to be given to the rights of a 'religious organisation',[110] it may be asked why certain privileges have been afforded only to the narrower category where the beneficiary is an 'organised religion'. This may actually infringe not only section 13, but also Article 9.

Secondly, the 'compliance' or 'non-conflict' principles must be engaged. Although these terms are new to the Equality Act, they are simply short-hand expressions to cover the reasons why the organised religion may discriminate (which remain largely unchanged). The compliance principle is engaged where the discrimination takes place 'so as to comply with the doctrines of the religion'.[111] The non-conflict principle is engaged where the discrimination takes place 'so as to avoid conflicting with the strongly held convictions of a significant number of the religion's followers'. In *R (Amicus MSF Section)* v. *Secretary of State for Trade and Industry*,[112] Richards J stated that these requirements imposed 'very real additional limitations' and suggested that both tests were objective.[113] To make use of the first basis, reference should not be made to the subjective 'motivation of the employer', but rather to 'an objective test whereby it must be shown that employment of a person not meeting the requirement would be incompatible with the doctrines of the religion'. Differing ideas concerning the interpretation and content of doctrine render this a complicated task.[114] Although Richards J conceded that the second basis is wider, he nevertheless claimed that it is 'hemmed about by restrictive language' and requires 'an objective, not subjective, test' which 'is going to be a very far from easy test to satisfy in practice'. Deciding whether a 'significant number' of followers may be offended is by no means a straightforward task. Indeed, in the case of some faiths it is further complicated by the lack of a definition of membership.[115]

---

[108] Equality Act 2010 Explanatory Notes para. 799.   [109] See discussion below.
[110] See Chapter 4.   [111] Equality Act 2010 Sch. 9 para. 2(5).
[112] [2004] EWHC 860.   [113] At para. 117.
[114] For instance, for discussion of the difficulties in determining the 'doctrine of the Church of England', see *Clergy Discipline (Doctrine)*, Report of a Working Group of the House of Bishops (London: GS 1554, 2004).
[115] See the findings of the Colloquium of Anglican and Roman Catholic Canon Lawyers in J. Conn, N. Doe and J. Fox (eds.), *Initiation, Membership and Authority in Anglican and Roman Catholic Canon Law* (Rome: Colloquium of Anglican and Roman Catholic Canon Lawyers, 2005); and P. Colton, 'The Pursuit of a Canonical Definition of membership of the Church of Ireland' (2007) 10(1) *Ecclesiastical Law Journal* 3–33.

Thirdly, the employer can discriminate either where the employee does not meet the requirement imposed or where the employer is not satisfied and it is reasonable for him not to be satisfied that that person meets it.[116] The importance of this reasonableness requirement was stressed in *Reaney* v. *Hereford Diocesan Board of Finance*,[117] in which the claimant had been denied the job of Diocesan Youth Officer in Hereford after the Bishop expressed his concern that Reaney had been in a committed same-sex relationship and refused to accept Reaney's assurance that he would remain celibate. The Bishop concluded that Reaney could not at the present time make a promise not to have a same-sex relationship in the future and therefore did not offer him the post. The Employment Tribunal found that the Bishop could not rely upon the exception. Although employment as a Diocesan Youth Officer was for the purposes of an organised religion and the Bishop had been permitted to apply a requirement related to sexual orientation on either of the grounds laid out in the regulations, the religious exception did not apply because Reaney did meet the requirement imposed and it was not reasonable for the Bishop to conclude otherwise.

The exception in paragraph 2 is materially the same as the old law. The main difference between the two separate employment exceptions formerly covering discrimination on grounds of sex[118] and of sexual orientation[119] and paragraph 2 is the naming of the 'compliance' or 'non-conflict' principles. Originally, however, the exceptions in the Equality Bill would have made two significant changes. The first was to require explicitly the application of the requirement to be proportionate. The second was to provide a definition of employment for the purposes of a religious organisation as employment that 'wholly or mainly involves leading or assisting in the observation of liturgical or ritualistic practices of the religion, or promoting or expanding the doctrine of the religion'. This would have reversed the finding in *Reaney* that employment as a Diocesan Youth Officer was for the purpose of an organised religion. Both of these changes were rejected in Parliament. However, this does not seem to be fully reflected in the Explanatory Notes to the Act, which seem to impose additional requirements that are not found in the text of the exception. They state that the organised religion may only discriminate where it is 'crucial to the post' to

---

[116] In relation to discrimination on grounds of marriage or civil partnership, the employer can only discriminate where the employee does not meet the requirement imposed: Equality Act 2010 Sch. 9 para. 2(8).

[117] [2007] Employment Tribunal, judgment 17 July 2007 (Case No: 1602844/2006).

[118] Sex Discrimination Act 1975 s. 19. Previously this was buttressed in the case of the Church of England by s. 6 of the Priests (Ordination of Women) Measure 1993, but s. 6 was repealed on grounds that it was not compatible with EU law since the Measure was not limited to reasons of religious conscience: Employment Equality (Sex Discrimination) Regulation 2005 reg. 20(2).

[119] Employment Equality (Sexual Orientation) Regulations 2003 reg. 7(3).

do so and it cannot be 'merely one of several important factors'.[120] More importantly, the Explanatory Notes also state that it 'must be a proportionate way of meeting the criteria'.[121] The text of paragraph 2 suggests that this is not the case – which raises the question of whether or not the exception is broader than that permitted under EU law. As the Explanatory Memorandum on the EU Directive makes plain,[122] a 'double test of a justified aim and proportionate means of reaching it . . . is required'. Paragraph 2 does not meet these requirements since it does not on its face require proportionality.

Paragraph 3 of Schedule 9 to the Equality Act 2010 provides a further exception allowing employers with an ethos based on religion or belief to discriminate on grounds of religion or belief. This replicates the exception previously afforded in the Employment Equality (Religion or Belief) Regulations 2003, making no material changes.[123] It applies where three criteria are met.

Firstly, a person with an 'ethos based on religion or belief' must conclude that being of a particular religion or belief is an occupational requirement. They must reach this conclusion having regard to that ethos and to the nature or context of the work which is carried out. The old law only provided for 'an employer' rather than 'a person', but paragraph 3 makes it clear that the discrimination needs to be 'in relation to work'. The Explanatory Notes state that: 'It is for an employer to show that it has an ethos based on religion or belief by reference to such evidence as the organisation's founding constitution.'[124] Secondly, requiring the person to be of a particular religion or belief must be 'a proportionate means of achieving a legitimate aim'. Thirdly, either the person to whom the requirement is applied must not be of the particular religion or belief required or the employer must have reasonable grounds for not being satisfied that the person does not meet the occupational requirement.

This exception is much broader than paragraph 2 and can be seen simply as an extension of the general occupational requirement.[125] Two cases concerning Prospects, a charity which provides housing and day-care for people with learning disabilities, have engaged the application of this exception.[126] Prospects decided that in principle all its posts should be filled by Christians and therefore assumed that it was covered by the exception. The tribunal concluded that this approach had been fatally flawed: the law required that

---

[120]   Equality Act 2010 Explanatory Notes para. 800.   [121] *Ibid.*
[122]   COM (2008) 426 2008/0140, 8.
[123]   Reg. 7(3).   [124] Equality Act 2010 Explanatory Notes para. 804.
[125]   Now found in Equality Act 2010 Sch. 9 para. 1.
[126]   *Louise Hender* v. *Prospects*, *Mark Sheridan* v. *Prospects* [2008] ET Cases nos. 2902090/2006 (Hender) and 2901366 (Sheridan) (13 May 2008).

each post should be considered separately. A job evaluation should have been carried out for every vacant post.

The following table provides a summary of the religious exceptions which apply in relation to employment:

Exception	Source of Law	Beneficiary	Terms of the Exception	Extent of the Exception
Exception from laws forbidding discrimination on grounds of sex in relation to employment.	Equality Act 2010 Sch. 9 para. 2.	The employment must be for the purposes of an organised religion.	The exception is applied either to comply with the doctrines of the religion or to avoid conflicting with the strongly held convictions of a significant number of the religion's followers.	The employer can discriminate either where the employee does not meet the requirement imposed or where the employer is not satisfied and it is reasonable for him not to be satisfied that that person meets it.
Exception from laws forbidding discrimination on grounds of sexual orientation in relation to employment.	Equality Act 2010 Sch. 9 para. 2.	(As above.)	(As above.)	(As above.)
Exception from laws forbidding discrimination on grounds of religion in relation to employment.	Equality Act 2010 Sch. 9 para. 3.	A person with an 'ethos based on religion or belief'.	The exception is applied either where being of a particular religion or belief is an occupational requirement. Requiring the person to be of a particular religion or belief must be 'a proportionate means of achieving a legitimate aim'.	(As above.)

Goods and services exceptions

In relation to goods and services discrimination, the main religious exception is now to be found in paragraph 2 of Schedule 23 to the Equality Act 2010. This provides a general exception for 'organisations relating to religion or belief' covering discrimination in relation to goods and services,[127] the disposal, management and occupation of premises[128] and discrimination by association.[129] Schedule 3 provides some further exceptions in respect of goods and services.

The general religious exception found in paragraph 2 permits discrimination on grounds of religion and sexual orientation. It allows an 'organisation relating to religion or belief' or anyone acting on its behalf or under its auspices lawfully to restrict the membership of the organisation, participation in its activities, the provision of goods, facilities or services or the use or disposal of premises[130] owned or controlled by the organisation on grounds of religion or belief or sexual orientation.[131] It replaces similar provisions previously found in section 57 of the Equality Act 2006 (in respect of religious discrimination) and Regulation 14 of the Employment Equality (Sexual Orientation) Regulations 2007. Although the exceptions for both religion and sexual orientation discrimination can now be found in the same paragraph, paragraph 2 is drafted so that the terms of the exception continue to differ, largely mirroring the old law. The exception applies where two criteria are met.

Firstly, the discrimination must be by 'an organisation relating to religion or belief'.[132] This is defined as:

. . . an organisation the purpose of which is –

(a) to practice a religion or belief,
(b) to advance a religion or belief,
(c) to teach the practice or principles of a religion or belief,
(d) to enable persons of a religion or belief to receive any benefit, or to engage in any activity, within the framework of that religion or belief, or
(e) to improve relations, or maintain good relations, between persons of different religions or beliefs.

This paragraph does not apply to an organisation whose sole or main purpose is commercial.

There is no legal articulation of the difference, if any, between an 'organisation relating to religion or belief' and the term used in the employment

---

[127] Prohibited in Pt 2 of the Equality Act 2010.
[128] Prohibited in Pt 4.   [129] Prohibited in Pt 8.
[130] See Equality Act 2010 Sch. 23 para. 2(12) for limits on this in relation to sexual orientation discrimination.
[131] Para. 2(3)–(4). A minister may also restrict participation in activities and the provision of goods, facilities or services carried on in the performance of his functions: see para. 2(5). For the definition of a minister, see para. 2(8).
[132] Para. 2(1)–(2).

exception, an 'organised religion'.[133] This is a matter of practical importance since with respect to discrimination on grounds of sexual orientation, for example, religious exceptions in relation to employment can be only be used for the purposes of an 'organised religion', while religious exceptions in relation to the provision of goods and services can only be relied upon by an 'organisation relating to religion or belief'. Although the High Court decision in *Amicus* predates the use of the term 'organisation relating to religion or belief', Richards J's judgment seems to suggest that the term 'organisation relating to religion or belief' is broader than the term 'organised religion'. Therefore, it may be said that whilst an 'organised religion' will always also be an 'organisation relating to religion or belief', an 'organisation relating to religion or belief' will not always be an 'organised religion'. However, the law remains silent as to the precise difference between the two. The only key difference is that 'organised religion' relates to 'religion' rather than 'religion or belief'. Perhaps another difference may be that rather than simply having one of the purposes of an 'organisation relating to religion or belief', an 'organised religion' is an entity which meets most of them. On that analysis, the word 'or' in the definition effectively becomes an 'and'. At present, however, this is mere speculation, since the relationship between these two terms is unknown. The difference between these terms and the phrase 'ethos based on religion or belief' is also unclear, although it might be suspected that the reference to 'ethos based on religion or belief' is broader. Unlike the terms 'organised religion' and 'organisation relating to religion or belief', the reference to 'ethos' does not presuppose the existence of a group.

In relation to sexual orientation discrimination, paragraph 2 provides that the definition of an 'organisation relating to religion or belief' is to be restricted. Part (e) is to be ignored.[134] An organisation whose purpose is 'to improve relations, or maintain good relations, between persons of different religions or beliefs' can discriminate on grounds of religion, but not on grounds of sexual orientation. Moreover, the exception does not apply to anything done 'on behalf of a public authority' and 'under the terms of a contract between the organisation and a public authority'.[135]

This explains why the exception cannot be enjoyed by Roman Catholic adoption agencies. Although these agencies are entitled to the exception in that they are 'organisations relating to religion or belief', they lose that exception when they contract with the State to provide their service. This proved

---

[133] R. Sandberg and N. Doe, 'Religious Exemptions in Discrimination Law' (2007) 66(2) *Cambridge Law Journal* 302, 310–12.

[134] Para. 2(11).

[135] The term 'public authority' is defined in s. 150 of the Act as those which are specified in Sch. 19.

controversial prior to the enactment of the Employment Equality (Sexual Orientation) Regulations 2007. Cardinal Cormac Murphy O'Connor, then head of the Roman Catholic Church in England and Wales, wrote to the Cabinet asking for an exception. However, while the then Prime Minister Tony Blair was reportedly in favour of an exception, he was out-manoeuvred by his Cabinet colleagues, leading to a compromise whereby faith-based adoption and fostering agencies would be given a specified time to adapt to the new regime. Regulation 15 of the 2007 Regulations provided an exception that ran until 31 December 2008. Since then, discrimination by such adoption agencies on grounds of sexual orientation has been unlawful.[136] The Charity Tribunal has held that a charity cannot seek to avoid this by changing their objects in order to rely upon an exception for charities.[137]

In addition to meeting the definition of 'an organisation relating to religion or belief', the would-be discriminator also needs to meet the second criterion. This is the requirement that the discrimination must be on certain grounds. These grounds differ between religion and belief discrimination and sexual orientation discrimination. The organisation can only discriminate on grounds of religion or belief 'because of the purpose of the organisation' or 'to avoid causing offence, on grounds of the religion or belief to which the organisation relates, to persons of that religion or belief'.[138] This mirrors the exception previously provided in section 57 of the Equality Act 2006. The organisation can only discriminate on grounds of sexual orientation 'because it is necessary to comply with the doctrine of the organisation' or 'to avoid conflict with the strongly held convictions' of a 'significant number of the religion's [or belief's] followers'.[139] This mirrors the exception previously found in Regulation 14 of the Employment Equality (Sexual Orientation) Regulations 2007. Interestingly, although the grounds mirror those for employment in relation to sexual orientation, the 'compliance' or 'non-conflict' labels are not used in this context.

Schedule 3 provides some further religious exceptions in respect of goods and services. Most notably,[140] paragraph 29 provides an exception for ministers allowing them to provide a service only to persons of one sex or separate

---

[136] The Conservative–Liberal Democrat Coalition Government has no plans to change this. See House of Lords Debate (2010–11) 8 July 2010 c 336.

[137] *Catholic Care (Diocese of Leeds)* v. *Charity Commission for England and Wales* [2009] Charity Tribunal CA/2008/0003 (1 June 2009). At the time of writing (August 2010), the case has been sent back to the Charity Commission.

[138] Equality Act 2010 Sch. 23 para. 2(6).   [139] Paras. 2(7)–(9).

[140] See also para. 18, which provides an exception from goods and services discrimination on grounds of religion or belief where decisions are taken in accordance with immigration rules.

services for persons of each sex. This applies when the service is done for the purposes of an organised religion at a place used for those purposes and it is necessary in order to comply with the doctrines of the religion or is for the purpose of avoiding conflict with the strongly held religious convictions of a significant number of the religion's followers. A minister is defined as 'a minister of religion, or other person, who performs functions in connection with the religion and holds an office or appointment in, or is accredited, approved or recognised for the purposes of, a relevant organisation in relation to the religion'. Paragraph 29 provides a definition of a 'relevant organisation in relation to a religion' which is identical to the definition of 'organisation relating to religion or belief', but for the omission of the word 'belief' on each line. This exception replaces a similar provision in section 35 of the Sex Discrimination Act 1975; some of the requirements have been modified in order to provide consistency within the Equality Act 2010.[141]

In the same way as *Amicus* emphasised the narrowness of religious exceptions in relation to employment, the Court of Appeal in *Ladele*[142] emphasised the narrowness of religious exceptions in relation to goods and services. Dyson LJ held that the exception now found in paragraph 2 of Schedule 23 of the Equality Act 2010 'identifies the relatively limited circumstances in which it is permissible to discriminate against anyone on grounds of sexual orientation on grounds of religion or belief'.[143] This means that where the exception does not apply, 'the prohibition of discrimination by the 2007 Regulations takes precedence over any right which a person would otherwise have by virtue of his or her religious belief or faith to practice discrimination on the ground of sexual orientation'.[144]

For Dyson LJ, 'the legislature has decided that the requirements of a modern liberal democracy, such as the United Kingdom, include outlawing discrimination in the provision of goods, facilities and services on grounds of sexual orientation, subject only to very limited exceptions'.[145] This is perfectly true; but the judgment in *Ladele* points to a broader trend where it seems to have been forgotten that the United Kingdom has also chosen to outlaw discrimination on grounds of religion or belief. There needs to be more recognition of the necessity to balance competing protected characteristics. The 'trumping' of rights is crude and unhelpful.[146]

The following table provides a summary of the religious exceptions which apply in relation to goods and services:

---

[141] Equality Act 2010 Explanatory Notes para. 752.   [142] [2009] EWCA (Civ) 1357.
[143] At para. 70.   [144] At para. 69.   [145] At para. 73.
[146] See further R. Sandberg, 'The Implications of the Court of Appeal Decision in *Ladele*', www.law.cf.ac.uk/clr/research/WorkingPapers.html.

Exception	Source of Law	Beneficiary	Terms of the Exception
Exception from laws forbidding discrimination on grounds of sexual orientation in relation to the provision of goods and services.	Equality Act 2010 Sch. 23 para. 2.	The discrimination must be done by 'an organisation relating to religion or belief'.	The exception is applied either because it is necessary to comply with the doctrine of the organisation or to avoid conflict with the strongly held convictions of a significant number of followers.
Exception from laws forbidding discrimination on grounds of religion in relation to the provision of goods and services.	Equality Act 2010 Sch. 23 para. 2.	The discrimination must be done by 'an organisation relating to religion or belief'.	The exception is applied either because of the purpose of the organisation or 'to avoid causing offence on grounds of religion or belief'.
Exception from laws forbidding discrimination on grounds of sex in relation to the provision of goods and services.	Equality Act 2010 Sch. 3 para. 29.	A minister providing a service for the purposes of an 'organised religion' at a place used for those purposes. The Minister must hold an office or appointment in, or is accredited, approved or recognised for the purposes of, 'a relevant organisation in relation to the religion'.	The exception is applied either because it is necessary in order to comply with the doctrines of the religion or is for the purpose of avoiding conflict with the strongly held religious convictions of a significant number of the religion's followers.

Conclusions

One of the most striking distinctions between twentieth-century religion law and that of the twenty-first century is the importance of provisions found in discrimination law. The interaction between discrimination law and religion is now at the heart of the study of law and religion. Although many of the key provisions predate the Equality Act 2010, that statute is now one of the most important in domestic religion law. It is unquestionably the case that the new discrimination provisions have furthered religious freedom in some instances, notably in relation to working hours and in some religious dress cases. However, the most significant effect of the new law has been an increase in litigation and the growing prevalence of the notion of religious rights.

Many aspects of the law remain clouded in uncertainty. For instance, whilst it is clear that the religious exceptions now found in the Equality

Act 2010 have not been as radically narrowed as they were in earlier drafts of that Bill, the ambit and scope of the exceptions remain unknown. This is shown in the almost comical way in which both those arguing for and against the changes to the Equality Bill insisted that their view was in line with the current law. The complexity of the provisions and the ambiguity of the language used will inevitably lead to further litigation. The only guidance to be derived from the cases to date is that the exceptions are to be interpreted narrowly. It is to be hoped that this guidance, buttressed by concerns raised by the European Commission, does not lead to a situation where the exceptions are routinely not applied. The application of these exceptions needs to be determined on a case-by-case basis. There should be no presumption (implicit or explicit) that they should not be applied because of their perceived narrowness. If the narrowness of the exceptions continues to be stressed, the risk is that they will narrow to the extent that they cease to exist.

This is not to say, however, that the current exceptions strike the correct compromise. The lines drawn may at times seem arbitrary. It would be easier to understand why certain exceptions are enjoyed by 'organised religions' and others by 'organisations relating to religion or belief' if it was known what those terms meant. Nevertheless, discrimination law does make some concession to religious groups and to religious employers whose religious beliefs clash with obligations placed on them. In contrast, religious individuals – such as religious employees – are in a very different legal position. They simply have to rely on the general terms of the law protecting religion. The cases of *Ladele*, *McFarlane* and *McClintock* illustrate the limits of the protection offered by the new law.

The cases to date on religion and belief discrimination show that claims for direct discrimination will rarely be successful. Given that direct discrimination cannot be justified, the restrictive approach employed here may not be a bad thing, always provided that other forms of legal redress are available to the claimant. Many of the direct discrimination claims made to date could and should have been argued under indirect discrimination. Direct discrimination claims ought to be made prudently. A tendency to argue 'everything but the kitchen sink' undermines the worth of the argument and is off-putting to the decision-maker.

Although a less restricted approach has been taken in relation to indirect discrimination claims, a number of recent decisions are cause for concern. Some cases seem to follow the trend found in the Article 9 case law and focus upon the question of interference rather than justification. This is unnecessary, because the claim could have been adequately dealt with by focusing upon the question of justification. Even if focusing upon interference does not alter the outcome of the case, this tendency is problematic in that it might not allow examination of the merits of the case. Focusing upon justification does not mean that the law provides claimants with a blank cheque. It does, however, allow nuanced fact-specific conclusions which will not constrain subsequent cases. This tendency to focus upon the question of interference points to a larger problem. The new religion law is being hampered by the restrictive approach that is being taken in relation to the interpretation of Article 9. This means that Article 9 is not seen as the heart of British religion law. If it were, then all other religious rights could be said to derive from the basic protection afforded under Article 9.

The last two chapters have highlighted the two main recent legal changes of twenty-first-century religion law. The changes reflect a complicated and conflicted move towards a multi-faith society where the State seeks to facilitate (and regulate) a religious free market by increasing the quantity and reach of regulation. The new 'two pillars' of religion law, Article 9 and the law prohibiting discrimination on grounds of religion, have resulted in new standards and expectations which may be used to critique older long-standing provisions of religion law. The next three chapters seek to explore this in greater depth. They investigate areas where law and religion have long interacted, examining how older provisions concerning religion are being challenged in the twenty-first century.

7

Religious offences

Introduction

The law on blasphemy[1] was perhaps the most well-known piece of religion law in England and Wales. However, following years of passionate debate about the future of the offence in a multicultural and religiously diverse society, the abolition of blasphemy was surprisingly low-key. Section 79 of the Criminal Justice and Immigration Act 2008 took just one sentence to abolish the offence. However, the abolition of blasphemy does not mean that the criminal law no longer engages with religion. This chapter is the story of how the dormant offence of blasphemy has been succeeded by an unworkable offence of stirring up religious hatred.

This chapter falls into two sections. The first examines the 'old' religious offences, focusing upon the offence of blasphemy and the events which led to its abolition. The second examines the 'new' religious offences, focusing upon the offences created by the Racial and Religious Hatred Act 2006, together with the new category of religiously aggravated offences. This chapter examines how the interaction between religion and English criminal law has long been, and remains, multi-faceted, perplexing and controversial.[2]

The old religious offences

English criminal law interacts with religion in various different ways.[3] Although there are examples of some religious exceptions from specific crimes,[4] there is no general defence of carrying out divine instructions[5]

---

[1] See, generally, D. Nash, *Blasphemy in the Christian World: A History* (Oxford: Oxford University Press, 2007).

[2] See also A. Jeremy, 'Religious Offences' (2003) 7 *Ecclesiastical Law Journal* 127; and J. G. Oliva, 'The Legal Protection of Believers and Beliefs in the United Kingdom' (2007) 9 *Ecclesiastical Law Journal* 66.

[3] This chapter does not discuss sentencing, on which see C. Bakalis and P. Edge, 'Taking Account of Religion in Sentencing' (2009) 29(3) *Legal Studies* 421.

[4] Under s. 139 of the Criminal Justice Act 1988, it is a defence to the charge of having a blade in a public place if the blade is carried 'for religious reasons'. Body modification, including ritual circumcision of males and religious flagellation with consent is an answer to a charge under the Offences against the Person Act 1861: *R. v. Brown* [1993] 2 All ER 75 (see, in particular, the comments of Lord Mustill); cf. Female Genital Mutilation Act 2003.

[5] *Blake* v. *DPP* [1993] Crim L. R 556.

or special protection for religious drug use.[6] Religious laws often contain provisions on discipline and, in the case of the Church of England, such laws are part of the law of the land.[7] However, even focusing solely upon religious offences, it is clear that there is a plethora of overlapping laws. The story does not begin, let alone end, with the law of blasphemy.

A number of provisions enacted in the nineteenth and early twentieth centuries protecting religious worship remain on the statute books. Under the Offences Against the Person Act 1861, it is an offence to obstruct any clergyman from celebrating divine service or otherwise officiating in any church, chapel, meeting house or other place of divine worship.[8] Similarly, in England and Wales[9] it is an offence to molest, disturb, vex or trouble[10] or to attack any clergyman or other minister who is engaged in a rite or duty.[11] It is an offence if a person knowingly and wilfully solemnises a marriage according to the rites of the Church of England or Church in Wales[12] falsely pretending to be in Holy Orders.[13]

Several offences protect the burial of the dead. It is an offence to obstruct by threats or force the lawful burial of the dead in any churchyard or other burial place[14] or interfere with any grave, vault, tombstone or other memorial or any flowers or plants.[15] Some of these provisions overlap with the offence of blasphemy. Most notably, under the Burial Laws Amendment Act 1880, it is an offence to 'bring into contempt or obloquy the Christian religion, or the belief or worship of any church or denomination of Christians, or the members or any minister of any church or denomination, or any other person'.[16] These blasphemy-like offences remain operative. Section 79 of the Criminal Justice and Immigration Act 2008 only abolished the 'offences of blasphemy and blasphemous libel[17] under the common law of England and Wales'.[18]

---

[6]   *R.* v. *Taylor* [2001] EWCA Crim 2263; *R.* v. *Andrews* [2004] EWCA Crim 947.

[7]   For discussion of clergy discipline in the Church of England, see M. Hill, *Ecclesiastical Law*, 3rd edn (Oxford: Oxford University Press, 2007), ch. 6.

[8]   Offences against the Person Act 1861 s. 36.

[9]   Although the offence of riotous behaviour under s. 2 of the Ecclesiastical Courts Jurisdiction Act does not extend to Scotland, the common law offence of breach of the peace (which is a much wider offence in Scotland than in England and Wales) provides the necessary protection to religious services: see Select Committee on Religious Offences in England and Wales: First Report of Session 2002–03 (HL 95–I) para. 27.

[10] Ecclesiastical Courts Jurisdiction Act 1860 s. 2.   [11] Criminal Law Act 1967 s. 1.

[12] Marriage Act 1949 s. 78.   [13] Marriage Act 1949 s. 75(1)(d).

[14] Offences against the Person Act 1861 s. 36; Criminal Law Act 1967 s. 1.

[15] Local Authorities' Cemeteries Order 1977 s. 18.   [16] Section 7.

[17] For convenience, the term 'blasphemy' is used to refer to both of these offences throughout this chapter.

[18] The Criminal Law Act 1967 abolished the statutory offence of blasphemy, repealing the Blasphemy Act 1697. Although the Criminal Justice and Immigration Act 2008 removed the references to blasphemous libel in the Criminal Libel Act 1819, and for eliminating blasphemy in the Law of Libel Amendment Act 1888, it does not affect other statutory religious offences.

The common law offence of blasphemy

The law of blasphemy protected the sanctity of Christian beliefs since those beliefs were regarded as being at the heart of society.[19] Originally dealt with by the Church courts, by the seventeenth century the offence became enforced by the ordinary criminal courts. Blasphemy was akin to treason. In *Taylor's Case*,[20] the Chief Justice of the day held that saying that 'Jesus Christ was a bastard, an impostor and a cheat' was 'not only an offence to God and to religion, but a crime against the laws, state and Government'. He reasoned that to undermine religion was 'to dissolve all those obligations whereby the civil societies are preserved'; since 'Christianity is parcel of the Laws of England', it followed that 'to reproach the Christian religion is to speak in subversion of the law'.[21]

The *actus reus*[22] of the offence was to publish 'blasphemous' material in any form.[23] Material was 'blasphemous' if the content was contrary to the tenets of the Church of England and couched in indecent or offensive terms likely to shock and outrage the feelings of the general body of believers. The extent to which the law extended beyond the Church of England was an open question. As noted in Chapter 2, after the Reformation the Church of England alone was the lawful religion. Even though other religions became tolerated over time, the terms 'Christianity' and the 'Church of England' were often regarded as being synonymous. This led to judicial pronounce-ments which today seem contradictory. In *Gathercole's Case*,[24] for instance, it was noted that a person could lawfully attack 'any sect of the Christian Religion (save the established religion of the country)' because the Church of England alone is 'the form established by law, and is therefore a part of the constitution of the country' and yet 'any general attack on Christianity is the subject of criminal prosecution, because Christianity is the established religion of the country'.

However, the question of whether or not the offence covered other forms of Christianity was largely academic because of the *Williams*[25] overlap

---

[19] The following develops arguments first made in R. Sandberg and N. Doe, 'The Strange Death of Blasphemy' (2008) 71(6) *Modern Law Review* 971; and M. Hill and R. Sandberg, 'Blasphemy and Human Rights: An English Experience in a European Context' IV (2009) *Derecho y Religión* 145.

[20] (1676) 1 Vent 293.

[21] See House of Lords Select Committee on Religious Offences in England and Wales, Volume I – Report (2003), Vol. I, App. 3, para. 2.

[22] In English criminal law, as a general rule it must be proved beyond reasonable doubt that the defendant has committed the *actus reus* of the offence with the needed *mens rea* and is not entitled to any defence. The *actus reus* is the external element which varies from offence to offence, but usually takes the form of conduct, circumstances or a state of affairs. The *mens rea* is the mental element, usually denoted by words such as 'intentionally', 'recklessly', 'maliciously' or 'negligently'.

[23] 'Blasphemous' material could be published in a written or verbal form. See *R. v. Gott* (1922) 16 Cr App R 87.

[24] (1838) 2 Lewin 237.   [25] (1797) 26 St Tr 654.

principle: attacks on other Christian denominations and other religions were protected 'to the extent that their fundamental beliefs are those which are held in common with the established Church'.[26] In *Williams*, a publication attacking the Old Testament was interpreted not merely as an attack upon Judaism: rather it was held that 'the Old Testament is so connected with the New that it was impossible that such a publication as this could be uttered without reflecting upon Christianity itself'. Other religious groups, Christian or not, were protected to the extent that their beliefs overlapped with those of the Church of England.[27]

The material also needed to be couched in indecent or offensive terms likely to shock and outrage the feelings of the general body of Church of England believers. Material was blasphemous if it was 'offensive to anyone in sympathy with the Christian religion, whether he be a strong Christian, or a lukewarm Christian, or merely a person sympathising with their ideas'.[28] Decent and reasonable criticism was not blasphemous. The mere publication of a anti-Christian work,[29] and the registration of a company promoting the principle that human conduct should be based upon natural knowledge and not supernatural belief,[30] were thus not caught by the blasphemy law.

The *mens rea* of the offence was only firmly established in the last successful prosecution. The House of Lords in *R. v. Lemon, R. v. Gay News*[31] held that the defendant must have intended to publish the blasphemous material. There was no requirement that the defendant had an intention to blaspheme; it was sufficient for the prosecution to prove that the publication had been intentional and that the matter was blasphemous. The *Gay News* case was the first successful prosecution for almost sixty years.[32] During that period, blasphemy was policed extra-legally. It was curtailed 'by the fears, anxieties and sensitivities of individuals' rather than by law:[33] copies of Siné's *Massacre*, a French cartoonist's book of anti-clerical cartoons (some of which had a sexual theme), were burned; permission was refused to make a film entitled *The Many Faces of Jesus* concerning Jesus' sex life; and moral campaigner Mary Whitehouse led a campaign against *Monty Python's Life of Brian*.[34] A similar moral panic led to the *Gay News* case itself in 1979, in which Whitehouse brought a private prosecution alleging that the publication of James Kirkup's poem, 'The Love That Dares to Speak its Name', was blasphemous. In 1991 an attempted private prosecution for blasphemy

---

[26] See also *R. v. Chief Stipendiary Magistrate, ex parte Choudhury* [1991] 1 QB 429.
[27] See also *House of Lords Select Committee* (above), Vol. 1, App. 3, para. 4.
[28] *R. v. Gott* (1922) 16 CR App R 87.   [29] *R. v. Ramsay and Foote* (1883) 15 Cox CC 231.
[30] *Bowman* v. *Secular Society Ltd* [1917] AC 406.   [31] [1979] AC 617.
[32] Since *R. v. Gott* (1922) 16 CR App R 87.
[33] See R. Webster, *A Brief History of Blasphemy* (Oxford: Orwell Press, 1990), ch. 1.
[34] R. Hewison, *Monty Python: The Case Against* (London: Eyre N Methuen Ltd, 1981), pp. 66–7.

against Salman Rushdie following the publication of *The Satanic Verses* failed: in *R. v. Chief Stipendiary Magistrate, ex parte Choudhury*,[35] the application was refused on the grounds that the common law offence of blasphemy applied only to the Christian religion and there was no justification for a court to extend this, not least since it was likely to do more harm than good.

The road to abolition

The *Choudhury* judgment that extending blasphemy was likely to do more harm than good could be seen as clear evidence that the abolition of blasphemy was inevitable. The private prosecution of *Gay News* proved exceptional. Later similar publications had passed unnoticed. 'The Love That Dares to Speak its Name' was broadcast on BBC television[36] and recited publicly without prosecution.[37] The offence of blasphemy had seemed to fall into desuetude. Commentators spoke of the offence as a 'dead letter'[38] and abolition was mooted by those who considered its removal as a mere tidying-up exercise.[39] In 1981, the Law Commission proposed abolition,[40] while in 2001, the then Home Secretary David Blunkett told the House of Commons that the Government's position was that 'there is a good case for revising and, indeed, removing existing blasphemy law'.[41]

During this time it was often asserted that the offence of blasphemy could not exist in a modern multi-faith society since it would be incompatible with the European Convention on Human Rights. In *Corway v. Independent Newspapers (Ireland) Ltd*,[42] the Irish Supreme Court concluded that a prosecution for the crime of blasphemy could not succeed in Ireland on grounds of freedom of religion and legal uncertainty. It was questionable whether the blasphemy law was compatible with the freedom of religion provision in Article 44.1 of the Constitution which places the duty on the State to respect and honour religion. Moreover, since blasphemy was undefined by

---

[35] [1991] 1 QB 429.

[36] During the course of the BBC2 television programme *Taboo* (broadcast 12 December 2001). The response from the BBC's Head of Programme Complaints Unit was that this 'was responsible and appropriate to the subject matter and the inclusion of part of the poem was justified. [The] change in public attitudes over time has extended the degree of tolerance'.

[37] In 2002, a group from the National Secular Society arranged a public recitation of 'The Love That Dares to Speak its Name' to commemorate the twenty-fifth anniversary of the prosecution. Advanced notice was provided in the press. Again, there was no police action.

[38] A. Denning, *Freedom Under Law – Hamlyn Lecture* (London: Stevens & Co, 1949), p. 46.

[39] See, e.g. R. Ahdar and I. Leigh, *Religious Freedom in the Liberal State* (Oxford: Oxford University Press, 2005), p. 368.

[40] Law Commission (1981) Offences against Religion and Public Worship (Working Paper No. 79).

[41] HC Deb Column 707 (26 November 2001).   [42] [1999] 4 IR 484.

the Irish Constitution or in its law,[43] it was 'impossible to say of what the offence of blasphemy consists'. Relying upon *Corway*, the House of Lords Select Committee on Religious Offences in England and Wales expressed the view that the offence of blasphemy was a dead letter, contending that 'any prosecution for blasphemy today . . . is likely to fail on grounds either of discrimination or denial of the right to freedom of expression'.[44] The Report contended that in addition to discrimination against non-Christian faiths, the law on blasphemy was uncertain in relation to whether the offence applied only to the Church of England. Similar concerns were also expressed at the report stage in the House of Lords of what was to become the Racial and Religious Hatred Act 2006. During this, Lord Averbury advanced what are now well-rehearsed arguments concerning legal certainty and discrimination against other faiths, together with fears concerning the perceived low level of *mens rea* required for a blasphemy prosecution and the concern that the enactment of the Racial and Religious Hatred Act without the abolition of blasphemy would lead to confusion.[45] These constant human rights concerns suggested that the road to abolition, although long, was inevitable.

However, this is a simplification. The absence of prosecutions could be seen as a sign of the success of the law, rather than its futility. Arguments concerning blasphemy made by the Irish Supreme Court, the House of Lords Select Committee and in Parliamentary debates on what was to become the Racial and Religious Hatred Act 2006 all rested upon the assumption that the offence was incompatible with the European Convention on Human Rights. Yet the European Court of Human Rights had repeatedly come to the opposite conclusion. In *Gay News Ltd* v. *United Kingdom,*[46] it was held that the law on blasphemy was compliant with both freedom of religion (Article 9) and freedom of expression (Article 10). Although the offence constituted a restriction on freedom of expression, the restriction was justified in order to protect the religious feelings of citizens and was legitimate and necessary in a democratic society, provided the principle of proportionality was respected. Strasbourg also upheld the right of public bodies to enforce the English law of blasphemy.[47] Articles 9 and 10 are to be balanced against one another. The freedom to manifest religion does not amount to a right to be

---

[43] The Defamation Act 2009 has subsequently made the publication of 'blasphemous matter' an offence under Irish law. The Act abolished the common law offences of criminal libel, seditious libel and obscene libel, but fixed the maximum fine for the new offence of publishing of blasphemous matter at €25,000. It provides a defence of 'genuine literary, artistic, political, scientific or academic value' in respect of allegedly blasphemous material.

[44] House of Lords Select Committee on Religious Offences in England and Wales, First Report (2002–3) App. 3, para. 9.

[45] HL Hansard, Col. 520 (8 November 2005), Cols. 521–2.

[46] (1983) 5 EHRR 123.   [47] *Wingrove* v. *United Kingdom* (1997) 24 EHRR.

exempt from all criticism,[48] while freedom of expression contains 'a duty to avoid expressions that are gratuitously offensive to others and profane'.[49]

It is also questionable whether the law of blasphemy would have been held to be incompatible with Convention standards on legal certainty (Article 7) or discrimination against other faiths (Article 14). In the *Gay News* case,[50] the House of Lords was able to review centuries-old authorities to reach the conclusion that the *mens rea* of the offence was certain. And the alleged lack of clarity as to whether the offence protected the Church of England specifically or Christianity generally was a moot point, given the *Williams*[51] overlap principle. The offence of blasphemy was no more uncertain than several other common law crimes such as manslaughter by gross negligence. To date, the courts have not held that these crimes are incompatible with Article 7.[52]

In relation to discrimination, it needs to be remembered that the Article 14 prohibition is not a free-standing right;[53] the discrimination must be within the ambit of another Convention Article.[54] If it was alleged that the offence was not Convention-compliant since it discriminated against non-Christian faiths, then the relevant other Convention Article would be Article 9. Such a claim was unsuccessful in *Choudhury* v. *United Kingdom*.[55] It was held that that 'no State authority or anybody under which the United Kingdom Government may be responsible under the Convention directly interfered in the applicant's freedom to manifest his religion or belief'. The current unwillingness of English courts to accept interference with Article 9,[56] especially in conjunction with Article 14,[57] suggests that even after the Human Rights Act 1998 the domestic courts would have reached a similar

---

[48]   *IA* v. *Turkey* (Application no. 42571/98), 13 September 2005, para. 28.

[49]   *Ibid.*, para. 24.

[50]   *Corway* v. *Independent Newspapers (Ireland) Ltd* (above) at para. 31.

[51]   (1797) 26 St Tr 654.

[52]   D. Ormerod, *Smith & Hogan Criminal Law*, 12th edn (Oxford: Oxford University Press, 2008), 26.

[53]   Article 1 of Protocol 12 would extend the right to 'any right set forth by law', but this has not been ratified in the UK.

[54]   This does not mean that a 'violation of a substantive Article needs to be established at all in cases involving discrimination' under Art. 14. As the Strasbourg Court held in *Case Relating to Certain Aspects of the Laws on the Use of Languages in Education in Belgium* (1979–80) 1 EHRR 252 at 282: 'a measure which in itself is in conformity with the requirements of the Article enshrining the right or freedom in question may however infringe this Article when read in conjunction with Article 14 for the reason that it is of a discriminatory nature'. See P. M. Taylor, *Freedom of Religion* (Cambridge: Cambridge University Press, 2005), pp. 182–3.

[55]   *Choudhury* v. *United Kingdom* (1991) 12 HRLJ 172.

[56]   See Chapter 5.

[57]   *Gallagher (Valuation Officer)* v. *Church of Jesus Christ of Latter-day Saints* [2008] UKHL 56. See R. Sandberg, 'Underrating Human Rights: *Gallagher* v. *Church of Jesus Christ of the Latter-Day Saints*' (2009) 11 *Ecclesiastical Law Journal* 75.

decision. As we will see, litigation concerning the broadcast of *Jerry Springer: the Opera* seems to indicate that this was the case.

Jerry Springer: the court case

It might seem that the High Court decision in *Green* v. *The City of West-minster Magistrates' Court*[58] is destined to be a historical footnote. At first glance, the case may be seen as yet another failed attempt to bring a prosecution for an offence that was clearly past its sell-by date. However, examined more closely, *Green* may be regarded as the last hurrah of the blasphemy offence. Contrary to the consensus that emerged in the Irish Supreme Court, the House of Lords Select Committee and in Parliamentary debates concerning the Racial and Religious Hatred Act, *Green* indicated that the law of blasphemy *was* compatible with the European Convention on Human Rights. The *Jerry Springer* litigation suggests that blasphemy was abolished because the offence was dormant rather than dead. Despite appearances to the contrary, *Green* is more than a historical footnote.

In 2005 the television broadcast of *Jerry Springer: The Opera* caused a furore, albeit one which was stirred up by certain pressure groups.[59] Two years later a member of one of the most vocal groups, Christian Voice, sought to bring a private prosecution for blasphemous libel against the producer of *Jerry Springer: the Opera* and the Director General of the BBC. When the District Judge sitting in the Magistrates' Court refused to issue a summons, on the grounds that prosecution was prevented by the Theatres Act 1968 and there was no prima facie case, Green applied for judicial review. The Divisional Court refused the application. Hughes LJ noted that although it was very rarely invoked, the offence of blasphemy still existed. The law could be accurately stated and was Convention-compliant because interference with freedom of expression is permitted under Article 10(2); and there would not normally be an interference with Article 9 rights since the right to hold and practise a religion was generally unaffected by such insults. This undermined the conventional view that blasphemy was not Convention-compliant.

However, the two grounds upon which Hughes LJ refused judicial review provided a more cogent rationale for abolishing the offence. Firstly, he held that the District Judge had not erred in her finding that there was no prima facie case to answer. The District Judge had been entitled to

---

[58] [2007] EWHC (Admin) 2785.

[59] The BBC received a record 55,000 complaints before transmission and 8,000 further complaints post transmission. Many commentators, including BBC News, attributed this high volume of complaints to an orchestrated campaign by various Christian groups – such as Christian Voice and The Christian Institute. Christian Voice published the home addresses of several BBC executives on their website, which led to one executive receiving death threats and having to leave their home for a while to protect their life and those of their children.

conclude that the play as a whole was not and could not reasonably be regarded as aimed at Christianity or at what Christians held sacred. It was apparent from the claimant's own description of the work (and confirmed by the Court's own brief viewing of a recording) that the target of *Jerry Springer: the Opera* was 'the tasteless "confessional" chat show, rather than the Christian religion'. Moreover, there was no evidence before the District Judge justifying a finding of prima facie damage to society or of the risk of civil strife. Since the facts were not in dispute, her conclusion was within the range of decisions properly open to her. Secondly, Hughes LJ held that section 2(4) of the Theatres Act 1968 prevented prosecution. The Act states that no one can be prosecuted against in respect of a play 'for an offence at common law where it is of the essence of the offence that the performance or, as the case may be what was said or done was obscene, indecent, offensive, disgusting or injurious to morality'. The Court held that this applied to the offence of blasphemy, which was a common law offence, the essence of which was such offensiveness as to be a danger to society in general. Although the Theatres Act 1968 did not apply to the broadcast by the BBC, the Broadcasting Act 1990[60] contained provisions identical to those in the Theatres Act applicable to broadcasts.

To put it mildly, it is surprising that provisions in the Theatres Act 1968 or the Broadcasting Act 1990 were not considered in previous judicial deliberations or academic writings concerning blasphemy. If the reasoning of the court is correct, then the post-*Green* offence of blasphemy was heavily curtailed. The recognition of the requirement for proof of societal damage in *Green*, although by no means new, had a similar effect. However, it was arguably Hughes LJ's *dicta* concerning the European Convention which were the most important. The judgment negatived many of the human-rights justifications assumed by those who advanced the abolition of blasphemy. And, for the reasons explained above, it was entirely correct to do so. The *Jerry Springer* litigation showed that although the prospect of a prosecution was small, the offence was sufficiently certain and Convention-compliant to be successfully invoked if necessary. Although the House of Lords refused to hear the case judicially, it was not long before Parliament consigned the offence of blasphemy to history.

The right to blaspheme

On 9 January 2008 on the floor of the House of Commons, Dr Evan Harris MP moved a new clause to the Criminal Justice and Immigration Bill to abolish what he called 'the ancient discriminatory, unnecessary, illiberal and non-human rights compliant offences of blasphemy and blasphemous libel'.[61] Dr Harris withdrew his amendment in response to an

---

[60] Schedule 15 para. 6.   [61] HC Deb (2008–09) (9 January 2008) c 442.

undertaking by the Government to bring forward its own new clause to like effect in the House of Lords, subject to a satisfactory outcome to consultations with the Church of England.[62] The Labour Government, contending that it was 'high time that Parliament reached a settled conclusion on the issue',[63] moved such an amendment on 5 March 2008 in the House of Lords.[64]

The Government's reasons for the amendment were said to be twofold. Firstly, it was held that there was now 'new legislation to protect individuals on the grounds of religion and belief'. Secondly, somewhat comically, it was argued that since the law 'has fallen into disuse', this 'runs the risk of bringing the law as a whole into disrepute'. This is questionable. The *Jerry Springer* litigation showed that the law was beginning to be used again. The dearth of prosecutions could be seen as a sign of the success rather than the failure of the law. The argument that a defective law on blasphemy had the potential to bring down the whole legal system is not worth engaging with. This warped rhetoric sought to mask the fact that the underlying factor, however, was the decision in *Green* or at least the reaction to it. It was the very finding in *Green* that blasphemy was not obsolete (as many had assumed) which galvanised the abolitionists. The High Court had showed that blasphemy was a sleeping giant. Although the giant would rarely be woken, he was dormant, not dead. The amendment was passed by 148 votes to 87 by the House of Lords and then by 378 votes to 57 in the House of Commons. The giant was dead.

However, the abolition of blasphemy does not mean that there is now a complete right to blaspheme. The only change is that the goalposts have moved. Under the blasphemy laws there was a criminal prohibition against publishing material outraging Christianity and offending Christians. Its abolition means that, in the absence of a criminal prohibition, there is now a legal freedom to publish such material. This is the space left by the 2008 Act. However, if a publication stirs up religious hatred or causes a public order disturbance, the new criminal law on religion will intervene. The major difference between blasphemy and the new criminal offences is that Christianity is now treated the same as all other religions. In other respects the offences are very similar; and some commentators have contended that certain provisions provide an effective replacement for the blasphemy offence.[65] More importantly, as we will see, many of the criticisms made of the old law of blasphemy may also be made of the new offences. It remains uncertain when a publication will step over the line and a criminal offence will be committed. The problem with blasphemy was that the law was largely symbolic and it was not clear when the criminal law should step

---

[62] *Ibid.*, cc 453–4.   [63] *Ibid.*, c 453.   [64] HL Deb (2008–09) (5 March 2008) c 1118.

[65] See N. Addison, *Religious Discrimination and Hatred Law* (Oxford: Routledge, 2007), p. 133, referring to s. 4A of the Public Order Act 1986.

in. As discussed below, the same is true of the offences enacted in the Racial and Religious Hatred Act 2006. Many of the laws are of largely symbolic importance.[66]

The new religious offences

From the last quarter of the twentieth century onwards, there has been a considerable growth in the number of public order offences.[67] A number of these general offences have been used to control both religious speech and speech that may offend religious believers.[68] The general provisions of the Public Order Act 1986 have been used to prosecute successfully the display of a poster in a window showing events of 9/11 and the words 'Islam out of Britain'[69] and the display of a sign by an elderly Evangelical protester saying 'Stop Immorality. Stop Homosexuality. Stop Lesbianism. Jesus is Lord'.[70] Unsuccessful prosecutions have been brought in respect of the publication of *The Satanic Verses*[71] and a notice denouncing a president of a Gurdwara as a hypocrite, liar and 'mad dog'.[72] The Protection from Harassment Act 1997 has been used to grant an injunction against an individual because of his continual harassment of members of the Mormon Church[73] and against a Sikh mother-in-law for badly treating her daughter-in-law following an arranged marriage.[74] Anti-Social Behaviour Orders (ASBOs)[75] have also been used in religious matters; but the extent to which they are used is difficult to quantify.[76]

In addition to these general public order offences sometimes used to regulate religion, there are two developments which together may be seen as representing the new criminal law on religion: new offences outlawing religious hatred and religiously aggravated offences. As with the new law on religious discrimination,[77] the new criminal law on religion extends laws which previously afforded protection on grounds of race to cover

---

[66] However, it could be said that, while the law of blasphemy was a nostalgic symbol of a Christian past, the new offences are symbolic of an attitude on the part of Government that religion is a social problem to be controlled.

[67] For an earlier example, see *Wise* v. *Dunning* [1902] 1 KB 167.

[68] The following develops arguments first made in N. Doe and R. Sandberg, 'The Changing Criminal Law on Religion' (2008) 161 *Law and Justice* 88.

[69] *Norwood* v. *DDP* [2003] EWHC Admin 1564.

[70] *Hammond* v. *DDP* [2004] EWHC Admin 69.

[71] *Horseferry Road Metropolitan Stipendiary Magistrate, ex parte Siadatan* [1991] 1 QB 260.

[72] *Dehal* v. *CPS* [2005] EWHC Admin 2154.

[73] *Christ of Latter Day Saints* v. *Price* [2004] EWHC Admin 325.

[74] *Singh* v. *Bhaker* [2006] Fam Law 1026.

[75] Under the Crime and Disorder Act 1998, Police Reform Act 2002 ss. 61–6 and the Anti Social Behaviour Act 2003 ss. 85–6.

[76] See N. Addison, *Religious Discrimination and Hatred Law* (Oxford: Routledge, 2007), pp. 137–8.

[77] See Chapter 6.

religion. This creates an equal playing-field. While previously Sikhs[78] and Jews[79] were protected as races, other religious groups such as Muslims were left unprotected.[80] A basic argument could be advanced reasoning that the extension of protection ought to be uncontroversial given that it seeks only to create this equal playing-field. However, the attractiveness of this simplistic logic should not detract from the fact that these developments *are* controversial. Leaving to one side the vexed question of whether religion is a comparable category to race,[81] important questions remain concerning the merit and effectiveness of these developments.

Religious hatred

These questions are particularly relevant in relation to the Racial and Religious Hatred Act 2006.[82] It took four attempts and five years to get offences outlawing religious hatred on the statute book and even then the content of the offences differed from what the Labour Government had intended.[83] The Act amended the Public Order Act 1986 to create Part 3A, entitled 'Hatred against persons on religious grounds'. Under the Criminal Justice and Immigration Act 2008,[84] this Part was expanded to include 'Hatred against persons on religious grounds or grounds of sexual orientation', following the trend in discrimination law whereby religion and sexual orientation are regulated similarly.[85]

Part 3A includes six criminal offences protecting groups of believers from being threatened in a way that is defined by reference to religious belief or lack of religious belief. For each offence the words, behaviour, written material, recordings or programmes must be threatening and intended to stir up religious hatred. This is contrary to the original intentions of the Government, which had wanted the offence to be extended to also include 'abusive or insulting' words or behaviour and had wanted a dual *mens rea* whereby the prosecution would need to prove *either* intention to stir up religious hatred *or* that the defendant was being reckless as to whether or

---

[78] *Mandla* v. *Dowell Lee* [1983] 2 AC 548.

[79] *Seide* v. *Gillette Industries Ltd* [1980] IRLR 427.

[80] *J. H. Walker Ltd* v. *Hussain and others* [1996] ICR 291. See also *Crown Suppliers (PSA) Ltd* v. *Dawkins* [1993] ICR 517, concerning Rastafarians.

[81] This question has also come to the fore in relation to discrimination law. See Chapter 6.

[82] For a full account, see I. Hare, 'Crosses, Crescents and Sacred Cows: Criminalising Incitement to Religious Hatred' [2006] *Public Law* 521; and K. Goodall, 'Incitement to Religious Hatred: All Talk and No Substance' (2007) 70(1) *Modern Law Review* 89.

[83] The House of Lords defeated the Government on many key points. Although the Government tried to get the Bill back to its original state in the House of Commons, it lost this by one vote when the then Prime Minister Tony Blair left early. The Bill thus passed into law with Commons supporting some of the Lords' amendments. See N. Addison, *Religious Discrimination and Hatred Law* (Oxford: Routledge, 2007), pp. 139–41.

[84] See s. 74 and Sch. 16.   [85] See Chapter 6.

not religious hatred would be stirred up. This would have extended the reach of the offences.

The offences cover 'every conceivable form of communication that hatred could be incited by'.[86] The new offences apply to the use of words or behaviour or display of written material, publishing or distributing written material, the public performance of a play, distributing, showing or playing a recording, broadcasting or including a programme in a programme service, and the possession of written materials or recordings with a view to display, publication, distribution or inclusion in a programme service. There is an inchoate form of the offence, by way of possession of inflammatory material, allowing law enforcement agencies to tackle those who harbour material with a view to committing one of the above communications. Unusually, however, there is no equivalent substantive offence.[87] Moreover, the need for these offences may be questioned. Most of the extreme types of incidents suggested in Parliament would have already been covered by existing criminal offences.[88]

The offences are further restricted in two ways: by the definition of 'religious hatred' and by the inclusion of a freedom of speech clause. Religious hatred is defined as 'hatred against a group of persons defined by reference to religious belief or lack of religious belief'.[89] Although the Explanatory Notes professed that the meaning of 'religious belief or lack of religious belief' was deliberately broad,[90] the reference to 'religious belief' seems narrower than the term 'religion or belief' used in human rights and discrimination law.[91] Whilst including those defined by a lack of religious belief, it would seem to exclude beliefs that are not religious. Moreover, the focus upon 'a group of persons' would seem to exclude individual believers who cannot be identified with a larger group. This mirrors trends in discrimination law.[92]

In response to numerous complaints on grounds of free speech by actors and comedians such as Rowan Atkinson, the Government introduced a clause on 'Savings for discussion, debate and criticism, etc'. The clause itself was a masterpiece of circular reasoning stating that a person was not guilty of an offence under that part of the Bill which was part of a discussion or debate, or consisted of insulting or ridiculing any religion, religious belief or religious practice 'unless he intends thereby to stir up religious hatred or is reckless as to whether religious hatred would be stirred up thereby'. In other words, a person was not to be liable for stirring up religious hatred

---

[86]   R. Clarke, 'Freedom of Speech, Religious Sensibilities and Inciting Hatred in English Law in N. Doe and R. Sandberg (eds.), *Law and Religion: New Horizons* (Leuven: Peeters, 2010), p. 95.
[87]   I. Hare, 'Crosses, Crescents and Sacred Cows: Criminalising Incitement to Religious Hatred' [2006] *Public Law* 521, 533.
[88]   See Hansard HC Deb vol. 435 c 668–762 (21 June 2005).   [89]   S. 29A.
[90]   Explanatory Notes, para. 12.   [91]   See Chapter 3.
[92]   *Eweida* v. *British Airways* [2010] EWCA Civ 80, discussed in Chapter 6.

unless he stirred up religious hatred. Unsurprisingly, this utterly meaningless provision was replaced by the House of Lords. The 'protection of freedom of expression' provision now reads:

> Nothing in this Part shall be read or given effect in a way that prohibits or restricts discussion, criticism or expressions of antipathy, dislike, ridicule, insult or abuse of particular religions or the beliefs or practices of their adherents, or of any other belief system or the beliefs of practices of its adherents, or proselytising or urging adherents of a different religion or belief system to cease practising their religion or belief system.[93]

This provision is yet to be considered judicially and so its worth is open to question. It may well be that the section, like section 13 of the Human Rights Act 1998,[94] is largely symbolic, serving simply as a reminder that competing rights do exist. The Explanatory Notes purported to explain the section by providing what was effectively a verbatim copy of the section. The reference to 'beliefs' in the section is of interest, given that the offence seemingly protects only 'religious beliefs'; criticism of a non-religious belief will not be restricted by any of the offences anyway. Moreover, the woolly 'protection of freedom of expression' provision can still be contrasted with the clear exception clause which states that '[n]othing in this Part applies to a fair and accurate report' of Parliamentary[95] or judicial proceedings. However, it remains the case that, for most commentators, the existence of this provision (together with the neutering of the offences) means that the likelihood of a successful prosecution under the Act is slim.[96] This may not be a bad thing. If the Labour Government had succeeded with its original plans for the offence, religious hatred would represent a significant and disproportionate limit upon free speech. However, the law as it currently stands amounts to little more than political posturing; a simple statement that religious hatred is wrong.

Religiously aggravated offences

The Crime and Disorder Act 1998 created a new category of racially aggravated offences and, following 9/11, the Anti-Terrorism Crime and Security

---

[93] Public Order Act 1986 s. 29J. Section 29JA now provides a separate freedom of expression in relation to sexual orientation (inserted by the House of Lords during the passage of the Criminal Justice and Immigration Act 2008). The Government sought to remove the section during the passage of the Coroners and Justice Act 2009, but this was again rejected by the House of Lords.

[94] See Chapter 4.

[95] Including the Scottish Parliament and now the Welsh Assembly (Criminal Justice and Immigration Act 2008 Sch. 16 para. 15).

[96] See A. Jeremy, 'Practical Implications of the Enactment of the Racial and Religious Hatred Act 2006' (2007) 9 *Ecclesiastical Law Journal* 187.

Act 2001 extended these to deal with religiously aggravated offences.[97] There are four categories of racially or religiously aggravated offences in England and Wales which 'piggy-back' onto existing criminal offences.[98] Section 29 of the Crime and Disorder Act 1998 covers racially or religiously aggravated assaults,[99] piggy-backing onto the offences of common assault,[100] actual bodily harm[101] and maliciously wounding or causing grievous bodily harm;[102] section 30 covers criminal damage;[103] section 31 covers several offences under the Public Order Act 1986;[104] while section 32 covers harassment.[105] If it is proved that the defendant commits one of the offences listed in that category and that it was racially or religiously aggravated, the offence carries a higher maximum punishment.[106]

In relation to all other offences,[107] section 145 of the Criminal Justice Act 2003 provides that racial or religious aggravation is a factor hightening the seriousness of the offence which may be taken into account at sentencing stage.[108] Thus, while there is no offence of religiously aggravated arson, if a person commits arson in a religiously aggravated manner, the sentence should be higher than it otherwise would have been.[109] The difference between the two is that the question of whether one of the offences found in sections 29 to 32 of the Crime and Disorder Act 1998 is religiously aggravated is a question of fact, determined usually by the jury By contrast, for all other offences, the question of religious aggravation is a question of sentencing, determined by the judge.[110]

Regardless of whether religious aggravation is a question of fact or a question of sentencing, there are two different ways in which an offence can be said to be religiously aggravated. Firstly, an offence is religiously aggravated if the offender demonstrates towards the victim hostility based

---

[97] See M. Idriss, 'Religion and the Anti-Terrorism Crime and Security Act 2001' [2002] *Criminal Law Review* 890; and R. Card, *Card, Cross and Jones Criminal Law*, 19th edn (Oxford: Oxford University Press, 2010), pp. 219–26.

[98] In Scotland, 'offences aggravated by religious prejudice' are governed by the Criminal Justice (Scotland) Act 2003. See also s. 50A of the Criminal Law (Consolidation) (Scotland) Act 1995.

[99] Although the marginal note uses the term 'assaults', it would be preferable to regard these as racially or religiously aggravated offences against the person since maliciously wounding or causing grievous bodily harm does not require proof of an assault. See *R. v. Savage & Parmenter* [1991] 4 All ER 698.

[100] Criminal Justice Act 1988 s. 39.   [101] Offences against the Person Act 1861 s. 47.

[102] Section 20.   [103] Criminal Damage Act 1971 s. 1(1).   [104] Sections 4, 4A and 5.

[105] Protection from Harassment Act 1997 ss. 2 and 4.

[106] *R. v. Rogers* [2007] UKHL 8 at para. 16, Baroness Hale.

[107] See, e.g. *R. v. Christian Murphy* [2009] EWCA Crim 2859. As with most of the reported cases, this case was concerned with racial rather than religious aggravation. However, it is likely that the principles apply just as much to religious aggravation.

[108] Section 146 provides for an increase in sentences for aggravation related to disability or sexual orientation, following the trend in discrimination law whereby religion and sexual orientation are regulated similarly.

[109] See N. Addison, *Religious Discrimination and Hatred Law* (Oxford: Routledge, 2007), p. 131.

[110] *R. v. Rogers* [2007] UKHL 8 at para. 16, Baroness Hale.

on the victim's membership of (or presumed membership of) a religious group.[111] This limb of the offence is concerned with the 'outward manifestation' of religious hostility.[112] This does not require proof that the defendant was motivated by religious hostility.[113] The test is that the defendant formed the view that the victim was a member of a religious group and that the defendant demonstrated hostility based on that membership.[114] The demonstration of hostility must be 'immediately' before or after the criminal offence: a demonstration twenty minutes after the act will not suffice.[115] Membership includes 'association with members of that group' and presumed membership means presumed by the offender.[116] A religious group is defined as 'a group of persons defined by reference to religious belief or lack of religious belief'.[117]

Secondly, an offence is religiously aggravated if it is motivated by hostility towards members of a religious group based on their membership of that group.[118] This limb of the offence is concerned with 'the inner motivation of the offender'.[119] It requires proof that the defendant was at least partly[120] motivated by religious hostility. This need not be towards the victim, but needs to be towards members of a religious group. Religious aggravation may exist regardless of whether the defendant is of the same religious group as the object of the offence.[121] The hostility may be established by evidence relating to what the defendant has said or done on other occasions.[122]

In both cases, it is immaterial whether or not the hostility of the offender is also based, to any extent, on any other factor other than religion.[123] This raises the question of where the line should be drawn between offences which are aggravated by religion and offences where the facts of the dispute just happened to concern religion. The law on racial aggravation shows that the question of where to draw the line is difficult. This is shown, for instance, by the case of *DDP* v. *M (A Minor)*,[124] in which following a dispute with the Turkish chef about whether he had paid for food, the defendant said the word 'bloody foreigners' before he committed an offence of criminal damage. He was found liable for a racially aggravated offence.

---

[111] Crime and Disorder Act 1998 s. 28(1)(a).

[112] *R. v. Rogers* [2007] UKHL 8 at para. 6, Baroness Hale.

[113] *DPP* v. *Green* [2004] EWHC (Admin) 1125.

[114] R. Card, *Card, Cross and Jones Criminal Law*, 19th edn (Oxford: Oxford University Press, 2010), p. 224. See *AG`s Reference (No. 4 of 2004)* [2005] EWCA Crim 889 (on racial aggravation).

[115] *Perry* v. *DPP* [2004] EWHC (Admin) 3112 (on racial aggravation). See R. Card, *Card, Cross and Jones Criminal Law*, 19th edn (Oxford: Oxford University Press, 2010), p. 225.

[116] Crime and Disorder Act 1998 s. 28(2).   [117] Section 28(5).

[118] Section 28(1)(b).   [119] *R. v. Rogers* [2007] UKHL 8 at para. 6, Baroness Hale.

[120] See R. Card, *Card, Cross and Jones Criminal Law*, 19th edn (Oxford: Oxford, University Press, 2010), p. 226.

[121] *White* [2001] EWCA Crim 216 (on racial aggravation).

[122] *G* v. *DDP* [2004] (Admin) EWHC 183 (on racial aggravation).

[123] Crime and Disorder Act 1998 s. 28(3).   [124] [2004] EWHC (Admin) 1453.

However, as Card has argued, the case could be said to be more to do with food served in a kebab shop than racial aggravation.[125] The House of Lords in *R. v. Rogers*[126] confirmed that 'the context will illuminate what the conduct shows'.[127] But this is not always clear. Language derived from certain religious traditions has now taken on a secular meaning. It is clear that calling someone 'Judas', for instance,[128] would not always equate to religious hostility – but working out when it does and when it does not is far from straightforward. In *R. v. Rogers*,[129] the House of Lords suggested that 'the statute intended a broad non-technical approach',[130] meaning that although an offence does not simply become racially aggravated because of the use of a particular word,[131] the use of the words 'bloody foreigners' could amount to racial aggravation in a certain context.[132] This would seem that generic anti-religious sentiments, such as a reference to 'superstitious nonsense', could amount to religious aggravation. The curt answer that 'it depends on the context' shows that the law here is as uncertain as the law on blasphemy ever was.

Many of the criticisms that apply to the religious hatred offences apply also in relation to religiously aggravated offences. It is unclear why these offences are needed and why existing criminal law offences could not be applied. If existing powers of sentencing are insufficient when there is religious hostility, then surely they are insufficient in other contexts and so the appropriate remedy would be to increase the maximum sentence. Moreover, it is strange and potentially discriminatory that these provisions apply only to religious groups and protect only religious beliefs and groups defined by the lack of such beliefs.[133] However, unlike the headline-grabbing provisions of the Racial and Religious Hatred Act, the existence of religiously aggravated offences is not merely symbolic posturing. It is to be expected that wherever there is any suggestion of religious aggravation, any criminal liability will be increased.

Conclusions

Given the abolition of blasphemy, the temptation is now to ignore any interaction of religion and criminal law. After all, most of the religion law litigation concerns human rights and discrimination law rather than the criminal law provisions discussed in this chapter. However, this would be misguided, not least because the reported cases only shed light on a small

---

[125] R. Card, *Card, Cross and Jones Criminal Law*, 19th edn (Oxford: Oxford University Press, 2010), p. 224.
[126] [2007] UKHL 8.   [127] Para. 14, Baroness Hale.
[128] P. W. Edge, 'Extending Hate Crime to Religion' (2003) 8 *Journal of Civil Liberties* 5, 23.
[129] [2007] UKHL 8.   [130] Para. 11, Baroness Hale.   [131] Para. 13.   [132] Para. 14.
[133] P. W. Edge, 'Extending Hate Crime to Religion' (2003) 8 *Journal of Civil Liberties* 5, 21.

area of activity. Religious offences remain a key part of our religion law. They are often misunderstood and their ambit is usually unknown.

Recent years have seen significant changes to the way in which English criminal law interacts with religion. The headline is that the dormant offence of blasphemy has been replaced by the unworkable offence of religious hatred. However, delving behind this headline shows that the interaction between religion and the criminal law has been far from straightforward: *Green* shattered common understandings about the offence of blasphemy, leading to its abolition, while the religious hatred provisions found on the statute books are drastically different from those intended by the Government. The precise effect of the freedom of expression provision, in particular, is unknown.

Delving beneath the headline, it is also important to note that the replacement of blasphemy by the religious hatred offences did not occur in isolation. Older provisions protecting religious worship are still operative and some of the general provisions are curiously blasphemy-like. Alongside these a plethora of modern public order offences can be and are used in relation to religion, often in unexpected ways. This is especially true of the use of ASBOs: the extent to which they are applied in religious matters is unknown. Moreover, although often forgotten, the provisions on religious aggravation have real bite: all offences can result in tougher penalties if religiously aggravated. Again, however, the law is unclear. There is an absence of reported decisions and it is uncertain how far the law extends.

The practical effect of religious offences is open to doubt. However, this ineffectiveness may not necessarily be a bad thing. An argument may be made here that the criminal law is the wrong vehicle to regulate religion. The criminal law provides the 'established state response'[134] seeking to punish wrongdoing, which is so severe that a prosecution needs to be brought on behalf of the State in the name of the Crown. It is too blunt an instrument to regulate religion. Human rights and discrimination law provisions provide better vehicles which can be driven not by the State, but by aggrieved parties. In *Percy* v. *DPP*,[135] the High Court accepted that 'there is a pressing social need in a multi-cultural society to prevent the denigration of objects of veneration and symbolic importance for one cultural group'. This is true. But a case could be made that this is a matter for individual believers, facilitated by the State, rather than a matter for the State. In other words, it is a matter for the civil rather than the criminal law. It is thus to be regretted that the civil cases on religious symbols have not adequately protected religious believers.[136] This is not to say that the criminal law should never be used in relation to religion. Rather, the criminal law should be used sparingly. And in the rare cases where the State needs to bring a

---

[134] J. Herring, *Criminal Law*, 6th edn (Hampshire: Palgrave Macmillan, 2009), p. 4.
[135] [2001] EWHC Admin 1125.   [136] See Chapters 5 and 6.

criminal prosecution, it is to be expected that the crime in question would be outlawed by the general criminal law. There should be no need for specific religious offences.

The ineffectiveness of the law does not mean that concerns about religiously offensive material do not occur. Moral panics will take place even when there is no chance of a successful prosecution. The lack of legal redress may serve to restrict rather than reinforce free speech. For instance,[137] in 2004 Birmingham Repertory Theatre's production of *Behzti*, a contemporary play by Sikh playwright Gurpreet Bhatti which explored issues of sexual abuse, manipulation and relationships inside a Gurdwara, a Sikh place of worship, led to violent protests. The windows of the theatre were broken. Threats were made against the director and actors. The play was immediately withdrawn from production, but no criminal charges were brought. Blasphemy was policed by mob-rule. Policing blasphemy by public pressure is inherently problematic, since the most active pressure groups may not be representative of society as a whole. Moreover, rule by pressure group ignores the democratic basis that underpins the law. The defects in the current criminal law on religion are therefore of concern. The current legal framework, while seeking to appease both believers and non-believers, actually fails to satisfy either. Current compromises are largely adequate. The next chapter will question whether the same is true of education law on religion, another area where law and religion have long interacted.

---

[137] See also the furore surrounding the television broadcast of *Jerry Springer: The Opera*, discussed above.

8

Religion in schools

Introduction

Although the contexts and specificities differ, school attendance is one of the few common experiences that most of the population have. It is this that makes the study of the relationship between religion, law and education especially important. With the possible exception of rites of passage such as marriage and funerals,[1] the closest many people get to religion is in school. While there are many different laws affecting the place of religion in the public sphere, such as the prison rules concerning religious observance[2] and rules concerning the provision of chaplaincy[3] (in prisons,[4] hospitals,[5] the armed forces[6] and universities[7]), it is the religion law provisions affecting schools which have the most effect upon the entire population.

This chapter examines the law concerning religious education and worship in schools and the legal status of faith schools.[8] It asks whether the current laws are sustainable in light of changing social norms, the increased legal protection of the rights of the child and the new legal framework concerning religion addressed in previous chapters. Are current, often long-standing, legal provisions compatible with twenty-first century religion law?

---

[1] See Chapter 4. [2] Prison Act 1952; Prison Rules 1999.
[3] See J. Rivers, *The Law of Organized Religions* (Oxford: Oxford University Press, 2010), ch. 7.
[4] See Chapter 4.
[5] The provision of spiritual care for patients and staff in hospitals is governed by health service guidelines which have the status of quasi-legislation. See, e.g. Department of Health, *Your Guide to the NHS: Getting the Most from your National Health Service* (2001); *NHS Chaplaincy: Meeting the Religious and Spiritual Needs of Patients and Staff* (2003). See the Department of Health website: www.dh.gov.uk.
[6] Army Chaplains Act 1868; Queen's Regulations for the Army 1961; Territorial Army Volunteer Regulations 1967; Queen's Regulations for the Royal Air Force 1964; Queen's Regulations for the Royal Navy 1967.
[7] Chaplaincy is largely a matter for the individual religious organisations and the individual universities; and its extent and nature vary widely between institutions because the institutions themselves vary so widely.
[8] The following develops research originally conducted for M. Hill, R. Sandberg and N. Doe, *Religion Law: United Kingdom* (The Netherlands: Kluwer Law International, 2010). I am indebted to Paul Barber, of the Catholic Education Office, who provided valuable comments upon that research.

The school system

There are many different types of schools in Great Britain.[9] This chapter distinguishes between those schools which have a religious character and those which do not. However, it is important to note that there is no simple distinction between 'faith schools' and 'State schools'. A great number of 'faith schools' receive a great amount of State funding, while 'State schools' are by no means secular. Indeed, Rivers has claimed that 'a case could be made that almost all schools in England and Wales are faith schools'.[10] The meaningful distinction is between schools which are maintained by the State and independent schools that are not so funded.[11] Both maintained and independent schools can have a religious character. Rather than talking of 'faith schools' and 'State schools', the distinction should be drawn between schools without a religious character and schools which are designated as having a religious character. The following will outline the differences between maintained and independent schools.

Maintained schools

As a general rule maintained schools are financially maintained by Local Education Authorities (LEAs), follow the National Curriculum and are subject to inspection by Ofsted.

Maintained schools include both those established by the State (LEAs and their predecessors) – about two-thirds of the total – and those established by voluntary bodies – about one-third. The voluntary body in question is typically religious; schools tend to be set up by churches and other religious communities.

Maintained schools are organised into five statutory categories laid out in section 20 of the School Standards and Framework Act 1998:

(a) community schools;
(b) foundation schools;
(c) voluntary schools, comprising –
    (i) voluntary aided schools, and
    (ii) voluntary controlled schools;
(d) community special schools; and
(e) foundation special schools.[12]

---

[9] The education system differs significantly in the different nations. Unless stated otherwise, the following relates only to education in England.

[10] J. Rivers, *The Law of Organized Religions* (Oxford: Oxford University Press, 2010), p. 234.

[11] See www.direct.gov.uk/en/Parents/Schoolslearninganddevelopment/ChoosingASchool/DG_4016312.

[12] Section 20(1).

There are three basic different types: community, voluntary and foundation schools.[13] Community schools are those established by the State, while voluntary schools are those established by voluntary bodies whose successors[14] normally own the school's land and buildings and appoint some members of the school's governing body. Voluntary schools are divided into voluntary aided and voluntary controlled schools. Foundation schools may be seen as a hybrid form. They are largely State-established schools, but a foundation school may acquire a formal relationship with a charitable trust and become known as a 'trust school'. The foundation school category also contains a significant number of voluntarily established schools which, like voluntary schools, already have trust arrangements in place.

The main differences between these categories are control and financing. Community and voluntary controlled schools are run by the LEA, which employs the staff and sets admission criteria. Foundation and voluntary aided schools are run by their governing bodies. Where a voluntary body has established a school, it will appoint 'foundation governors' whose duty is to preserve and develop the religious character of the school and to ensure that it is conducted in accordance with its trust deed. These are in the minority in voluntary controlled and foundation schools, but in the majority in the case of voluntary aided schools. In voluntary aided schools the governors, rather than the LEA, are responsible for capital expenditure, but usually with the assistance of a 90 per cent grant from central government.

Independent schools

In contrast to these maintained schools, independent schools are funded by fees paid mainly by parents. Just over one-half of independent schools have charitable status.[15] They are largely free to run their own affairs, including setting their own curricula and admission policies, but need to be registered with the Government Department responsible for education and are subject to inspection either by Ofsted or by an inspectorate approved by the

---

[13] Community special schools and foundation special schools cater for children with special educational needs.

[14] A charitable trust known as a 'foundation' in education law: School Standards and Framework Act 1998 s. 21.

[15] It is commonly understood that the effect of the Charities Act 2006 is that it is no longer presumed that charities for the advancement of education are for the public benefit. Instead, public benefit needs to be proven. A number of independent schools believe they will lose charitable status unless they meet the charity commission's checklist or 'guidance'. See the reports by the Charity Commission and the recent update on progress at www.charity-commission.gov.uk/RSS/News/pr_pb_update.aspx. See also P. Luxton, *Making Law? Parliament* v. *The Charity Commission* (London: Politeia, 2009).

Secretary of State. The distinction between maintained schools and independent schools is not watertight. For instance,[16] Academies,[17] City Technology Colleges and City Colleges for the Technology of the Arts fall between the two different models.[18] These are, technically, independent schools, set up by a private or charitable 'sponsor', but funded fully by central government by means of a funding agreement with the sponsor. This forbids the charging of fees to pupils and obliges the school to operate within some of the same constraints applicable to maintained schools.

The important point to note is that both maintained and independent schools may have some form of religious character. The following section focuses upon maintained schools which have not been designated as having a religious character. This is then followed by an examination of schools that have a religious character, distinguishing between maintained schools with a religious character and independent schools.

Schools without a religious character

Religion is far from absent in those maintained schools which do not have a religious character. Historically, education grew out of the work of both the established and non-established churches. This was true of the universities.[19] Until the nineteenth century, it was impossible for those who were not members of the Church of England to obtain a university degree in England because both Oxford and Cambridge imposed a religious test.[20] Non-conformists either attended the so-called 'Dissenting Academies' or went to study in Scotland. The first avowedly secular Higher Education institution, University College, London, was established by Jeremy Bentham in 1826. The religious test at Oxford and Cambridge was not removed until the passing of the Universities Tests Act 1871 – and even so, for some time afterwards it was retained for students and teachers of theology.

The same trend can be seen in relation to schools. These were first formed by religious bodies with State involvement deepening throughout

---

[16] Non-maintained special schools are a further exception. These are schools established by charitable trusts and approved by the Secretary of State. They cater for children with special educational needs, and are funded by contracts with LEAs who place children with them: Education Act 1996 s. 342.

[17] See the Academies Act 2010.   [18] Education Act 1996 s. 482; Education Act 2002 s. 68.

[19] See F. Cranmer, 'La Présence Religieuse dans l'Enseignement Supérieur au Royaume-Uni' in A. Fornerod (ed.), *Assistance spirituelle dans les Services publics* (Strasbourg: Strasbourg University Press), forthcoming.

[20] At Cambridge, non-Anglicans could attend the University but not proceed to a degree, while at Oxford they were simply not admitted at all: A. Kadish and K. Tribe, *The Market for Political Economy: The Advent of Economics in British University Culture, 1850–1905* (London: Routledge, 1993), p. 22.

the nineteenth century. In England and Wales,[21] Parliamentary grants for voluntary schools for the poor were available from 1833.[22] The genesis of the current law can be found in the Elementary Education Act 1870 (the 'Forster Act'), which established local School Boards in areas where there were insufficient voluntary schools. Section 7 of the Act was the 'Cowper-Temple Clause' that 'no religious catechism or religious formulary distinctive of any particular denomination' was to be taught in these new schools. Over time, free compulsory elementary education became the norm[23] and the responsibilities of School Boards were passed to municipal councils, which became the LEAs.[24]

The Education Act 1944 (the 'Butler Act') was a watershed. It provided free secondary schooling for all in grammar, secondary modern and technical schools.[25] The Act made Religious Instruction (RI) and worship compulsory in all schools which received State funding, although parents could withdraw children on grounds of conscience. The Act also provided for Standing Advisory Councils for Religious Education (SACREs) – local regulatory bodies – and for voluntarily aided schools which would receive some State funding but be under denominational control. The current law, which is to be found in the Education Act 1996 and the School Standards and Framework Act 1998, remains very similar to that outlined in the Butler Act.

Religious Education

Religious Education (RE), as opposed to Religious Instruction (RI), continues to be compulsory in maintained schools. However, RE does not form

[21] In Scotland, the Church of Scotland had a major part to play in the establishment of a national system of education. In 1616 an Act of the Privy Council commanded every parish to establish a school; this was followed by the Education Act 1633, which levied a tax for their support on local landowners, and the Education Act 1696, which governed education until the passing of the Education (Scotland) Act 1872. Under the 1872 Act, the State took over responsibility for schooling from the Church of Scotland and it finally became compulsory for all children aged between five and thirteen. Although Roman Catholic voluntary schools were at first outside the State funding system, this was remedied by the Education (Scotland) Act 1918. The current law can be found in the Education (Scotland) Act 1980, as amended.

[22] From 1838 these were administered by a Special Committee of the Privy Council established by Order in Council. See C. Birchenough, *History of Elementary Education in England and Wales* (London: University Tutorial Press, 1938), p. 53.

[23] Fees were finally abolished by the Education Act 1918.

[24] Education Act 1902. The Scottish equivalent is Education Authority.

[25] Pupils were graded by the 'eleven-plus' exam into these three different schools. In practice, very few technical schools were set up. In 1965, a Labour Government Circular instructed LEAs to reorganise secondary education on comprehensive lines, for all children from a particular area irrespective of gender, ethnicity or social class, without any differentiation as to the type of school. While most LEAs completed this reorganisation, some only did so partially, and others did not do so at all, leading to the current patchy provision.

part of the National Curriculum. The Education Reform Act 1988, which introduced the National Curriculum, stated that RE was to be compulsory, but also provided that the content of RE would continue to be determined locally. The LEA, the governing body and the head teacher are under a legal obligation to ensure that RE is given in accordance with the local agreed syllabus.[26]

During the passage of the Education Reform Act 1988, a number of amendments in the House of Lords sought to secure the centrality of Christianity. This resulted in a requirement that RE had to 'reflect the fact that the religious traditions in Great Britain are in the main Christian'.[27] This remains the law; but there have been attempts to recognise religious plurality. Subsequent guidance insisted that RE syllabuses should not be based solely on Christianity and should include material on all 'principal religions'.[28] The current law reflects this, but remains based on the premise that Christianity is the norm. It states that the syllabus must 'reflect the fact that the religious traditions in Great Britain are in the main Christian whilst taking account of the teaching and practices of the other principal religions represented in Great Britain'.[29] However, despite the Christian starting-point, it is also stressed that RE is the study *of* religion rather than a study *in* religion. It is still forbidden for RE to be given to pupils 'by means of any catechism or formulary which is distinctive of a particular religious denomination (but this is not to be taken as prohibiting provision in such a syllabus for the study of such catechisms or formularies)'.[30]

The current law therefore seems to walk a tightrope: it begins from a presumption that Christianity is the norm, but that religious education also needs to embody religious neutrality while recognising religious plurality. The precise balance is determined at a local level. The locally agreed syllabus is determined by the SACRE.[31] It is compulsory for every LEA to establish a SACRE, which consists of 'representative groups' and other 'persons co-opted as members of the council by members of the council'. The 'representative groups' must include 'a group of persons to represent such Christian denominations and other religions and denominations of such religions

---

[26] School Standards and Framework Act 1998 s. 69. The syllabus may be different for different schools, classes or pupils.

[27] Section 8(3).

[28] The 'Non-Statutory Framework for Religious Education', published by the Qualifications and Curriculum Authority in 1994, said that RE ought to include Christianity and 'other principal religions' named as Buddhism, Hinduism, Islam, Judaism and Sikhism. It also recommended that there be an opportunity to study other religious traditions and secularist philosophies.

[29] Education Act 1996 s. 375(3).

[30] Schedule 19 to the School Standards and Framework Act 1998.

[31] The syllabus is adopted after receiving the advice of a periodic conference convened for that purpose. The membership requirements for the Conference are the same as those for the SACRE: Education Act 1996 Sch. 31.

as, in the opinion of the authority, will appropriately reflect the principal religious traditions in the area' and, in England, there must be 'a group of persons to represent the Church of England'.[32] This arguably provides an often-overlooked but potentially influential incident of establishment.[33] The reference to 'religious traditions' follows the trend in religious offences whereby protection is afforded only to religion and not to other beliefs.[34] This is out of sync with developments in human rights and discrimination law.[35] If discriminating against someone who has a belief in climate change can constitute religious discrimination,[36] then surely persons representing that belief should be allowed to influence the content of religious education. Most problematic, however, is the requirement that before appointing such a religious representative, 'the authority shall take all reasonable steps to assure themselves that he is representative of the religion, denomination or associations in question'.[37] This seems to allow LEAs to make a value judgment as to whether someone is genuinely representative of a religious group.

In addition to taking into account local factors, the law also provides for the accommodation of the religious beliefs of parents. Section 9 of the Education Act 1996 states that in exercising their powers LEAs should 'have regard to the general principle that pupils are to be educated in accordance with the wishes of their parents, so far as that is compatible with the provision of efficient instruction and training and the avoidance of unreasonable public expenditure'.[38] This ensures that domestic law is compatible with ECHR standards.[39] In practice, this means that if a parent requests that a pupil 'be wholly or partly excused' from receiving RE, the pupil is to be so excused until the request is withdrawn.[40] A pupil may be withdrawn from the school to receive RE elsewhere if the pupil 'cannot with reasonable convenience' be sent to school where religious education of that kind is provided.[41] There is also recognition of the religious freedom of teachers. No teacher can be required to give religious education, nor is he or she to 'receive any less remuneration or be deprived of, or disqualified for, any promotion or other advantage . . . by reason of the fact that he does

---

[32] Education Act 1996 s. 390.   [33] See Chapter 4.   [34] See Chapter 7.
[35] See Chapters 5 and 6.   [36] *Grainger Plc* v. *Nicholson* [2009] UKEAT 0219/09/ZT.
[37] Education Act 1996 s. 392(b).   [38] Section 9.
[39] Under Art. 2 of the First Protocol of the ECHR, the State must respect the right of parents to ensure for their children education conforming to the parents' own religious convictions. The United Kingdom has entered a reservation in relation to this accepting it only insofar as it is compatible with the provision of efficient instruction and training and the avoidance of unreasonable public expenditure.
[40] School Standards and Framework Act 1998 s. 71.
[41] Section 71(3). A pupil may not be withdrawn unless the LEA is satisfied that the arrangements proposed are such as will not interfere with the attendance of the pupil at school on any day except at the beginning or end of a school session: s. 71(4).

or does not give religious education'.[42] It may be noted that the only person whose religious freedom is not explicitly provided for is that of the pupil. This now seems at odds with the shift towards protecting the rights of the child[43] as well as the fact that the courts have entertained religious freedom and discrimination claims from schoolgirls.[44]

Religious worship

The law on religious worship in maintained schools is similar to that in relation to religious education. It remains compulsory for schools to hold a daily act of collective worship.[45] This will normally be held on school premises,[46] but it does not have to be held at the beginning of the day; and separate acts of worship may be held for pupils in different age or school groups.[47]

As with RE, the provisions on religious worship in the Education Reform Act 1988 are still reflected in the law; but the current law provides some degree of additional nuance. Under the 1988 Act, collective worship was to be 'wholly or mainly of a broadly Christian character'.[48] However, in *R. v. Secretary of State for Education, ex parte R and D*,[49] McCullough J held that worship which 'reflected Christian sentiments' complied with the Education Reform Act 1988 even if there 'was nothing in [it] which was explicitly Christian'. It was held that worship 'must in some sense reflect something special or separate from ordinary school activities. [It] should be concerned with reverence or veneration paid to a being or power regarded as supernatural or divine and . . . the pupil at his or her level, should be capable of perceiving this'.[50]

The current law is found in Schedule 20 to the School Standards and Framework Act 1998. This still states that 'the required collective worship shall be wholly or mainly of a broadly Christian character'. However, it clarifies that collective worship is of a broadly Christian character 'if it reflects the broad traditions of Christian belief without being distinctive of any particular Christian denomination'. Moreover, not every required act of collective worship needs to be of broadly Christian character, 'provided

---

[42] Section 59(3).
[43] This is in line with the principle in the Children Act 1989 that the welfare of the child is paramount.
[44] See Chapters 5 and 6.   [45] School Standards and Framework Act 1998 s. 70.
[46] However, if the governing body is of the opinion that it is desirable for worship on a special occasion to take place elsewhere than on the school premises, it may make arrangements after consultation with the head teacher.
[47] School Standards and Framework Act 1998 Sch. 20.   [48] Section 7(1).
[49] [1994] ELR 495.   [50] At 502.

that, taking any school term as a whole, most such acts which take place in the school do comply'.

Again, the precise balance is determined at a local level. One of the functions of the SACRE is to advise the LEA on 'such matters connected with ... religious worship in community schools or in foundation schools'.[51] The SACRE has the power to disapply the requirement in prescribed schools, for particular classes or for particular descriptions of pupils. This occurs on the application of the head teacher after consulting the Governing Body, which should take appropriate steps to consult parents.[52] In determining this, the SACRE should 'have regard to any circumstances relating to the family backgrounds of the pupils at the school, or of the pupils of the particular class or description in question, which are relevant for determining the character of the collective worship appropriate in their case'.[53] The SACRE is required to give the head teacher written notification of its decision on the application.[54]

The law also provides for the religious freedom of parents, teachers and, in this context, sixth-formers. Parents have a right to withdraw their children and sixth-formers have a right to withdraw themselves from daily worship.[55] If the parent of a pupil other than a sixth-form pupil requests that a child may be wholly or partly excused from attendance, that pupil shall be so excused until the request is withdrawn. Likewise, a sixth-form pupil making such a request shall be so excused. The religious freedom of teachers is also expressly provided for. No person is to be disqualified from being a teacher at a school or being employed or engaged for any other purpose at the school by reason of his or her religious opinions or for attending or omitting to attend religious worship.[56] And no teacher 'shall receive any less remuneration or be deprived of, or disqualified for, any promotion or other advantage . . . by reason of his religious opinions or of his attending or omitting to attend religious worship'.[57]

A satisfactory compromise?

On the face of it, the current law seems to strike a flexible, nuanced approach whereby the precise balance is determined locally, with emphasis given to the religious freedom of parents. However, the influence of the Education Reform Act 1988 continues to shape the law. The starting point remains Christian. It may be argued that this reflects both historical and sociological reality. As the sociologist of religion Davie has written:

---

[51] Education Act 1996 s. 391.   [52] Education Act 1996 s394(1), (5), (6).
[53] Section 394(2).   [54] Section 394(3).
[55] School Standards and Framework Act 1998 s. 71, 71A.
[56] *Ibid.*, s. 59(2).   [57] Section 59(4).

Christian nominalism remains a more prevalent phenomenon than secularism. Nor should the fact that belief in this country derives primarily from a Christian and largely Protestant culture be taken for granted. Christian assumptions and Christian vocabulary remain important even if the content has altered quite significantly.[58]

However, such views are by no means uncontested.[59] For instance, another sociologist of religion, Bruce, has argued that although 'the culture of a once-Christian society still possesses a few remnants, a few reminders of its past', the interest in religion is 'becoming weaker and more rare'.[60] Although the social historian Brown is right to say that 'the British have not replaced a certainty of religious faith with a certainty of atheistic faith',[61] it is questionable whether the religious underpinning found in education law reflects social reality. Legal assumptions that Britain is 'mainly' or 'broadly' Christian seem outmoded.

Indeed, given the abolition of blasphemy,[62] a case could be made that the laws on religious education and worship are now the clearest examples of the favouring of Christianity in religion law. However, as we saw in relation to blasphemy, there is no reason why the current law should automatically be considered to be incompatible with human rights standards. As Strasbourg has stated, preferential treatment towards one religion is not in itself incompatible with the ECHR. Incompatibility only arises if that special treatment prevents the religious freedom of those who do not conform to that religion.[63] Moreover, Strasbourg jurisprudence on Article 2 of the First Protocol indicates that the setting and planning of curricula fall within the competence of States, which enjoy a wide margin of appreciation. Strasbourg jurisprudence only draws the line at indoctrination.[64] The State 'must take care that information or knowledge included in the curriculum is conveyed in an objective, critical and pluralistic manner'.[65] The compatibility of the current law with both human rights and discrimination law standards is underscored by the fact that refusals to allow teachers time off during school

---

[58] G. Davie, *Religion in Britain since 1945* (Oxford: Blackwell, 1994), p. 76. See also G. Davie, *The Sociology of Religion* (London: Sage, 2007).

[59] This is a simplification of a multifaceted debate between Davie, Bruce and other sociologists of religion. A fuller account is given in R. Sandberg, 'Religion, Society and Law: An Analysis of the Interface between the Law on Religion and the Sociology of Religion' (Doctoral Thesis, Cardiff University, 2010).

[60] For Bruce, it is the lack of interest in religion that explains why self-conscious atheism and agnosticism remains rare. He notes that avowed atheists and agnostics are features of religious cultures and were at their height in the Victorian era: S. Bruce, *Religion in the Modern World: From Cathedrals to Cults* (Oxford: Oxford University Press, 1996), p. 38.

[61] C. G. Brown, *Religion and Society in Twentieth-Century Britain* (Harlow: Pearson, 2006), p. 314.

[62] See Chapter 7.

[63] *Darby* v. *Sweden* (1991) 13 EHRR 774. See Chapter 4.

[64] *Kjeldsen, Busk Madsen and Pederson* v. *Denmark* (1979) 1 EHRR 71.

[65] *Valsamis* v. *Greece* (1997) 24 EHRR 294.

hours to attend prayers have been upheld by courts as being consistent with the ECHR[66] and the law prohibiting religious discrimination.[67]

However, calls for change will not be abated just because the law is technically compatible with the ECHR. As we saw in Chapter 7, human rights and discrimination concerns led to the abolition of blasphemy even though the offence was compatible with ECHR standards. The problem was that the underpinning premises of the blasphemy law were different from those which underpin twenty-first-century religion law. The blasphemy law began from the premise that Britain is a Christian country and that the law ought to protect religion as such. These premises are not shared by the new religion law. And that ultimately is why blasphemy had to go. The same can be said of the laws concerning religion in schools without a religious character. The Christian starting point of the law jars with the expectation of religious neutrality expressed in the new law. Even though that Christian starting point may well be ECHR-complaint in that it does not lead to disadvantages for other religions or beliefs, the references to Christianity seem outmoded. Moreover, the emphasis on local and parental choice does not sit easily with the notion of religious freedom as an individual right. The extension of protection to sixth-formers is a step in the right direction, but is inadequate in an age where schoolchildren regularly appear in court trying to enforce their religious rights and when courts respond by saying that a child who wants to manifest his or her religious freedom in a different way can change school.[68]

Schools with a religious character

The existence, and Government encouragement of, so-called 'faith schools' represents one of the most controversial ways in which religion and the State interact. In addition to being a particular bugbear for secularists, the gen-uineness of faith schools is routinely undermined by frequent media reports of parents becoming 'religious' so that their children can attend what they perceive to be better schools. This section seeks to explore the legal reality, uncovering how the regulation of faith schools differs from those schools which do not have a religious character (discussed above). Throughout the discussion the legally accurate phrase 'schools with a religious character' will be used in preference to the colloquial phrase 'faith schools'. Although the phrase 'faith schools' is now commonly used to describe all religious schools, the term is a contested one which is resisted by many of the providers

---

[66] *Ahmad* v. *Inner London Education Authority* [1978] QB 36.

[67] *Mayuuf* v. *Governing Body of Bishop Challoner Catholic Collegiate School and another* [2005] Employment Tribunal Case no. 3202398/04 (21 December 2005).

[68] See Chapter 5 for a discussion of *R. (on the application of Begum)* v. *Headteacher and Governors of Denbigh High School* [2006] UKHL 15 and the subsequent case law.

of schools with a religious character.[69] Schools with a religious character are not new. As we have seen, originally they were the only schools. The subsidising of religious schools, which began in the nineteenth century, continues to this day. The two main types of religious school established by religious communities are maintained schools and independent schools. The following will examine both types in turn, with reference to their legal status and the application of the rules concerning religious education and worship.[70]

State-maintained schools with a religious character

Any foundation or voluntary school may be designated by the Secretary of State as having a religious character where he or she is satisfied that the school was established by a religious body or for religious purposes.[71] The designation must state the religion or religious denomination of the school.[72] The main legal advantages of designation are that such schools are able in prescribed circumstances to discriminate on grounds of religion or belief and are subject to different rules as to religious education and worship in schools and the respect given to the religious freedom of teachers.

The most important advantage is that a school designated as having a religious character can lawfully restrict entry based on religion or belief.[73] Three requirements must be met. Firstly, the school must be over-subscribed.[74] Secondly, the school's actions must fall within the exception afforded to schools so designated under the Equality Act 2010. The exception, now found in paragraph 5(a) of Schedule 11 to the 2010 Act,[75] exempts schools designated as having a religious character from the usual rules forbidding discrimination in admissions.[76] This exception also exempts designated

---

[69] Until the 1990s, the term 'church schools' was frequently used.

[70] See also P. Petchey, 'Legal Issues for Faith Schools in England and Wales' (2008) 10 *Ecclesiastical Law Journal* 174.

[71] School Standards and Framework Act 1998 s. 69(3).

[72] Section 69(4). Where more than one religion or religious denomination is so specified, this is to be construed as including a reference to any of those religions or religious denominations (s. 142). The procedure is governed by the Religious Character of Schools (Designation Procedure) Regulations 1998.

[73] However, attendance or abstaining from attending a Sunday school or a place of worship cannot be required as a condition of attending a maintained school: Education Act 1996 s. 398. Exceptions are also provided for LEAs and other public authorities: see Equality Act 2010 Sch. 3 para. 11. The previous law was found in the Equality Act 2006 ss. 51–2.

[74] Schools Admission Code for 2007, paras. 2.41–3. Section 84 of the School Standards and Framework Act 1998 provides that admission authorities must act in accordance with this Code. See J. Rivers, *The Law of Organized Religions* (Oxford: Oxford University Press, 2010), p. 255.

[75] The new provisions replicate those previously found in the Equality Act 2006 s. 50(1)(a).

[76] Equality Act 2010 s. 85(1).This covers the refusal to admit a person as a pupil as well as the arrangements and terms concerning admissions.

schools from the usual rules forbidding discrimination by schools in how they provide education.[77] However, the exception does not extend to other rules prohibiting discrimination by excluding pupils from school or by subjecting pupils to any other detriment.[78] Schools that have a religious character are not exempt from the general law on these matters – which means that they could not subsequently exclude a pupil or disadvantage him if he or his parents subsequently changed or lost their faith.[79]

The third requirement that needs to be met before a school with a religious character can lawfully restrict admission is that the school's actions must be on grounds of religion or belief. The exception found in paragraph 5(a) of Schedule 11 to the Equality 2010 Act only applies in relation to religion or belief discrimination. Schools with a religious character cannot discriminate on any other ground, such as on grounds of race or ethnicity. This is problematic, since often a watertight distinction cannot be drawn between race and religion. Where the line is drawn can have important ramifications. If admission is seen to be refused on grounds of religion, it is lawful; if admission is seen to be refused on grounds of race, it is unlawful. In *R (on the application of E)* v. *JFS Governing Body*,[80] the Supreme Court were asked to determine whether the school's admission requirement stipulating a restricted definition of Jewishness in accordance with the teaching of the Office of the Chief Rabbi was a test of ethnicity or a religious test. The Supreme Court Justices were divided. The majority held that it was a test of ethnicity and was therefore unlawful. Five considered that there had been direct discrimination on the grounds of race, while two concluded that there had been indirect discrimination that could not be justified. The minority held that there had been no racial discrimination at all; instead, the school had made a legitimate selection on the ground of religion in accordance with doctrine.[81]

In addition to different rules concerning admissions, schools designated as having a religious character also benefit from different rules concerning religious education and worship. In relation to religious education, a distinction is drawn between foundation and voluntary controlled schools with a religious character on the one hand and voluntary aided schools with a religious character on the other hand. The basic difference is that voluntary aided schools enjoy more freedom.[82]

---

[77] Section 85(2)(a)–(d). This includes the ways in which it does not provide education and affords and does not afford the pupil access to a benefit, facility or service.

[78] Section 82(2)(e)–(f).

[79] N. Addison, *Religious Discrimination and Hatred Law* (Oxford: Routledge, 2006), p. 94.

[80] [2009] UKSC 15.

[81] See further F. Cranmer, 'Who is Jew? Faith Schools and the Race Relations Act 1976' (2010) 164 *Law & Justice* 275; and P. Barber, 'State Schools and Religious Authorities: Where to Draw the Line?' (2010) 12(2) *Ecclesiastical Law Journal* 224.

[82] P. Petchey, 'Legal Issues for Faith Schools in England and Wales' (2008) 10 *Ecclesiastical Law Journal* 174, 177.

In a foundation or voluntary controlled school with a religious character, the rules are similar to those which apply to schools without a religious character. Religious education must be in accordance with an agreed syllabus, but the difference is that the agreed syllabus is one adopted for the school or for a class of pupils.[83] As with schools without a religious character, the agreed syllabus must be non-denominational.[84] However, while the general law affecting schools without a religious character provides a parental right to opt out, the law in relation to foundation or voluntary controlled schools with religious character provides a parental right to opt in. Where parents request that their children receive religious education in accordance with the religion or religious denomination specified in relation to the school, the governors are under an obligation to 'make arrangements for securing that such religious education is given to those pupils in the school during not more than two periods in each week' unless special circumstances render it unreasonable for them to do so.[85]

In voluntary aided schools with a religious character, the rules are closer to what one might expect of a faith school. Religious education must be in accordance with the trust deed or with the tenets of the religion or religious denomination specified in relation to the school.[86] There is a parental right to opt out of this denominational education.[87] This takes the form of a request that their child receive the kind of non-denominational RE that would be found in other schools. The governing body of a voluntary aided school with a religious character is under an obligation to make such arrangements where parents request that their children receive religious education in accordance with any agreed syllabus and it is not reasonably convenient for the parents to send the children to a school at which that syllabus is in use.[88] If the LEA is satisfied that the governing body is unwilling to make such arrangements, then they shall be made by the LEA.[89]

In relation to worship, no distinction is made between foundation, voluntary aided and voluntary controlled schools with a religious character. The daily act of collective worship must be in accordance with the trust deed or with the tenets of the religion or religious denomination specified in relation to the school.[90] In this respect, all schools with a religious character are in a very different position from schools without a religious character

---

[83] School Standards and Framework Act 1998 Sch. 19 para. 3.   [84] Para. 2(5).
[85] Para. 3(3).   [86] School Standards and Framework Act 1998 Sch. 19 para. 4.
[87] This is not to say that other faiths are not studied. In 2006 faith leaders entered into a non-statutory agreement with the Department of Education for religious schools to teach about other religions, primarily to demonstrate the need to understand other faiths and to combat ignorance and prejudice. See Department for Children, Schools and Families, *Faith in the System* (2007).
[88] Para. 4(3)–(4).   [89] Para. 4(5).
[90] School Standards and Framework Act 1998 Sch. 20 para. 5.

(at least in terms of legal provisions). The governing body of any voluntary or foundation school with a religious character are under an obligation to ensure that any denominational education given to pupils and the content of the school's collective worship are inspected.[91]

Different rules also apply in relation to teachers.[92] Once again, voluntary aided schools with a religious character enjoy more freedom. In foundation or voluntary controlled schools which have a religious character, different rules only apply in relation to 'reserved' teachers. Provided that there are more than two teachers, 'reserved' teachers can be appointed who are selected for their fitness and competence to give the required religious education and are specifically appointed to do so.[93] The number of such 'reserved' teachers must not exceed one-fifth of the total number of teachers, including the head teacher.[94] In the case of 'reserved' teachers, preference may be given in connection with the appointment, remuneration or promotion of teachers at the school to persons whose religious opinions are in accordance with those of the school, who attend religious worship in accordance with those tenets, and who give or are willing to give religious education at the school in accordance with those tenets.[95] Regard may be had, in connection with the termination of the employment or engagement of any reserved teacher at the school, to any conduct on his or her part which is incompatible with the precepts, or with the upholding of the tenets, of the specified religion or religious denomination.[96] In connection with the appointment of the head teacher, where the head teacher is not to be a reserved teacher, 'regard may be had to that person's ability and fitness to preserve and develop the religious character of the school'.[97]

All of the other teachers are governed by the same rules which apply to schools which do not have a religious character.[98] No teacher is to be required to give religious education.[99] They cannot be dismissed, paid less or not promoted because they do not give RE lessons, because of their religious opinions or because of their absence from religious worship.[100] No teacher 'shall receive any less remuneration or be deprived of, or disqualified for, any promotion or other advantage by reason of the fact that he does not give religious education or by reason of his religious opinions or of his attending or omitting to attend religious worship'.[101]

---

[91] Education Act 2005 ss. 48–50.
[92] L. Vickers, 'Religion and Belief Discrimination and the Employment of Teachers in Faith Schools' (2009) 4(2–3) *Religion & Human Rights* 137.
[93] School Standards and Framework Act 1998 s58(2).   [94] Section 58(3).
[95] Section 60(3), (5)(a).   [96] Section 60(3), (5)(b).   [97] Section 60(4).
[98] Section 60(2).   [99] Section 59(3).
[100] Section 59(2), (4).   [101] Section 59(4).

In voluntary aided schools which have a religious character, the rules which apply to reserved teachers in other schools with a religious character may be applied to all teachers.[102] All of the schools with a religious character may also be able to rely upon exceptions provided in discrimination law,[103] but these exceptions do not apply automatically or universally. They will need to show that in the particular case the terms of the exception are met.[104]

Independent schools with a religious character

Parents are placed under a legal duty to ensure that children of compulsory school age receive 'efficient full-time education . . . either by regular attendance at school or otherwise'.[105] They may decide that their children are to be educated at home or at an independent school instead of their attending any school maintained by the LEA.[106] Independent schools can be set up by any group. However, they must be registered[107] and are subject to inspection[108] against the Independent School Standards.[109]

Independent schools can be designated as having a religious character in the same way as a foundation or voluntary school. The order must state the religion or religious denomination in accordance with whose tenets education is provided at the school or the school is conducted.[110] The procedure is governed by separate secondary legislation.[111] Once designated, independent schools enjoy the same right to discriminate on grounds of religion in relation to school admissions as enjoyed by other designated maintained schools.[112]

Independent schools are not bound to follow the National Curriculum and requirements as to religious education and collective worship. However, the Independent School Standards must be met.[113] These provide requirements as to the quality of education provided, as well as the spiritual, moral, social and cultural development of pupils. For example, the school must promote principles that 'enable pupils to distinguish right from wrong and

---

[102] Section 60(5).   [103] See Chapter 6.
[104] *Glasgow City Council* v. *Mcnab* [2007] UKEAT 0037 06 1701 (17 January 2007).
[105] Education Act 1996 s. 77. For Scotland, see Education (Scotland) Act 1980. LEAs are under a duty to make arrangements to enable them to establish (so far as it is possible to do so) the identities of children who are not receiving suitable education otherwise than at a school: Education Act 1996 s. 436A.
[106] Education Act 1996 s. 463.   [107] Education Act 2002 ss. 158, 159.
[108] Sections 162A, 162B. For Wales, see ss. 163, 164.   [109] Sections 157, 165.
[110] School Standards and Framework Act 1998 s. 124B.
[111] Religious Character of Schools (Designation Procedure) (Independent Schools) (England) Regulations 2003.
[112] Equality Act 2010 Sch. 11 para. 5(b).
[113] Education Act 2002 Pt 10; Education (Inspection School Standards) (England) Regulations 2003 Sch.

to respect the law'; they must 'provide pupils with a broad general knowledge of public institutions and services'; and must 'assist pupils to acquire an appreciation of and respect for their own and other cultures in a way that promotes tolerance and harmony between different cultural traditions'.[114] These standards seem to go further than the courts, which have held that primarily equipping a child for life within their community rather than the country as a whole would be acceptable, provided that it does not foreclose the child's options in later years.[115] In respect of media concerns that schools with a religious character do not encourage pupils to be tolerant of other faiths, it might be observed that the regulation of independent schools in this matter is tighter than in relation to voluntary aided schools with a religious character.

The rules concerning the employment of teachers in independent schools designated as having a religious character are in line with voluntary aided schools. Independent schools may give preference in connection with the appointment, remuneration or promotion of teachers at the school to persons whose religious opinions are in accordance with that of the school, who attend religious worship in accordance with those tenets and who give or are willing to give religious education at the school in accordance with those tenets. Regard may be had, in connection with the termination of the employment or engagement of any teacher at the school, to any conduct on his or her part which is incompatible with the precepts, or with the upholding of the tenets, of the specified religion or religious denomination.[116]

Conclusions

The law concerning religion in schools is characterised by a number of complexities and contradictions. The letter of the law suggests that schools without a religious character have to be more 'religious' than one might have expected. Not only are religious education and worship compulsory, but the law requires them to be mainly Christian. Flexibility is, however, provided both through the powers given to local SACREs and the deference given to parental choice. In contrast, the letter of the law suggests that schools that are designated with a religious character are less religious than expected. As the table below indicates, this varies greatly depending upon type of school:

---

[114] Education (Inspection School Standards) (England) Regulations 2003 Sch. para. 2.
[115] *Secretary of State for Education and Science, ex parte Talmud Torah Machzikei Haddass School Trust* (1985) *The Times*, 12 August 1985.
[116] School Standards and Framework Act 1998 s. 124A.

Type of School	Admissions	Religious Education	Religious Worship	Teaching Staff
All schools without a religious character.	Cannot discriminate on grounds of religion.	Compulsory. Content determined by SACREs. Must be 'in the main Christian'. Parental right to opt out.	Compulsory. SACRE to advise and may disapply. Must be 'wholly or mainly of a broadly Christian character'. Parental/sixth-former right to opt out.	Not obliged to take RE or attend worship. Must not suffer disadvantage because of this or their religious views.
Foundation or voluntary controlled schools with a religious character.	May discriminate on grounds of religion.	Compulsory. In accordance with agreed syllabus for school or class. Must be non-denominational. Parental right to opt in to RE in accordance with religious character of school.	Compulsory. In accordance with religious character of school.	'Reserve' teachers can be appointed, disadvantaged and dismissed on grounds of their religion or belief and appointed to give RE. In relation to all other staff, same rules as apply in relation to schools without a religious character apply.
Voluntary aided schools with a religious character.	May discriminate on grounds of religion.	Compulsory. In accordance with religious character of school. Parental right to opt out of denominational RE.	Compulsory. In accordance with religious character of school.	All teachers may be treated as 'reserve' teachers.
Independent schools with a religious character.	May discriminate on grounds of religion.	Not compulsory. Independent School Standards must be complied with.	Not compulsory. Independent School Standards must be compiled with.	Teachers can be appointed, disadvantaged and dismissed on grounds of their religion or belief and appointed to give RE.

Although worship in all designated schools may be in accordance with the religious character of the school, rules as to religious education and the employment of staff differ greatly between the different types. It is only voluntary-aided schools and independent schools that live up to popular stereotypes concerning faith schools. And even in these schools, there are safeguards in place to ensure that pupils are taught respect for other faiths.

The letter of the law suggests that many popular fears concerning faith schools may be misplaced. However, the extent to which the letter of the law is observed is, of course, a different question.

Two conclusions can be made. Firstly, the law concerning religion in schools, although technically compliant with the ECHR, appears to be outmoded in the same way in which the law of blasphemy was. There is a tension between the letter of the law and the expectations of the new religion law. Secondly, there appears to be a significant distance between the popular fears found in the media and the letter of the law. This is similar to the law on religious offences, where popular fears concerning the religious hatred offences are out of step with the legal reality.[117] In both contexts the existence of a significant gulf between public fears and the letter of the law suggests that the legal framework is misunderstood. This is unsurprising given its complexity and the frequent changes made. The next chapter will address how similar misunderstandings have also come to the fore concerning religious law and religious courts.

---

[117] In that, despite media fears to the contrary, the actual provisions enacted by the Racial and Religious Hatred Act 2006 are toothless.

9

Religious law

Introduction

As Chapter 1 proposed, the study of law and religion can be understood as the study of two elements. The first, 'religion law', comprises the external temporal laws affecting religious individuals and groups which are made by State legislatures (and certain supra- and sub-State institutions). The second, 'religious law', comprises the internal spiritual laws made by religious groups themselves. The argument was made that the study of law and religion in England and Wales must be seen as requiring *at least* the study of these two overlapping elements. However, much of this book and much of the law and religion literature has been concerned with religion law rather than religious law. The detailed study of religious law has largely been left to experts in particular religious law systems, such as experts in Islamic law,[1] Jewish law,[2] Hindu law,[3] Roman Catholic canon law[4] or the ecclesiastical law of the Church of England.[5]

However, this has begun to change. There have been a number of important comparative studies.[6] Moreover, a number of writers have begun to focus more upon questions concerning the status and application of religious laws.[7] This has been provoked in part by a lecture on the relationship between Islam and English law by the Archbishop of Canterbury on 7th

---

[1] See, e.g. W. B. Hallaq, *An Introduction to Islamic Law* (Cambridge: Cambridge University Press, 2009).

[2] See, e.g. N. S. Hecht *et al.* (eds.). *An Introduction to the History and Sources of Jewish Law* (Oxford: Clarendon Press, 1996).

[3] See, e.g. W. Menski, *Hindu Law: Beyond Tradition and Modernity* (Oxford: Oxford University Press, 2003).

[4] See, e.g. J. A. Coriden, *An Introduction to Canon Law* (London: Continuum, 2004).

[5] See, e.g. M. Hill, *Ecclesiastical Law*, 3rd edn (Oxford: Oxford University Press, 2007).

[6] See, e.g. N. Doe, *The Legal Framework of the Church of England* (Oxford: Clarendon Press, 1996); A. Huxley (ed.), *Religion, Law and Tradition: Comparative Studies in Religious Law* (London: Routledge, 2002); G. Arthur, *Law, Liberty and Church: Authority And Justice in the Major Churches In England* (Aldershot: Ashgate, 2006); J. Neusner and T. Sonn, *Comparing Religions Through Law* (London: Routledge, 1999).

[7] See, e.g., S. Bano, 'In Pursuit of Religious and Legal Diversity: A Response to the Archbishop of Canterbury and the "Sharia Debate" in Britain' (2008) 10(3) *Ecclesiastical Law Journal* 283; F. Cranmer, 'The Archbishop and Sharia' (2008) 160 *Law & Justice* 3; B. Jackson, '"Transformative Accommodation" and Religious Law' (2009) 11 *Ecclesiastical Law Journal* 131; and a number of the essays in R. Grillo *et al.* (eds.), *Legal Practice and Cultural Diversity* (Aldershot: Ashgate, 2009) and the articles in (2010) 164 *Law and Justice*.

February 2008, in which he tentatively suggested that 'we have to think a little harder about the role and rule of law in a plural society of overlapping identities' and spoke of 'a scheme in which individuals retain the liberty to choose the jurisdiction under which they will seek to resolve certain carefully specified matters'.[8] The lecture provoked much heat, causing an animated but generally ill-informed debate in the media concerning the extent to which English law should accommodate religious legal systems, such as Sharia law.

The purpose of this chapter is to begin to convert this heat into light.[9] The first section discusses whether religious law is an appropriate object of study within law and religion. It questions whether it is possible and desirable to develop a category of 'religious law' and whether the study of this should be a matter for law or theology. The second section examines the reality behind the fears raised by the media. It questions the extent to which English law already recognises and enforces religious law.

Defining religious law

Like all social groups, religious groups are not only regulated by the law of the State, but also by their own internal laws, rules and procedures.[10] The term 'religious law' can be used to describe both the rules found in sacred texts and also the more practical rules developed by religious groups themselves. Many aspects of these rules differ from religious group to religious group. Beckford and Richardson contrast the highly formal religious laws of the Roman Catholic Church with Islam, Hinduism and Buddhism, which 'lack single authoritative organisations for regulating their national and transnational

---

[8] R. Williams, 'Civil and Religious Law in England – A Religious Perspective' (2008) 10 *Ecclesiastical Law Journal* 262, 271, 274. See also Lord Phillips of Worth Matravers, 'Equality Before the Law' (2008) 161 *Law and Justice* 75.

[9] The study of the actual content of systems of religious law is outside the scope of this chapter. This chapter will include brief and selective reference to systems of religious law found in England and Wales. Room permits only a preliminary and rudimentary study. Most of the examples used in this section will relate to Christianity with some comparative references to other systems of religious law in order to discuss the universality of given characteristics. For a fuller study (although confined to Christianity), see N. Doe, 'Modern Church Law' in J. Witte Jr and F. S. Alexander (eds.), *Christianity and Law* (Cambridge: Cambridge University Press, 2008), p. 271; and N. Doe, *Contemporary Principles of Christian Law* (Cambridge: Cambridge University Press, forthcoming).

[10] Analogies can be drawn with both the regulation of sport and that of families. James draws a distinction between the 'national sports law' found in Acts of Parliament and case law and the 'domestic sports law' created by the sporting organisations themselves through their national governing bodies: M. James, *Sports Law* (London: Palgrave Macmillan, 2010), pp. 6–8. In relation to family law, although this is commonly understood only to include national and international law affecting families, the work of Wood and Beck analyses the spoken and unspoken rules which are developed internally by families: D. Wood and R. Beck, *Home Rules* (Maryland: Johns Hopkins University Press, 1994), as discussed by W. Twinning and D. Miers, *How To Do Things with Rules*, 5th edn (Cambridge: Cambridge University Press, 2010), p. 24.

activities'.[11] This section will ask whether despite these differences it is possible and desirable to speak of 'religious law'. The key question is whether, in addition to categories such as Islamic law, Jewish law and Hindu law, it is possible to speak meaningfully of an umbrella category called 'religious law'. This section will attempt to devise a working definition of religious law by looking at its purposes and functions, sources and subject matter as well as asking whether and in what ways it can be regarded as law.

It is worth stressing at the outset that there is no corresponding term to Islamic law, Jewish law and Hindu law used in the context of Christianity.[12] Although the term 'canon law' is sometimes employed to provide the Christian equivalent of systems of religious law such as Islamic law and Hindu law,[13] the term is often reserved for the Roman Catholic, Anglican and Orthodox churches. Even in that context, the term is problematic,[14] being employed in various ways – some very narrow,[15] some very wide.[16] Other Christian groups, such as the Free Churches, do not generally use the term 'canon law'. However, as Arthur concluded, 'the Methodist[17] and United Reformed Churches have set up structures of varying flexibility that act like Canon Law'.[18] Even though Arthur concludes that there is no equivalent to canon law in the Baptist Church, where issues of church discipline are the responsibility of the local church, Doe has included Baptists in his study of 'Modern Church Law', pointing out that the Baptist Union of Great Britain and Ireland and the Baptist World Alliance both have constitutions.[19] In that study Doe reaches the tentative conclusion that 'it may be possible to

---

[11] J. A. Beckford and J. T. Richardson, 'Religion and Regulation' in J. A. Beckford and N. J. Demerath (eds.), *The Sage Handbook of the Sociology of Religion* (London: Sage, 2007), pp. 396, 399.

[12] See Chapter 1 for an assessment of the usefulness of the term 'ecclesiastical law'.

[13] See, for instance, S. Ferrari, 'Canon Law as a Religious Legal System' in A. Huxley (ed.), *Religion, Law and Tradition: Comparative Studies in Religious Law* (London: Routledge, 2002), p. 49, which focuses purely on the law of the Roman Catholic Church.

[14] See N. Doe, *The Legal Framework of the Church of England* (Oxford: Clarendon Press, 1996), pp. 12–13.

[15] For example, 'the expression "canon law" is used restrictively to mean the Canons of the Church of England': M. Hill, *Ecclesiastical Law*, 3rd edn (Oxford: Oxford University Press, 2007), p. 2.

[16] See, for instance, the assertion that canon law is 'so much of the law of England as is concerned with the regulation of the affairs of the Church of England'. Its sources include: theology (embracing divine law); the common law of England; and Acts of Parliament: T. Briden and B. Hanson, *Moore's Introduction to English Canon Law*, 3rd edn (London: Mowbrays, 1992), p. 4.

[17] See also in relation to the Methodist Church, G. Powell, *Towards a Definition of Global Methodism: A Comparative Study of the Canon Laws of Methodist Churches* (Doctoral Thesis, Cardiff University, forthcoming).

[18] G. Arthur, *Law, Liberty and Church: Authority and Justice in the Major Churches in England* (Aldershot: Ashgate, 2006), p. 172. See also F. Cranmer, 'Regulation in the Religious Society of Friends' (2003) 7 *Ecclesiastical Law Journal* 176.

[19] N. Doe, 'Modern Church Law' in J. Witte Jr and F. S. Alexander (eds.), *Christianity and Law* (Cambridge: Cambridge University Press, 2008), pp. 274, 275, 277.

construct a category "Christian law" from the similarities between the regulatory systems of churches of different traditions' on the basis that 'there seem to be principles of law common to all churches':[20]

> For all of them, law expresses a theological self-understanding of a church. Laws function predominantly in the public sphere of church life. Scripture is a key material source for church law. Law should reflect the revealed will of God. Ecclesiastical persons and bodies should act in accordance with law. Finally, law is the servant of the church in its mission.

The debate as to whether it is useful to talk of 'Christian law' as an umbrella category may shed light upon the usefulness of the term 'religious law' as an umbrella category. Indeed, Doe argues that one of the purposes of constructing the category of 'Christian law' is that it 'provides a point of comparison for scholars working in the fields of Islamic, Jewish and Hindu law (for example)'.[21] This parallel is useful. As Menski has noted, both Hindu and Islamic law are 'pluralist' legal systems rather than 'a solidly uniform legal system'.[22] However, this does not mean that there is no such thing as Hindu or Islamic law; it simply means that the category Islamic law is as multifaceted and diverse as Doe's concept of Christian law. Menski talks of 'Hindu law', but with a qualifier: 'Hindu law must be understood as a complex living system with many intangible and invisible elements, rather than a single tangible fossilised relic'.[23] The same is true of other systems of religious law and of the umbrella term 'religious law' itself.

The following will suggest how the umbrella category of religious law can be understood by reference to its purposes, sources and subject matter and also by reference to how it is studied. The discussion also addresses whether it is seen as law at all or rather as a species of theology. Use of the category of religious law would not presuppose or even contend that different religious laws are homogeneous, but would suggest that they have some basic similarities (and quite a few significant differences)[24] which makes it meaningful to study 'religious law' as part of law and religion.

A purpose-based definition

The first method is to say that religious law can be defined by its particular purpose or function. The purpose of religious law is to provide order for

---

[20] *Ibid.*, pp. 288–9.   [21] *Ibid.*, p. 289.

[22] W. Menski, *Hindu Law: Beyond Tradition and Modernity* (Oxford: Oxford University Press, 2003), p. 47, fn. 33.

[23] *Ibid.*, p. 546.

[24] One such difference is that Islamic, Jewish and Hindu law are more pervasive than Christian law. Neusner and Sonn note that, although it is emphatically not the case that 'Christianity took the position of indifference to public policy or left law outside its realm of governance', there are significant differences between 'religio-legal systems' and Christianity: J. Neusner and T. Sonn, *Comparing Religions Through Law* (London: Routledge, 1999), p. 5.

the religious group and to facilitate religious life. Doe distinguishes between the 'facility' and the 'order' theories of ecclesiastical regulation.[25] The order theory 'focuses on internal regulation as disciplinary or coercive, a juridical expression of the values of ecclesiastical order and control', while the facility theory sees the 'primary function' of church law as being 'to serve the purposes for which the church exists, to enable the people of God to fulfil their mission to society'.[26]

Religious law provides order and control. As Madrid has noted in relation to Catholic Canon Law, the Church 'needs canon law the way a freeway needs lane stripes'.[27] The notion that religious law provides the basic standards to order religious life was underlined by Pope John Paul II at the time of promulgating the 1983 Code of Canon Law. He noted that a Code of Canon Law[28] was 'absolutely necessary for the Church' because:

> Since the Church is established in the form of a social and visible unit, it needs rules, so that its hierarchical and organic structure may be visible; that its exercise of the functions divinely entrusted to it, particularly of sacred power and of the administration of the sacraments, is properly ordered; that the mutual relationships of Christ's faithful are reconciled in justice based on charity, with the rights of each safeguarded and defined; and lastly, that the common initiatives which are undertaken so that Christian life may be ever more perfectly carried out, are supported, strengthened and promoted by canonical laws.[29]

This means, in the words of Örsy, 'canon law imposes obligations; that is, it establishes legal bonds from which rights and duties flow'.[30] The same is true of other systems of religious law.[31] In his foreword to *The Principles of Canon Law*, a document particularly useful in this context providing as it does a description of general patterns of the juridical forms of church life

---

[25] Most notably, N. Doe, *The Legal Framework of the Church of England* (Oxford: Clarendon Press, 1996), pp. 33–47; but see also N. Doe, 'A Facilitative Canon Law: The Problem of Sanctions and Forgiveness' in N. Doe (ed.), *Essays in Canon Law* (Cardiff: University of Wales Press, 1992), p. 69 and N. Doe, *The Law of the Church in Wales* (Cardiff: University of Wales Press, 2002), pp. 21–2.

[26] N. Doe, *The Legal Framework of the Church of England* (Oxford: Clarendon Press, 1996), pp. 33–47.

[27] P. Madrid, 'Foreword' in P. Vere and M. Trueman, *Surprised by Canon Law* (Cincinnati: St Anthony Messenger Press, 2004), p. vii.

[28] Although his comments do not seem to be directed at a code as opposed to any other type of instrument.

[29] John Paul II, Apostolic Constitution, reproduced in *The Code of Canon Law* (London: Collins, 1983), p. xiv. See also J. A. Coriden, *Introduction to Canon Law* (London: Cassell Publishers, 1991), pp. 5–6.

[30] L. M. Örsy, 'Theology and Canon Law' in J. P. Beal, J. A. Coriden and T. J. Green (eds.), *New Commentary on the Code of Canon Law* (Mahwah: Paulist Press, 2000), p. 7.

[31] E.g.'The sacred Law of Islam is an all-embracing body of religious duties, the totality of Allah's commands that regulate the life of every Muslim in all its respects': J. Schacht, *An Introduction to Islamic Law* (Oxford: Clarendon Press, 1964), p. 1. That said, this is rather different from canon law. Canon law is not entirely theocratic. Elements of it are, but it also consists of humanly created rules.

found in the global Anglican Communion,[32] the Archbishop of Canterbury noted that Canon Law 'seeks clarity about what and who is responsible to whom'; and 'Canon Law is a necessary aspect of exercising authority and holding responsibility in the Church'.[33] As Massey H. Shepherd Jr, the architect of ECUSA's *Prayer Book 1979*, so memorably observed, the basic principle of the canon law of the Episcopal Church is 'to protect the people from their clergy and the clergy from their bishops': in short, separation of powers.[34]

The purpose of religious law is therefore subtly different from any other type of law. Religious law is not simply a secular phenomenon law, which is utilised in the religious sphere on grounds of necessity.[35] In addition to fulfilling the purpose of order (which may be seen as being a characteristic of law per se), religious law also fulfils the deeper purpose of facilitating religious life. This is clearly shown in the *Principles of Canon Law*, which state that 'Law is not an end in itself,'[36] but 'exists to assist a church in its mission and witness to Jesus Christ'.[37] As Principle 3(5) of the *Principles of Canon Law* puts it:

> Law in a church exists to uphold the integrity of the faith, sacraments and mission, to provide good order, to support communion amongst the faithful, to put into action Christian values, and to prevent and resolve conflict.

As Örsy writes: 'The *purpose* of canon law is to assist the Church in fulfilling its task which is to so reveal and communicate God's saving power to the world.'[38] The purpose of religious law, providing order for and facilitating religious life, may be seen as a definitional attribute of religious law. Religious law may be defined, at least in part, by purpose.

A source-based definition

A second method of definition is a source-based approach. In the same way as religious law shares some of the same purposes as other forms

---

[32] *The Principles of Canon Law Common to the Churches of the Anglican Communion* (Anglican Communion Office, 2008). See N. Doe, 'The Contribution of Common Principles of Canon Law to Ecclesial Communion in Anglicanism' (2008) 10 *Ecclesiastical Law Journal* 71.

[33] R. Williams, 'Foreword' in *The Principles of Canon Law Common to the Churches of the Anglican Communion* (Anglican Communion Office, 2008), p. 11.

[34] See F. Cranmer, 'Church Governance and Separation of Powers' (2004) 153 *Law and Justice* 128.

[35] On which see, e.g. J. A. Coriden, *Introduction to Canon Law* (London: Cassell Publishers, 1991), p. 5 and S. Zubaida, *Law and Power in the Islamic World* (London: I B Tauris, 2003), p. 1.

[36] Principle 1(3).

[37] Principle 1(1). See also Principle 2(1) ('Law is the servant of the church') and Principle 1(2) ('A church needs within it laws to order, and so facilitate, its public life and to regulate its own affairs for the common good').

[38] L. M. Örsy, 'Theology and Canon Law' in J. P. Beal, J. A. Coriden and T. J. Green (eds.), *New Commentary on the Code of Canon Law* (Mahwah: Paulist Press, 2000), p. 2.

of law (in terms of order and discipline), but also has distinctive purposes of its own (facilitating religious life), so too can it be noted that
religious law has some sources that are similar to other forms of law
and other sources that are distinctive. In the Anglican context, this difference is elucidated in the *Principles of Canon Law*, which distinguish
between 'fundamental authoritative sources of law', namely 'Scripture, tradition and reason', and 'formal sources', such as 'constitutions, canons,
rules, regulations and other instruments'.[39] Although the 'formal sources'
of religious law have much in common with other forms of law,[40] the
'fundamental authoritative sources' of religious law may be seen as being
distinctive.

In particular, it may be said that a distinctive characteristic of religious
law is that it generally includes not only human law, but also, uniquely,
divine law. The notion that religious law has both divine and human origins
is expressed in a number of religious traditions. It is a common theme in
Roman Catholic canon law; for instance, as Örsy comments, canon law
'springs from the will of Christ, but its minute and detailed rules come
from human agents . . . that is, the pope and the bishops'.[41] The same is true
of Anglicanism: Principle 2(2) of the *Principles of Canon Law* states that:
'Law should reflect the revealed will of God.'[42] Moreover, for Baderin, the
distinction in Islamic law between the *Sharia*, 'the source from which the
law is derived', and *Fiqh*, 'the method by which law is derived and applied',
may also be seen in this light: while *Sharia* 'is divine in nature and thus
immutable', *Fiqh* 'is a human product that may change according to time
and circumstances'.[43] However, the relationship between divine law and
human law in religious law is complex. For instance, while Ferrari states
that divine law 'is eternal and cannot be changed by any human authority',
he also notes that it is generally thought that divine law is not directly
operative unless it is embedded in a human law and therefore 'while the
rules and principles of divine law are immutable, the legal provisions which
give concrete expression to these rules and principles can change', meaning

---

[39] Principles 4(1) and 4(2). These are often buttressed by less formal means of achieving order
and facilitating religious life: see J. A. Beckford and J. T. Richardson, 'Religion and Regulation'
in J. A. Beckford and N. J. Demerath (eds.), *The Sage Handbook of the Sociology of Religion*
(London: Sage, 2007), pp. 396, 397.

[40] Note, for instance, the existence of constitutions and the growth of legislation by regulation.
See N. Doe, 'Ecclesiastical Quasi-Legislation' in N. Doe, M. Hill and R. Ombres (eds.), *English
Canon Law* (Cardiff: University of Wales Press, 1998), p. 93.

[41] L. Örsy, 'Towards a Theological Conception of Canon Law' in J. Hite and D. J. Ward (eds.),
Readings, Cases, Materials in Canon Law (New York: Collegeville, 1990), pp. 10, 11.

[42] See also Article 20 of the Thirty-Nine Articles of Religion: 'It is not lawful for the Church to
ordain any thing that is contrary to God's Word written'.

[43] M. A. Baderin, *International Human Rights and Islamic Law* (Oxford: Oxford University Press,
2003), pp. 33–4. However, such a clear-cut distinction is controversial. See S. Zubaida, *Law and
Power in the Islamic World* (London: I B Tauris, 2003), p. 10.

that it is always possible to invoke a better and fuller knowledge of divine law.[44]

At a more general level, it may be argued that the formal sources of religious law are distinctive, in that such laws are generally made by religious collectives themselves. However, even this claim merits further analysis. It is simply not the case that a watertight distinction can be made between religious law made by religious groups and religion law made by the State. This is true, for instance, even in the case of the Roman Catholic Church, which seems prima facie exclusively to regulate itself chiefly by means of its Code of Canon Law. As Coriden observes, State law[45] and concordats[46] are also sources of Canon Law alongside the Canons.[47] Moreover, in the context of England and Wales, a number of pieces of religion law provide the Roman Catholic Church with statutory recognition sometimes by general instruments, such as the Trustee Appointment Act 1850, and sometimes by specific instruments, such as the Roman Catholic Relief Act 1791 and the Roman Catholic Charities Act 1832. This is even more pronounced, of course, in relation to religious communities that are established by law, such as the Church of England and the Church of Scotland.[48] As we have seen, the State plays a significant role in the creation of the Measures and Canons of the Church of England.[49] This undermines any definition of religious law as laws made by a religious group itself, if this is taken to mean that such laws are created in isolation from the State. It follows that religious law cannot be defined by only a source-based approach. However, a source-based definition, if suitably nuanced, may prove useful in conjunction with other definitional methods.

A subject-based definition

Religious law can also be defined by reference to the subjects it covers. The subjects that religious laws cover tend to be different from other laws because religious groups tend to face unique, and to a degree common, issues. As Doe notes, there is 'considerable but not exact convergence between [Christian]

---

[44] S. Ferrari, 'Canon Law as a Religious Legal System' in A. Huxley (ed.), *Religion, Law and Tradition: Comparative Studies in Religious Law* (London: Routledge, 2002), p. 51.

[45] Often termed 'civil law' in this context.

[46] That is, formal international agreements between the Holy See and national governments. For details of concordats operational in Europe, see R. Sandberg and N. Doe, 'Church-State Relations in Europe' (2007) 1(5) *Religion Compass* 561, 567–9.

[47] J. A. Coriden, *Introduction to Canon Law* (London: Cassell Publishers, 1991), p. 31. See Canon 3 of the 1983 Code.

[48] The State influence is also pronounced in relation to religious communities which were formerly established by law such as the Church in Wales. On which see Chapter 4 above and N. Doe, *The Law of the Church in Wales* (Cardiff: University of Wales Press, 2002), ch. 1.

[49] See Chapter 4.

churches as to the subjects treated by their regulatory instruments'.[50] This
is neatly encapsulated in the Anglican context by Principle 3(5) of *The
Principles of Canon Law*, which states that for the churches of the Anglican
Communion:

> The principal subjects with which laws deal are ecclesiastical government, min-
> istry, discipline, doctrine, liturgy, rites, property, and ecumenical relations.

Suffice to say, not all pieces of religious law deal with all of these subjects, but
generally a focus on these subjects distinguishes religious laws from State
law or the rules of any other group.[51] Beckford and Richardson identify 'the
codification of beliefs, tests of orthodox, the training and certification of
leaders, and the disciplining of deviants' as 'forms' of what they refer to as
'religious self regulation'.[52]

However, it may be observed that many of the subjects dealt with by
religious law are not uniquely the preserve of religious law. Looking at the
Roman Catholic Church, it may be observed that although the titles of
some of the seven books that constitute the *Code of Canon Law* (such as
'The Teaching Function of the Church' and 'The Sanctifying Function of
the Church') would not be found in a non-religious context, the title of
other Books (such as 'Temporal Goods', 'Penal Law' and 'Procedural Law')
would not look out of place in a code of State laws.[53] Indeed, the Code
'does not, for the most part, regulate liturgical matters',[54] something that
is of unique concern to religious groups. Moreover, the Church does not
live in social isolation: many religious laws concern subjects that are also
dealt with under State law. It was noted in *Daly* v. *Commissioners of Inland
Revenue*[55] that: 'The government of the Church, the acquisition of property
by the Church, the administration of Church property and income, and
the rights and duties of priests, are regulated by . . . canon law.' Some, if
not all, of these matters are also regulated by State law. The considerable
overlap between the subject-matter of religious law and that of other forms
of regulation, such as State law, undermines the appeal of this approach.

---

[50] N. Doe, 'Modern Church Law' in J. Witte Jr and F. S. Alexander (eds.), *Christianity and Law*
(Cambridge: Cambridge University Press, 2008), pp. 271, 277.

[51] The laws of Christian churches are likely to be narrower than the laws of other world religions.
For instance, Islamic law is 'an overarching guide to every day conduct, a way that will lead the
believer to the benefits afforded by Allah', as well as being 'a living system of everyday
adjudication': L. Rosen, *The Justice of Islam* (Oxford: Oxford University Press, 2000), p. ix.

[52] J. A. Beckford and J. T. Richardson 'Religion and Regulation' in J. A. Beckford and N. J.
Demerath (eds.), *The Sage Handbook of the Sociology of Religion* (London: Sage, 2007), pp. 396,
397.

[53] For a fuller description of the contents, see, e.g. P. Vere and M. Trueman, *Surprised by Canon
Law* (Cincinnati: St Anthony Messenger Press, 2004), pp. 5–6.

[54] J. A. Coriden, *Introduction to Canon Law* (London: Cassell Publishers, 1991), p. 40. See Canon
2 of the 1983 Code.

[55] [1934] 18 Tax Cas 641.

There are two further problems with relying upon a subject-matter-based definition of religious law. The first problem is that the precise subject-matter of religious laws will vary across time and space in response to changing historical conditions,[56] as with other forms of law. Religious law, like other forms of law, is a political, cultural and historical product. It is often a pragmatic creature and its content may often be shaped by non-religious influences. The second problem is that the more general the description of the religious law subject matter, the less distinct it becomes. In sum, it appears that the extent to which it is possible to outline a distinctive subject-matter of religious law largely corresponds to the extent to which it is possible to articulate a distinctive purpose of religious law. Again, it seems that a subject-matter-based definition of religious law can only be used in conjunction with other definitional approaches.

A pedagogical definition

The three definitional methods discussed above have suggested that religious law may be an appropriate object of study. They point to the existence of something unique about religious law which means that it can be examined by law and religion scholars. However, it has also been suggested that categories of religious law (such as Islamic law, Jewish law, etc.) can also be defined as a field of study. For instance, in relation to Roman Catholic canon law, Coriden has noted that:

> 'Canon law' describes a system of rules for the church, an area of academic study, and a body of scientific literature.[57]

Defining Roman Catholic canon law as an area of academic study is fairly straightforward since, as Doe has noted, 'the Roman canonist had the tradition of centuries to which reference may be made for the method by which he/she discusses canon law; a method of scholarship, learning, exposition and criticism which had been distilled and handed down by generations of canonists'.[58] By contrast, he notes that for Anglican canonists, there is 'a wealth of sources to hand', but there is 'no immediate native or indigenous method, or style of approach, to which appeal may be made'.[59] Nevertheless, the Archbishop's Commission boldly asserted that: 'The Church needs not

---

[56] *The Canon Law of the Church of England, Being the Report of the Archbishop's Commission on Canon Law* (London: SPCK, 1947), p. 5.

[57] J. A. Coriden, *Canon Law as Ministry* (New York: Paulist Press, 2000), p. 1.

[58] N. Doe, 'Toward a critique of the role of theology in English ecclesiastical and canon law' (1992) 2 *Ecclesiastical Law Journal* 328.

[59] *Ibid.*

only laws but a science of law, its own system of jurisprudence, if it is to do its work.'[60]

However, the view that the study of religious law should be seen as a legal science does not attract universal approval. Other analyses place less emphasis upon the legal elements of religious law, but place greater stress upon its religious elements. In the Anglican context, Principle 2(3) of the *Principles of Canon Law* states that: 'Law has a historical basis and a theological foundation, rationale and end.' The relationship between religious law and theology in particular has produced much debate, especially among Roman Catholic canonists.[61] For some the study of religious law has more in common with theology than law. For Coriden, since canon law is 'the theology of the church put into practice', it follows that:

> Canon Law is a subset of theology, not a subset of law or juridical science. Canon Law is applied theology. It expresses in norms and rules that the church believes and teaches about itself.[62]

However, this seems to be a false choice. These characteristics do not mean that systems of religious law cannot be law. Indeed, it could be said that State law expresses in norms and rules what the State believes and teaches about itself. State law could be seen as applied politics: State law could simply be seen as politics written up; in the same way that religious law could be seen as theology written up. It seems that a preferable interpretation is to say that canon law in particular, or religious law generally, is not *just* a juridical science, is not *just* law.

Moreover, as Coriden himself concedes: 'Canon law does present a juridical aspect.'[63] The study of religious law is both a theological and legal enterprise. For Ombres, this means that: 'Canon law can only be done by the theologically sensitive and not just the legally proficient.'[64] It may also be argued that the reverse is true – that religious law can only be studied by those who are legally sensitive as well as theologically proficient. This is expressed well by Doe, applying these ideas to Anglican canon law, who noted that although in tapping into the 'rich canonical traditions of the past' the Anglican canonist may draw upon 'the canonical tradition of subjecting the rules of canon law to a rigorous analysis against the central Christian theological doctrines', they may also draw upon the analysis that

---

[60] *The Canon Law of the Church of England, Being the Report of the Archbishops' Commission on Canon Law* (London: SPCK 1947), p. 5.

[61] The debate concerning whether the study of canon law is primarily a legal or theological discipline has led to the identification of several schools of thought in relation to Roman Catholic canon law, which have set out to establish the relationship between law and theology. See J. A. Coriden, *Canon Law as Ministry* (New York: Paulist Press, 2000), pp. 13–19 and M. Örsy, 'Theology and Canon Law' in J. P. Beal, J. A. Coriden and T. J. Green (eds.), *New Commentary on the Code of Canon Law* (Mahwah: Paulist Press, 2000), pp. 3–5.

[62] J. A. Coriden, *Canon Law as Ministry* (New York: Paulist Press, 2000), p. 142.

[63] *Ibid.*, p. 152.   [64] R. Ombres, 'Why then the law?' [1974] *New Blackfriars* 296, 302.

subjects canonical rules 'against the rules of other legal systems (principally, traditionally, Roman law)'.[65]

However, the interaction between religious law and State law is not the only reason why religious law requires legal analysis. Religious law can be seen as 'law' in its own right. Writings on legal pluralism[66] suggest that 'any conception of law that is restricted to municipal law of nations states and classic public international law is misleading'.[67]

Indeed, religious law seems to fulfil the same basic functions as other forms of law. Religious laws perform Robert S. Summers' 'five basic techniques', by which 'law' discharges social functions: religious law remedies grievances, prohibits forms of antisocial behaviour, regulates socially desirable activities, regulates the provision of services and provides for the private arranging of affairs.[68] It also accomplishes Karl Llewellyn's four 'law-jobs' or basic functions of law: religious law provides the orderly resolution of disputes, the preventive channelling and reorientation of conduct and expectations to avoid conflict, the allocation of authority in the group and what Llewellyn called the 'net drive', that is, the organisation and harmonisation of group activity to provide direction and incentive to group members.[69] Indeed, religious law is often included in typologies of different forms of law provided by legal theorists.[70] This might suggest that religious law can be defined as a field of study which requires both theological and legal research methods.

Huxley's OWL

It is therefore suggested that, although it is not possible to define religious law solely by reference to its purposes, sources, subject-matter or the way in which it is studied, a fusion of these methods points to the existence of religious law as an object and field of study. The term 'religious law' is of use. However, this conclusion is contentious. Throughout Huxley's edited

---

[65] N. Doe, 'Toward a Critique of the Role of Theology in English Ecclesiastical and Canon Law' (1992) 2 *Ecclesiastical Law Journal* 328, 330–1.

[66] See E. Ehrlich, *Fundamental Principles of the Sociology of Law* (New York: Transaction Publishers, 2002), p. 39; and the growing modern literature on legal pluralism, such as P. Shah, *Legal Pluralism in Conflict: Coping with Cultural Diversity in Law* (Oxford: Routledge, 2005); and I. Yilmaz, *Muslim Laws, Politics and Society in Modern Nation States* (Aldershot: Ashgate, 2005).

[67] W. Twining, *Globalisation & Legal Theory* (London: Butterworths, 2000), pp. 139–40. For a narrower perspective on the definition of law, see, e.g. H. Kelsen, 'The Law as a Specific Social Technique' (1941) 9 *University of Chicago Law Review* 78.

[68] R. S. Summers, 'The Technique Element in Law' (1971) 59 *Californian Law Review* 733.

[69] K. N. Llewellyn, 'The Normative, the Legal and the Law Hobs: The Problem of Juristic Method' (1940) 49 *Yale Law Journal* 1355.

[70] See, e.g. W. Twining, *Globalisation & Legal Theory* (London: Butterworths, 2000), pp. 139–40; and H. P. Glenn, *Legal Traditions of the World*, 3rd edn (Oxford: Oxford University Press, 2000).

volume *Religion, Law and Tradition: Comparative Studies in Religious Law*,[71] a question mark hangs over whether the terms 'religious law' and 'religious legal system' are helpful. Huxley, for instance, argues that the label 'religious law' cannot capture the common elements which link the different studies in his book, namely that:

> All are at least a thousand years old. All are written traditions, structured as an exegesis of an old text containing timeless truth. All emanate from Eurasia. And all continue to influence twenty-first century legal behaviour.[72]

The label he prefers instead is the acronym OWL, 'which stands for *Old World Law texts* and for *Obsolescent Written Law*'. He further notes that emphasis is to be given to the 'O' word in both of these formulations, since 'what critically differentiates these . . . systems from the normal Comparative Law fodder is oldness, obsolescence or, if you prefer, history'.

It seems that Huxley is thinking of religious law as the rules found in sacred texts rather than the more practical rules developed by religious groups themselves. This means that his OWL classification cannot cover many modern systems of religious law. In the same volume, Silvio Ferrari puts forward a different view of what religious law is, which stresses neither age nor obsolescence:

> Religions (and religious laws) are born and die every day: it is a dynamic phenomenon, rooted in the present as well as the past. Jehovah's Witnesses law, the law of the Church of Scientology, Mormon law . . . There are a lot of new religious movements and some of them are not young offsprings of old religions but something really new.[73]

Ferrari's view seems preferable. Huxley's OWL classification appears to provide an easy justification for religious law to be relegated to what Menski called 'a bin for outdated rubbish marked "religious systems of law"'.[74] It follows that Huxley's OWL classification is not preferable to the term 'religious law'. Given that the subtitle of Huxley's collection is *Comparative Studies in Religious Law*, this suggests that the advantages of the term outweigh the disadvantages. On the cover of the book, Huxley answers the question that dominates the book: in short, yes, 'religious law' is a term that is easily understandable enough to merit its use.

In sum, it appears that religious law is an appropriate object of study within law and religion. It is possible and desirable to talk about religious law and its study requires both law and theology. Religious law provides a framework for believers which is so encompassing that for most of the time

---

[71] A. Huxley (ed.), *Religion, Law and Tradition: Comparative Studies in Religious Law* (London: Routledge, 2002).

[72] A. Huxley, 'Introduction' in *ibid.*, p. 6.

[73] S. Ferrari, 'Religious Law: A Discussion' in *ibid.*, p. 155.

[74] W. Menski, 'Hindu Law as a "Religious" System' in *ibid.*, p. 110.

they will be unaware of its existence. It includes not just age-old standards and rules rooted in sacred texts, but also the 'rules of the game' which allow religious groups to function. The sociologists of religion Beckford and Richardson have argued that the study of how religious groups regulate themselves 'is particularly interesting from a sociological perspective for what it reveals about the variety of ways in which religions seek to control their practices and practitioners'.[75] The study of religious law is also of importance for those who specialise in law and religion. The rules and regulations developed by religious groups inform and shape their interaction with the State. The next section explores this in more depth, looking at how religious law is often recognised and sometimes enforced by State legal mechanisms.

The recognition of religious law

The initial media and political reactions to the Archbishop of Canterbury's lecture[76] provided a clear reason why religious law ought to be ignored. It was commonly suggested that the current law gave no recognition to Islamic law or other systems of religious law. For instance, the then Prime Minister Gordon Brown was said to be clear that 'in Britain, British laws based on British values applied',[77] while the then Culture Secretary Andy Burnham commented, on BBC 1's Question Time on the same day, that: 'You cannot run two systems of law alongside each other. That would be a recipe for chaos.' These comments suggested that giving *some* recognition to Islamic law was impossible: the choice was simply between completely recognising all aspects of Islamic law or giving no accommodation at all.

However, once the initial hullabaloo had calmed down, it became clear that the choice was by no means this stark. Religious law is already recognised in England and Wales in several different ways. As discussed in Chapter 4, the rules and structures of religious associations are binding on assenting members through the doctrine of 'consensual compact'. Moreover, religious laws and practices are free to operate where the law of the State is silent.[78] For instance, some family lawyers have claimed that the silence of the law allows polygamous religious marriages because the offence of bigamy is restrictively drafted to cover only civil legal marriages and not

---

[75] J. A. Beckford and J. T. Richardson, 'Religion and Regulation' in J. A. Beckford and N. J. Demerath (eds.), *The Sage Handbook of the Sociology of Religion* (London: Sage, 2007), pp. 396, 398.

[76] R. Williams, 'Civil and Religious Law in England – A Religious Perspective' (2008) 10 *Ecclesiastical Law Journal* 262.

[77] 10 Downing Street afternoon press briefing on 7 February 2008 available at www.pm.gov.uk/output/Page14504.asp.

[78] This is the 'negative' approach to religious freedom, discussed in Chapters 2 and 5.

religious ones.[79] In addition to this negative freedom, there are four main ways in which English law may be said 'positively' to recognise religious laws.[80]

Recognition as a matter of fact

Religious law may enter the courtroom as part of the facts of the case[81] and may be introduced into the courtroom by expert witnesses.[82]

Recognition through state law

Pieces of State law may give effect to provisions of religious law or, more typically, religious practices. For instance, pieces of State law accommodate Muslim and Jewish laws concerning animal slaughter[83] and allow Islamic banks, *Sharia*-compliant mortgages and Islamic Bonds.[84] Perhaps the clearest example of State law recognising religious law is through the Divorce (Religious Marriages) Act 2002, which sought to solve problems in the Jewish community which arose where husbands refused to provide their estranged wives with a bill of divorce known as a '*get*'. This refusal meant that the wife could not marry again in accordance with Jewish rites, even if she obtained a civil divorce. The 2002 Act enables courts to require the granting of a religious divorce before a civil divorce can be granted.[85]

However, such solutions are not perfect. State law is a blunt instrument often incapable of dealing with the nuances found within faith communities. This can be shown in relation to the Divorce (Religious Marriages) Act 2002. The Act only applies to marriages which have been solemnised in accordance with the usages of the Jews or any other prescribed religious usages. Although other groups, such as Muslims,[86] could request inclusion as a prescribed religious usage; this is problematic in terms of working out who is representative of whom. The Divorce (Religious Marriages) Act 2002 was enacted to deal with a specific problem concerning the Jewish

---

[79] R. Hammond-Sharlot and P. Booth, 'Islamic Law in the UK' (2008) *Family Law* 362.

[80] The following develops arguments first presented as a public lecture organised under the auspices of the Centre for the Study of Islam in the UK at Cardiff University (9 February 2010). The text was subsequently published as R. Sandberg, 'Islam and English Law' (2010) 164 *Law & Justice* 227.

[81] Menski asserts that: 'Some British judges, virtually every day, have to decide matters of Muslim law and are grateful for expert advice, while others resent expert involvement' (W. Menski, 'Law, Religion and Culture in Multicultural Britain' in R. Mehdi *et al.* (eds.), *Law and Religion in Multicultural Societies* (Copenhagen: DJØF Publishing, 2008), p. 43.

[82] For an example of this, see *Uddin* v. *Choudhury and others* [2009] EWCA Civ 1205.

[83] Welfare of Animals (Slaughter or Killing) Regulations 1995.

[84] R. Hammond-Sharlot and P. Booth, 'Islamic Law in the UK' (2008) *Family Law* 362. See also the provisions of the Finance Act 2007.

[85] The law is now contained in s. 10A of the Matrimonial Causes Act 1973.

[86] The situation is particularly pressing in Islam, the Muslim *Talaq* being similar to the Jewish *Get*.

community and as a result was drafted narrowly. This is typical of the approach under English law. As Menski has noted:

> In Britain we make exceptions in certain cases, and thus move from case to case, in typical common law fashion. The result is, for some, a terrible mess, because almost everybody feels now that certain groups are receiving better treatment than others.[87]

Menski suggests that the ad hoc piecemeal approach of English law results from a reluctance on the part of the State to admit that different religious traditions may require different legal treatments. He asserts that the State 'shies away from admitting plurality-conscious awareness' using 'technical legal language, trying to keep out of ethnic politics, while working on practical solutions'.[88] This may be true, but surely the important thing is that practical solutions are being worked upon. The benefit of pragmatism is that it enables the legislature to avoid difficult larger issues raised concerning the relationship between religious law and State law. The reaction to the Archbishop's lecture illustrated how emotive these issues can be. However, that it not to say that the current pragmatic approach is uncontroversial. Very often there is an underpinning feeling being that any recognition is a 'favour' on the part of the State.[89]

Recognition by the Arbitration Act 1996

The Arbitration Act 1996, although a piece of State law which enables the recognition of religious law, merits separate examination. While the provisions examined above deal with specific religious problems by extending the protection and reach of State law, the Arbitration Act 1996 allows for disputes to be determined by religious courts and for their decisions to be recognised under State law. The 1996 Act[90] is the latest in a long line of statutes concerning arbitration. And like its forerunners, the Act focuses not upon courts, but upon people. Section 1 provides that:

> The parties should be free to agree how their disputes are resolved, subject only to such safeguards as are necessary in the public interest.

People can decide how civil disputes between them are to be resolved and once the parties decide to be bound by that decision, the secular courts will enforce that decision under the secular law of contract.[91] However, this is

---

[87] W. Menski, 'Law, Religion and Culture in Multicultural Britain' in R. Mehdi *et al.* (eds.), *Law and Religion in Multicultural Societies* (Copenhagen: DJØF Publishing, 2008), p. 43.

[88] *Ibid.*, p. 54.

[89] A. Bradney and F. Cownie, *Living Without Law* (Aldershot: Ashgate, 2000), p. 17.

[90] In Scotland, the law is updated and consolidated by the Arbitration (Scotland) Act 2010.

[91] See s. 82. Despite media fears to the contrary, the Arbitration Act does not deal with criminal matters. In English criminal law the 'dispute' is between the Crown and the defendant, not between the parties.

subject to a major limitation: as stated in section 1, the secular courts will not enforce a decision if the 'public interest' requires them not to.[92] Moreover, an agreement to arbitrate is just like any other contract: it is necessary to show a genuine agreement to arbitrate by both parties.[93] Contracts obtained by duress or those formed with minors or the incapacitated will not be enforced. The agreement to arbitrate must be in writing.[94] The arbitrator also has to comply with certain standards. Section 33 of the Arbitration Act 1996 states the general duty of the arbitrator and includes the duty to 'act fairly and impartially as between the parties, giving each party a reasonable opportunity of putting his case and dealing with that of his opponent'. An arbitration award can be set aside by the English courts[95] if the arbitrator does not fulfil this duty or if the agreement suffers from a 'serious irregularity'.[96]

The importance of this limitation is shown in the Court of Appeal decision in *Soleimany* v. *Soleimany*.[97] In that case two Iranian Jewish merchants were exporting Persian carpets. This breached Iranian law. The two merchants fell out and took their dispute to the Jewish court, the Beth Din. The Beth Din considered the illegality irrelevant under the applicable Jewish law and made an arbitration award. The Court of Appeal recognised this arbitration award made by the Beth Din as 'a valid agreement',[98] but refused to enforce it on grounds that public policy would not allow an English court to enforce an illegal contract.[99] This did not affect the Court's conclusion that the Beth Din had jurisdiction.[100] The Court held: 'An award, whether domestic or foreign, will not be enforced by an English court if enforcement would be contrary to the public policy of this country.'[101]

Although largely used for commercial purposes, the Arbitration Act 1996 can also be used for religious purposes.[102] Technically, it is not used *as such* by religious courts like the Beth Din, but rather by people who want to take their dispute to a religious court. The key fact about arbitration is that it allows the parties to decide what law the arbitrators will use to decide their dispute. This extends to systems of religious law. Section 46 of the Arbitration Act 1996 enables parties to choose for disputes to be decided 'in accordance with other considerations' rather than 'in accordance with law'. For these purposes 'law' has generally been understood to mean the law of

---

[92]   *Kohn* v. *Wagschal and others* [2007] EWCA Civ 1022 at para. 18.

[93]   R Blacklett, 'The Status of Religious "Courts" in English Law' [2009] *Disputes and International Arbitration Newsletter* 11, 13.

[94]   Arbitration Act 1996 s. 5.   [95]   Section 68(2)(a).

[96]   Section 68(2). The right to appeal from an arbitration award is limited. See s. 69.

[97]   *Soleimany* v. *Soleimany* [1999] QB 785.   [98]   At 798.   [99]   At 800.

[100]   At 799. See also *London Export Corporation Ltd* v. *Jubilee Coffee Roasting Co. Ltd* [1958] 1 WLR 271, 277–8, Diplock J.

[101]   At 799.

[102]   A. Tucker, 'The Archbishop's Unsatisfactory Legal Pluralism' [2008] *Public Law* 463, 466.

a State.[103] 'Other considerations', however, can extend to other systems of law that are not the law of the State, such as religious law.[104] Section 46 thus allows parties to choose for their dispute to be decided in accordance with systems of religious law. Therefore, parties may take a dispute to a religious court and enter into a contract to be bound by that court's decision.

There are numerous examples of the decisions of religious courts being enforced under the Arbitration Act – particularly the Beth Din.[105] There are fewer examples in respect of Islamic courts and there is evidence of at least one case where the decision of the Islamic Shari'a Council of London (ISC) was not so enforced, the decision in *Al-Midani* v. *Al-Midani*.[106] However, it is important not to extrapolate too simplistic a conclusion from that case, since on the facts the parties had not agreed to arbitration by the ISC. Whilst it is true that other Islamic courts and tribunals have generally not operated under the Arbitration Act,[107] this does not mean they cannot. There is now at least one clear example of an Islamic court operating under the Arbitration Act 1996: the Muslim Arbitration Tribunal (MAT).[108] The MAT website makes it clear that it operates under the Arbitration Act 1996.[109] It deals with all areas of civil and personal religious law, but not divorce proceedings (other than a religious divorce), child custody and criminal matters.

The Arbitration Act 1996 is a facilitative piece of legislation, giving the parties the choice to agree to resolve their disputes outside the courtroom. If an agreement is made to arbitrate a dispute, rather than considering the dispute itself, the court enforces the decision made by the arbitrator. Once an agreement is made to arbitrate any other legal proceedings may be paused.[110] The parties are free to agree on the number of arbitrators to form the tribunal and whether there is to be a chairman or umpire.[111] They are also free to decide upon the procedure for appointing the arbitrator or arbitrators.[112] However, the decision of the Court of Appeal in *Jivraj* v.

---

[103] L. Collins (ed.), *Dicey, Morris and Collins on the Conflict of Laws*, 14th edn (London: Sweet & Maxwell, 2006), paras. 16–050–5. See the discussion in *Halpern* v. *Halpern* [2007] EWCA Civ 291 and *Sayyed Mohammed Musawi* v. *R.E. International (UK) Ltd* [2007] EWHC 298.

[104] Section 46(2) states that: 'For this purpose the choice of laws of a country shall be understood to refer to the substantive laws of the country and not its conflict of laws rules.' Religious law could be therefore recognised as 'law' rather than 'another consideration' if that religious law is a substantive law in a country. See R. Blacklett, 'The Status of Religious "Courts" in English Law' [2009] *Disputes and International Arbitration Newsletter* 11, 13.

[105] See, e.g. *Cohen* v. *Baram* [1994] 2 Lloyd's Rep 138; and *Kohn* v. *Wagschal and others* [2007] EWCA Civ 1022. See S. Knights, *Freedom of Religion, Minorities and the Law* (Oxford: Oxford University Press, 2007), p. 75.

[106] [1999] CLC 904.

[107] In *Al-Midani* v. *Al-Midani*, the High Court explained this by reference to what they termed the position of 'strict' *Sharia* law summarising it in the following manner: 'an arbitration agreement to arbitrate future disputes is not valid, since it is uncertain; however, an agreement to arbitrate a specific dispute which has arisen is valid, but can be revoked before award': at 911.

[108] See, further, R. Sandberg, 'Islam and English Law' (2010) 164 *Law & Justice* 227.

[109] www.matribunal.com.   [110] Arbitration Act 1996 ss. 9(2),(4).

[111] Section 15.   [112] Section 16.

Hashwani[113] suggests that arbitration agreements which make distinctions on grounds of religion may fall foul of religious discrimination laws.

The case concerned an arbitration agreement entered into in 1981 which required that all arbitrators were to come from the Ismaili community. When Hashwani appointed an arbitrator from outside this community, Jivraj asserted that this was invalid under the terms of the agreement. However, Hashwani contended that, although the requirement that all arbitrators must come from the Ismaili community had been lawful when the agreement was made, it had been rendered unlawful by new laws prohibiting discrimination on grounds of religion or belief in relation to employment.[114] The Court of Appeal agreed.[115] Moore-Bick LJ held that the law prohibiting religious discrimination in relation to employment applied to arbitrators because employment was defined as meaning 'employment under a contract of service' and the nature of the arbitration was contractual.[116] Moreover, Jivraj could not rely on the religious exception that permits a person with an 'ethos based on religion or belief' to insist that being of a particular religion or belief is an occupational requirement of a job.[117] Since the arbitration agreement required the arbitrators to resolve the dispute in accordance with English law, it had not been shown that it was necessary for arbitrators to be members of the Ismaili community.[118] This suggests that parties who wish for their disputes to be determined by representatives of a particular religious tradition must ensure that they have shown that this is a genuine occupational requirement. The long-term implications of the Court of Appeal's judgment upon the use of the Arbitration Act for religious purposes is unknown. As with other cases concerning religious exceptions, it is notable that the narrowness of the religious exception was stressed[119] and that no attention was given to Jivraj's religious freedom as protected by Article 9.

More generally, arbitration agreements must comply with human rights standards concerning the right to a fair trial. States may be liable if basic standards are not met.[120] The European Court of Human Rights has insisted that states are under an obligation to ensure that religious courts meet the

---

[113] [2010] EWCA Civ 712.

[114] Employment Equality (Religion or Belief) Regulations 2003. The law is now to be found in the Equality Act 2010. See Chapter 6.

[115] Compare the decision of the High Court, which held that neither the Employment Equality (Religion or Belief) Regulations 2003 nor the Human Rights Act 1998 applies to the selection, engagement or appointment of arbitrators (unless a party to the particular arbitration agreement is a public authority): [2009] EWHC (Comm) 1364.

[116] [2010] EWCA Civ 712 at para. 14.

[117] Employment Equality (Religion or Belief) Regulations 2003 Reg. 7(3). The exception is now to be found in the Equality Act 2010 Sch. 19 para. 3. See Chapter 6.

[118] [2010] EWCA Civ 712 at para. 29.   [119] See para. 28.

[120] At the level of the United Nations, Art. 14 of the International Covenant on Civil and Political Rights protects the right to a fair trial. This right applies to arbitration by religious courts. See the Human Rights Committee in General Comment 22 (23 August 2007) at para. 24.

standards necessary to comply with the right to a fair trial. In *Pellegrini* v. *Italy*,[121] the Strasbourg Court considered Roman Catholic annulment proceedings in an ecclesiastical court where the applicant was not told the nature of proceedings in advance and was not allowed to read her husband's witness statements. The Italian courts had made operative the Vatican court's declaration of nullity and the European Court of Human Rights held that the proceedings in the ecclesiastical courts violated Article 6 of the ECHR in that the applicant's right to fair trial had been 'irremediably compromised'. Since the Vatican is not party to the Convention, the claim was made against the Italian State: the Court held that since the Italian courts had made operative the Vatican court's declaration of nullity, the State was in breach of Article 6; the Court 'should have refused to confirm the outcome of such unfair proceedings' and had 'failed in their duty to check . . . that the applicant had enjoyed a fair trial in the ecclesiastical proceedings'. It follows that the United Kingdom would be in breach of Article 6 if a religious court failed to meet Article 6 standards as to right to a fair trial and that decision was enforced under the Arbitration Act 1996.

The Arbitration Act does not, of course, cover all the functions performed by religious courts. Even religious courts which use the Act, such as the Beth Din and the MAT, also operate *outside* the Arbitration Act. A distinction is sometimes drawn between their 'legal' functions under the Arbitration Act and 'religious' functions. For instance, a study of the Beth Din by the Centre for Social Cohesion states that: 'The Beth Din serves two distinct functions for members of the Jewish communities in the UK.' Firstly, 'Jewish courts function as legally binding arbitration tribunals for civil cases'. Secondly, '[t]he Beth Din also functions as a religious – and not legal – authority [ruling] in a variety of religious matters', such as designating religious holidays or granting religious divorces'.[122] Such statements often suggest that where religious courts do not use the Arbitration Act, they are operating extra-legally and their decisions are not legally binding at all. However, this is not the case. The doctrine of 'consensual compact' means that the rules and structures of voluntary associations are binding on assenting members. Furthermore, the courts of the State will exceptionally intervene to enforce the laws of a religious group where there is a financial interest and in relation to the disposal and administration of property.[123] The ways in which religious courts operate outside the Arbitration Act are largely unknown. Further research is needed on the operation of religious courts and the binding effect of these religious functions.[124]

---

[121] (2002) 35 EHRR 2.

[122] *The Beth Din: Jewish Courts in the UK* (Centre for Social Cohesion, 2009), p. 4.

[123] *Forbes* v. *Eden* (1867) LR 1 Sc & Div 568.

[124] Research at Cardiff University funded by the Arts and Humanities Research Council and the Economic and Social Research Council represents a step in the right direction. The project, 'Social Cohesion and Civil Law: Marriage, Divorce and Religious Courts', brings together

Recognition through private international law

The fourth way in which English law may be said to recognise religious laws is through private international law.[125] A typical example of this would be the recognition of marriages conducted overseas. The key test is the same as under the Arbitration Act: whether the recognition complies with public policy.[126] This was underlined by the Court of Appeal decision of *KC and another* v. *City of Westminster Social & Community Services Dept*,[127] concerning a marriage by telephone link between England and Bangladesh and lack of mental capacity of one party. The Court of Appeal held that it was a valid marriage under Islamic law and Bangladeshi law, but was not valid under English law: the marriage was sufficiently offensive to the conscience of the English court that it should refuse to recognise it.

Conclusions

This chapter has sought to contextualise fears that arose in the aftermath of the Archbishop's lecture by examining what is meant by religious law and the extent to which it is recognised in England and Wales. Two conclusions may be reached. Firstly, the study of religious law is important. The various methods of defining religious law highlight that it is both possible and desirable to talk about religious law as an umbrella category. The study of religious law requires both law and theology: religious law *is* law, but is not *just* law. The many different ways in which English law currently recognises religious laws underscores the importance of religious law within the academic study of law and religion.

Secondly, as with the religious hatred offences discussed in Chapter 7 and the law on faith schools discussed in Chapter 8, it seems that many of the popular fears concerning religious courts seem to result from a misunderstanding of the letter of the law. This is particularly so in relation to courts operating under the Arbitration Act 1996. The 1996 Act places a

researchers at Cardiff Law School, the Centre for Law and Religion and the Centre for the Study of Islam in the UK at Cardiff University. It examines the workings of three religious courts in detail: a Jewish Beth Din; a matrimonial tribunal of the Roman Catholic Church; and a Muslim Shariah Council. The project asks 'What is the legal status of these courts?' and 'How do they operate in relation to marriage, divorce and remarriage?' The project began in April 2010 and runs until May 2011. For further information, see the Centre for Law and Religion website (www.law.cf.ac.uk/clr).

[125] The term 'international law' is often used to describe systems of law which govern the relationship between states, such as the legal instruments of the United Nations. However, technically this is known as 'public international law'. And this is compared with 'private international law', which is the part of the national law of a country that establishes rules for dealing with cases involving the laws of other countries – foreign law. 'Private international law' is also known as conflict of laws.

[126] M. Robe, 'Shari'a in a European Context' in R. Grillo *et al.* (eds.), *Legal Practice and Cultural Diversity* (Aldershot: Ashgate, 2009), pp. 93, 96–7.

[127] [2008] EWCA Civ 198.

great emphasis upon the choice of the parties, but provides a number of safeguards to avoid abuse. However, there is a clear need for further research into how religious courts operate, especially how they operate outside the Arbitration Act. Both of these conclusions support the need for the study of religious law to become a firm part of the legal sub-discipline of law and religion. There needs to be a greater dialogue between those who specialise in systems of religious law (such as Islamic law, Jewish law or Roman Catholic Canon law) and those who specialise in religion law. Moreover, there is a need for this academic dialogue to reach out to the general public, correcting popular misconceptions and fears. These goals will be easier to achieve if law and religion blossoms as a recognisable legal sub-discipline with an identifiable voice found in specific conferences, publications and associations.

10

The clash of arms

Introduction

Although historically this country is part of the Christian west, and although it has an established church which is Christian, I sit as a secular judge serving a multi-cultural community of many faiths in which all of us can now take pride, sworn to do justice 'to all manner of people'. Religion – whatever the particular believer's faith – is no doubt something to be encouraged but it is not the business of government or of the secular court. So the starting point of the law is an essentially agnostic view of religious beliefs and a tolerant indulgence to religious and cultural diversity. A secular judge must be wary of straying across the well-recognised divide between church and state. It is not for a judge to weigh one religion against another. All are entitled to equal respect, whether in time of peace, or, as at present, amidst the clash of arms.

Munby J, *Sulaiman* v. *Juffali*[1]

Every generation thinks that the challenges they face are unique. They think that the underlying political, social and moral problems they encounter are on a scale previously unseen and require radical and unorthodox solutions. This inevitably leads to the enactment of new law. In the early years of the twenty-first century, this has occurred in relation to religion. The Al-Qaeda terrorist attacks in New York on 11 September 2001 and in London on 7 July 2005 have changed the 'rules of the game'.[2] In the twentieth century, a cosy consensus developed concerning the place of religion in the public sphere. It was widely anticipated that the effect of the Enlightenment was the triumph of reason over religion, and that this would result in the retreat of religion to the private sphere like any other leisure activity.[3] However, events simply proved these expectations wrong.[4] Debates concerning the place of religion

---

[1] [2002] 2 FCR 427 at para. 47.

[2] To quote the words of Tony Blair in the aftermath of the London terrorist attacks of 7 July 2005. See www.number-10.gov.uk/output/Page8041.asp.

[3] As Hoffmann J commented in 1993, 'the attitude of the English legislator to racing is much more akin to his attitude to religion . . . it is something to be encouraged but not the business of government': *R.* v. *Disciplinary Committee of the Jockey Club, ex parte Aga Khan* [1993] 1 WLR 909 at 932.

[4] At least in part. Elements of the secularisation thesis continue to be persuasive. Most notably, church attendance figures continue to dwindle.

in the public sphere now dominate the domestic and international news agenda. Arguments concerning religious dress, courts and schools are ever-present and ever-divisive, stirring up passion on both sides of the debate. And there are now more laws concerning and affecting religion than ever before.

Although a number of the legal points made by Munby J in the extract above are questionable to say the least,[5] the quote is helpful in reminding us of the context in which the law operates and evolves. Modern religion law exists 'amidst the clash of arms'. The new laws and their interpretation both shape and are shaped by profound social and political changes. The new religion law is both a product and a cause of wider political and societal trends. This is nothing new. Conflicts concerning religion are a constant presence in British history and, as Chapter 2 has shown, they have affected the law. Many of the concerns associated with Islam today were foreshadowed by previous concerns about Roman Catholicism. In both cases, anxieties were raised by violent acts apparently in the name of religion and the loyalties that adherents were presumed to give to powers which were outside the nation State. The fear of religious difference runs deep.

However, there is something unique about the current situation. As Chapter 2 showed, there have long been laws affecting religion. Yet, the current law represents a marked shift. Just as toleration marked a substantial shift from post-Reformation discrimination, the Human Rights Act 1998 and new laws prohibiting discrimination specifically on grounds of religion or belief have encapsulated a considerable shift from passive toleration to the active promotion of religious liberty as a right. There is now a new body of law concerning religion which places a great emphasis upon religious rights.

This final concluding chapter falls into two sections. The first draws upon the earlier chapters in order to gather together the main trends. The second section identifies three particular pressure points which have emerged and suggests possible ways forward. The chapter then concludes by returning to the three sets of questions outlined in Chapter 1, focusing on the question of whether law and religion can and should now be seen as a distinct legal sub-discipline.

---

[5] For instance, claimants such as Playfoot and Eweida may dispute the notion that English law treats all religions equally 'whatever the particular believer's faith' (see Chapter 6). Moreover, is it really the case that there is 'a well-recognised divide between church and state' (see Chapter 4)? Most of the quotation is also unoriginal. The reference to religion not being the business of the judiciary or the legislature derives from *R* v. *Disciplinary Committee of the Jockey Club, ex parte Aga Khan*, quoted above, while the reference to the alleged Church-State divide can also be found in *R.* v. *Chief Rabbi, ex parte Wachmann* [1992] 1 WLR 1036 at 1043, which is discussed above in Chapter 4.

Emerging trends

This book has sought to tell the story of how law and religion interact in twenty-first century Britain. Whilst it is true that the last half of the twentieth century saw a number of piecemeal developments protecting religious freedom, these simply foreshadowed more wide-ranging developments that occurred in the twenty-first century. Two key trends may be identified. Firstly, there has been an increase in the regulation of religion. This increase in the quantity and reach of legislation and litigation may be referred to as the 'juridification of religion'. Secondly, a body of law affecting religion has developed, which this book has referred to as 'religion law'. This section will explore these trends in greater depth, drawing upon previous chapters.

The juridification of religion

The significant changes in the way in which the law regulates religion may be summed up in the phrase the 'juridification of religion'.[6] As Blicher and Molander note: 'Juridification is an ambiguous concept.'[7] They identify a number of different dimensions of juridification, three of which seem to describe to the changes in relation to the regulation of religion traced in previous chapters.

The first dimension of juridification refers to 'legal explosion',[8] a process 'through which law comes to regulate an increasing number of different activities'.[9] This includes what Habermas referred to as the '*expansion* of law, that is, the legal regulation of new, hitherto informally regulated social matters'.[10] This has clearly occurred in relation to religion. The last decade has seen a great deal of legislation concerning religion and a great deal of litigation. This is unsurprising. As Chapter 2 explained, the European Court of Human Rights has made plain that the State is now expected to facilitate religious freedom within the religious market place.[11]

---

[6] This term 'juridification' is often used to describe similar trends in sports law: see M. James, *Sports Law* (London: Palgrave Macmillan, 2010), pp. 5–8; and S. Gardiner *et al.*, *Sports Law*, 3rd edn (London: Cavendish, 2006), pp. 84–8.

[7] L. C. Blicher and A. Molander, 'Mapping Juridification' (2008) 14(1) *European Law Journal* 36.

[8] See G. Teubner, 'Juridification – Concepts, Aspects, Limits, Solutions' in G. Teubner (ed.), *Juridification of Social Spheres* (Berlin: Walter de Gruyter, 1987), pp. 3, 6–7.

[9] L. C. Blicher and A. Molander, 'Mapping Juridification' (2008) 14(1) *European Law Journal* 36, 38–9.

[10] J. Habermas, *The Theory of Communicative Action* (New York: Beacon Press, 1987), p. 359, cited by L. C. Blicher and A. Molander, 'Mapping Juridification' (2008) 14(1) *European Law Journal* 36, 42.

[11] The obligations placed upon the State are most clearly expressed by the Grand Chamber in *Refah Partisi* v. *Turkey* (2003) 37 EHRR 1 at para. 91. For discussion of the religious 'free market', see J. A. Beckford and J. T. Richardson, 'Religion and Regulation' in J. A. Beckford and N. J. Demerath (eds.), *The Sage Handbook of the Sociology of Religion* (London: Sage, 2007), pp. 396, 411.

A second and related dimension of juridification is the 'process whereby conflicts increasingly are being solved by or with reference to law'.[12] This again has clearly occurred in relation to religion law. The 'two pillars' of modern religion law – the right to religious freedom incorporated into domestic law by the Human Rights Act 1998 and the right not to be discriminated against on grounds of religion or belief – have led to a new emphasis upon the legal protection of religious rights. The codified rights they provide may long have been implicit in the common law, but the form these rights now take and the awareness and promotion of these rights have led to an increase in litigation concerning religion, as seen in Chapters 5 and 6. The starting point of the law is now that people have a right to religious freedom. This aspect of the juridification of religion is shown further in the way in which bodies that regulate religion are increasingly adopting a juridical approach.[13]

A third dimension of juridification refers to 'legal framing', that is the process 'by which people increasingly tend to think of themselves and others as legal subjects'.[14] This describes the 'awareness of an individual of their status, or potential, as a legal actor, the increased propensity for individuals and groups to see courts as the appropriate forum for the resolution of social disputes, and perhaps even simply an increased use of legal terminology in discourse'.[15] It also describes the way in which reference to law is used outside the courtroom both as a way of solving conflict and also shaping policy.[16] These developments seem to have occurred in relation to the regulation of religion. The Human Rights Act 1998 and the new law prohibiting religious discrimination have led to greater knowledge of religious rights. Moreover, the modern religion law has influence outside the courtroom. A quick internet search reveals the number of courses, guidelines and policies which employers and public authorities now have concerning religion, most of which include some reference to the legal framework. The language of religious rights has begun to enter into the public discourse, as a result of the new legal obligations and the media reporting of litigation.

The usefulness of the concept of juridification in relation to the regulation of religion is further shown by Rubin's account of the juridification

---

[12] L. C. Blicher and A. Molander, 'Mapping Juridification' (2008) 14(1) *European Law Journal* 36, 39.

[13] See P. W. Edge and J. M. Loughrey, 'Religious Charities and the Juridification of the Charity Commission' (2001) 21 *Legal Studies* 36.

[14] L. C. Blicher and A. Molander, 'Mapping Juridification' (2008) 14(1) *European Law Journal* 36, 39.

[15] R. Masterman, 'Labour's "Juridification" of the Constitution' (2009) 62(3) *Parliamentary Affairs* 476, 477.

[16] L. C. Blicher and A. Molander, 'Mapping Juridification' (2008) 14(1) *European Law Journal* 36, 44.

of military law,[17] which is strikingly similar to the main trends in the development of religion law. Rubin describes how military law was previously characterised by autonomy and judicial abstention: 'from the mid-nineteenth to the mid-twentieth century, the civil courts adopted a "hands off" approach to military disputes'.[18] The judiciary followed 'a policy of absenteeism . . . except in rare and egregious cases'.[19] Although this began to change in the second half of the twentieth century, these piecemeal changes have been 'complemented in recent years by more radical shifts'. And the most notable of these are the Human Rights Act and a number of 'equal opportunities and equal treatment cases before employment tribunals'.[20] This has meant that 'military law has ceased to be the narrow preserve of military lawyers'.[21] Previous chapters have described the same trends in relation to religion law. Although the judiciary are still reluctant to adjudicate religious disputes within religious groups,[22] they are now expected to adjudicate disputes brought to them under human rights and discrimination laws. The term 'juridification of religion law' may therefore be used as a convenient shorthand to describe the significant shift by which the passive tolerance of religious difference has been superseded by the prescriptive regulation of religion and the active promotion of religious liberty as a right.

The rise of religion law

However, the increase in the quantity and reach of laws affecting religion does not necessarily lead to the conclusion that a new body of law affecting religion has developed, known as 'religion law'. Alternatively, it may be said that the legal developments are best understood within the context of existing areas of law. Developments in human rights law and discrimination law could be said to be precisely that: the cases on Article 9 could be best understood in the context of human rights law, while the provisions on religion or belief in the Equality Act 2010 could be best understood as part of discrimination law. However, the previous chapters have argued against this conclusion. The legal developments are best understood as resulting in a new body of law which may be called religion law.

This was shown in Chapters 3 and 4. At first glance, the materials explored in Chapter 3 seemed to support the conclusion that a new body of law had not been formed. Different definitions of religion continue to exist in relation to registration and charity law, human rights and discrimination law. However, closer analysis showed an increasing homogeneity between these definitions, as religious discrimination cases began referring to the

---

[17] G. R. Rubin, 'United Kingdom Military Law: Autonomy, Civilisation, Juridification' (2002) 65 (1) *Modern Law Review* 36.
[18] *Ibid.*, 38. [19] *Ibid.*, 37. [20] *Ibid.*, 36. [21] *Ibid.* [22] See Chapter 4.

human rights jurisprudence.[23] Indeed, the effect of the Employment Appeal Tribunal decisions in *Greater Manchester Police Authority* v. *Power*[24] and *Grainger PLC* v. *Nicholson*[25] is the wholesale adoption of the human rights definition of 'belief' in discrimination law. The rule that a belief 'must satisfy some modest, objective minimum requirements'[26] is no longer limited to human rights law. Now it can and should be seen as a proposition of religion law.[27]

Similarly in Chapter 4, the establishment of the Church of England appeared to challenge the argument that a body of religion law now existed. The 'incidents of establishment' show how the Church of England remains in a different legal position from all other non-established religious groups. This may suggest that the law affecting the Church of England may be best seen as separate from the law affecting other religious bodies; as 'ecclesiastical law' not religion law, a conclusion which seems to be supported by the language of the Welsh Church Act 1914. However, as Chapter 4 argued, the differences between the legal position of the Church of England and all other non-established religious groups does not necessarily undermine the usefulness of religion law as a label. The Church of England remains shaped by broader pieces of religion law. Increasingly the incidents of establishment are challenged by EU law, the ECHR and pieces of domestic religion law. And even if we chose to retain the term 'ecclesiastical law' to describe the law affecting the Church of England, we can still say that this ecclesiastical law is part of religion law.[28] Moreover, the development of a distinct law concerning non-established religious groups – based upon the doctrine of consensual compact, the principle of non-interference and the *Forbes* v. *Eden*[29] exception – provides further evidence of the emergence of a distinct body of law.[30] The judgment in *HH Sant Baba Jeet Singh Maharaj* v. *Eastern Media Group Ltd*,[31] in particular, seems to point to a recognition on the part of the courts that the regulation of religious matters requires a particular approach. The case law that elucidates that approach may be described as part of religion law.

---

[23] The Charity Commission has also taken to citing Article 9 as a matter of course.

[24] [2009] EAT 0434/09/DA (12 November 2009).

[25] [2009] UKEAT 0219/09/ZT (3 November 2009).

[26] *R.* v. *Secretary of State for Education and Employment and others, ex parte Williamson* [2005] UKHL 15 at para. 23.

[27] And this conclusion can be used to criticise restrictive definitions found in other areas of religion law. The exclusion of non-religious beliefs in religious offences and education provisions (see Chapters 7 and 8) seems outmoded and discriminatory.

[28] We can also recognise that parts of ecclesiastical law are best understood as religious law; this might be a valuable way of recognising the autonomy of the established church.

[29] (1867) LR 1 Sc & Div 568.

[30] As does the material examined in J. Rivers, *The Law of Organized Religions* (Oxford: Oxford University Press, 2010).

[31] [2010] EWHC (QB) 1294.

Further evidence of the development of religion law can be seen in the tendency of decided cases to routinely cross-refer to other areas of religion law, developing propositions of religion law. The clearest evidence of this trend can be found in the Employment Appeal Tribunal decision in *McClintock* v. *Department of Constitutional Affairs*,[32] which suggested that evidence that a disadvantage was justified under indirect discrimination would satisfy the question of whether the interference was justified for Article 9 purposes. And this was not an isolated case. Article 9 is now regularly discussed in religious discrimination law disputes,[33] meaning that the case law on religious discrimination cannot be understood by reference to discrimination law alone; it requires knowledge of the Article 9 case law. Moreover, as Chapter 7 discussed, Article 9 and religious discrimination concerns[34] influenced the abolition of blasphemy. Older pieces of religion law, such as the education provisions discussed in Chapter 8, now need to be considered in the light of the expectations found in Article 9 and the law prohibiting religious discrimination. It is increasingly the case that in order to understand individual pieces of law affecting religion it is necessary to have wider knowledge of religion law.[35]

Pressure points

These swift changes in the way in which the law regulates religion have led to a number of anxieties. Although it is clear that the legal framework has changed, it is less certain whether the new laws have led to greater protection being afforded to religious individuals and groups.

This can be shown in relation to the new laws prohibiting religious discrimination, which have led to a great deal of litigation. Although the new laws have clearly extended protection in some respects, most notably in relation to claims about working hours and holy days[36] and some religious dress cases,[37] most claims have been unsuccessful. This in itself is not a bad thing. The courts are right to refuse what the Archbishop of Canterbury

---

[32] EAT, Appeal No. UKEAT/0223/07CEA (22 October 2007) at paras. 60–1.

[33] It was considered in all three Court of Appeal decisions concerning religious discrimination: *Ladele* v. *London Borough of Islington* [2009] EWCA (Civ) 1357; *Eweida* v. *British Airways* [2010] EWCA Civ 80; and *McFarlane* v. *Relate Avon Ltd* [2010] EWCA Civ 880.

[34] Raised in relation to Art. 14 of the ECHR.

[35] For instance, *New Testament Church of God* v. *Stewart* [2007] EWCA Civ 1004 shows how Article 9 has been influential upon the long-running debate as to whether or not ministers of religion should be seen as employees for the purposes of employment law.

[36] *Khan* v. *G & S Spencer Group* ET, Case Number: 1803250/2004 (12 January 2005); *Williams-Drabble* v. *Pathway Care Solutions* ET, Case Number: 2601718/2004 (2 December 2004); and *Fugler* v. *MacMillan – London Hairstudios Ltd* ET, Case Number: 2205090/2004 (21–3 June 2005).

[37] *R. (on the application of Watkins-Singh)* v. *The Governing Body of Aberdare Girls' High School* [2007] EWCA Civ 1004; *Noah* v. *Sarah Desrosiers (Wedge)* [2008] ET, Case Number: 2201867/07 (29 May 2008).

referred to as 'vexatious appeals to religious scruple'.[38] And a tendency in some cases to argue 'everything but the kitchen sink' may suggest that such claims are undeserving. However, the sheer number of unsuccessful cases questions the effectiveness of the new law.[39] Although on paper there have been significant changes, in practice the law seems to have been interpreted restrictedly.

The case of *McFarlane* v. *Relate Avon Ltd*[40] illustrates the level of concern that now exists.[41] The case was supported by a witness statement by the former Archbishop of Canterbury, Lord Carey of Clifton, in which he argued for 'a specially constituted Court of Appeal of five Lords Justices who have a proven sensibility to religious issues',[42] expressing concern that:

> Recent decisions of the Courts have illuminated insensitivity to the interests and needs of the Christian community and represent disturbing Judgments. The effect of these decisions is to undermine the religious liberties that have existed in the United Kingdom for centuries'.[43]

Lord Carey's concern deserves more attention than his proposed solution. In *McFarlane*, Laws LJ was quite right to reject flatly Lord Carey's call for a specially constituted Court of Appeal, a proposal which showed a complete lack of understanding of the judicial process.[44] However, Laws LJ was also correct in his judgment that it was appropriate to focus on what Lord Carey was arguing, given Carey's 'seniority in the Church and the extent to which others may agree with his views'.[45] This section will examine three of the main pressure points which have come to the fore in previous chapters and have resulted in the situation which so alarmed the former Archbishop.

The curse of *Begum*

The first pressure point is the way in which the newly codified religious rights are being interpreted restrictively by the English judiciary. As Chapters 5 and 6 explained, claims are being dismissed on the grounds that there is no interference with the right rather than because the interference was justified. The House of Lords decision in *Begum*[46] provided the turning

---

[38] R. Williams, 'Civil and Religious Law in England – A Religious Perspective' (2008) 10 *Ecclesiastical Law Journal* 262, 267.

[39] At the very least, the law seems to be creating false impressions about religious rights.

[40] [2010] EWCA Civ 880.

[41] For further analysis of the judgment, see R. Sandberg, 'Laws and Religion: Unravelling *McFarlane* v. *Relate Avon Ltd*' (2010) 12 *Ecclesiastical Law Journal* 361.

[42] Para. 17.　　[43] See para. 6 of the Witness Statement.

[44] See M. Hill, 'Judges Should not be Handpicked' *Church Times* Issue 7675 (23 April 2010).

[45] Para. 16.

[46] *R. (on the application of Begum)* v. *Headteacher and Governors of Denbigh High School* [2006] UKHL 15.

point. The majority gave general effect to the 'specific situation rule' developed at Strasbourg, noting in broad terms that 'interference is not easily established'.[47] The result of *Begum* is that Article 9 is now moribund. The legal arguments used in *R (on the application of Watkins-Singh)* v. *The Governing Body of Aberdare Girls' High School*[48] indicates the extent to which litigants will now argue anything but Article 9. Subsequent lower court and tribunal decisions have relied upon *Begum* to dismiss claims on the basis that there is no interference with religious rights where claimants are free to manifest their religion elsewhere.[49]

This reliance upon the question of interference is unnecessary because more often than not such claims could have been adequately dealt with by focusing upon the question of justification. Increasingly high barriers seem to be placed in front of those who wish to enforce what they believe to be their religious rights.[50] And the tendency to focus upon semantic questions of interference might not allow the court to examine the merits of the case. Cases concerning religious rights require nuanced, fact-specific judgments, which are best reached by focusing upon the question of justification. The current case law indicates that the judiciary are uncomfortable dealing with religious rights, clinging to questions of interference to deal swiftly with claims.[51] This is not to say that the 'religion or belief' argument always needs to win. However, the 'religion or belief' argument needs to be considered seriously and treated as being as important as other rights. And this does not seem to be the case at the moment.

The solution to this problem would be for courts to focus upon the question of justification rather than that of interference. However, if this is not to occur, at the very least the courts ought to be consistent in the way in which they apply the filters. At the moment, while courts have prevented believers from bringing faith into secular situations on the grounds that the believer has voluntarily entered the secular environment, they have never developed this to cover the converse situation. The specific situation rule should be accompanied by the 'religious situation rule'.[52] This would cover the situation where a non-believer voluntarily submits to a religious situation. If a non-believer enters a place of worship, faith school or religious

---

[47] Lord Bingham, paras. 23–4.   [48] [2008] EWHC (Admin) 1865.
[49] E.g. *R. (on the application of X)* v. *Y School* [2006] EWHC (Admin) 298; and *R. (on the Application of Playfoot (A Child)* v. *Millais School Governing Body* [2007] EWHC Admin 1698.
[50] The judgment in *Eweida* v. *British Airways* [2010] EWCA Civ 80 is particularly troubling, suggesting that fringe beliefs held by a few individuals (including beliefs held by a minority of believers within a larger religious group) will be denied protection.
[51] Further evidence of this can be found in the way in which the narrowness of the exceptions from discrimination law granted to religious groups is constantly stressed: *R. (Amicus MSF Section)* v. *Secretary of State for Trade and Industry* [2004] EWHC 860; and *Ladele* v. *London Borough of Islington* [2009] EWCA (Civ) 1357 at paras. 69–73.
[52] The following develops arguments first made in R. Sandberg, 'A Sign of the Times' (2010) *e-International Relation* www.e-ir.info/?p=3831.

bookstore, then surely their voluntary submission should be an answer to any claim that the religious setting breaches their Article 9 rights. One of the major concerns implicit in modern religion law is the extent to which religious groups are expected to live up to secular standards. This underpins the conflicts concerning exceptions in discrimination law and the existence of faith schools. The religious situation rule would help to address this, underlining the autonomy of religious groups by asserting that when someone voluntarily enters the religious realm they cannot automatically insist on secular standards.[53] It would be particularly helpful in the context of religious exceptions from discrimination law.

Judging religious doctrine

The second, and related, pressure point is the increasing tendency of the secular courts to examine questions of religious doctrine. The High Court decision in *HH Sant Baba Jeet Singh Maharaj* v. *Eastern Media Group Ltd*[54] is the latest in a long line of judgments which has stressed 'the well-known principle of English law to the effect that the courts will not attempt to rule upon doctrinal issues or intervene in the regulation or governance of religious groups'.[55] However, while the courts have followed this doctrine of non-interference in order to avoid adjudicating disputes within religious groups (unless the *Forbes* v. *Eden*[56] exception applies), courts *have* adjudicated on questions of faith and doctrine in cases where claimants have sought to assert their religious rights using the new religion law.[57]

This paradox can be explained by juxtaposing paragraphs 22 and 23 of Lord Nicholls of Birkenhead's speech in *Williamson*.[58] In paragraph 22, his Lordship asserts that 'emphatically, it is not for the court to embark on an

---

[53]   That said, it is important that the religious situation rule does not become a blunt instrument which allows courts to avoid the complex factual issues. Unlike the specific situation rule following *Begum*, it must remain the case that the religious situation rule is not of universal application. The rule should only apply in the rare situation where someone has clearly voluntarily submitted themselves to a system of norms, usually by means of a contract.

[54]   [2010] EWHC (QB) 1294.

[55]   Para. 5. This is strikingly similar to the concept of 'methodological agnosticism' used in the sociology of religion. This requires, in the words of Simmel, a distinction to be drawn between the 'metaphysical event that is readily capable of implying or forming the basis of religion' and 'the subjective attitude of human beings'. Methodological agnosticism requires the making of that distinction and the bracketing aside of the question of the status of religious claims: G. Simmel, 'Contributions to the Epistemology of Religion' in G. Simmel, *Essays on Religion* (New Haven: Yale University Press, 1917), p. 121.

[56]   (1867) LR 1 Sc & Div 568.

[57]   See the decisions in *Playfoot* [2007] EWHC Admin 1698, *Eweida* [2010] EWCA Civ 80 and *Ghai* [2009] EWHC (Admin) 978, discussed in Chapters 5 and 6.

[58]   *R.* v. *Secretary of State for Education and Employment and others, ex parte Williamson* [2005] UKHL 15.

inquiry into the asserted belief and judge its "validity" by some objective standard such as the source material upon which the claimant founds his belief or the orthodox teaching of the religion in question or the extent to which the claimant's belief conforms to or differs from the views of others professing the same religion' because '[f]reedom of religion protects the subjective belief of an individual'. However, in paragraph 23, he makes a different point, holding that 'when questions of "manifestation" arise . . . a belief must satisfy some modest, objective minimum requirements'. As Cranmer has argued, these propositions 'seem slightly at odds with each other': Lord Nicholls is effectively saying that 'we will not normally judge the validity of a belief but sometimes, in order to decide whether or not a particular manifestation is to be protected, we may well have to do just that'.[59]

The key word here is 'sometimes'. Lord Nicholls' speech suggests that the word 'sometimes' should read 'exceptionally'. He said that 'too much should not be demanded in this regard'.[60] And his Lordship was adamant that:

> The relevance of objective factors such as source material is, at most, that they may throw light on whether the professed belief is genuinely held.[61]

However, the judgments in *Playfoot*, *Eweida* and *Ghai* have gone significantly beyond this. In those cases, there was no question that the belief was not genuinely held. The courts applied objective tests to hold that the claimant was under no obligation by reason of their faith's doctrine to manifest their religion in the way they claimed. If freedom of religion 'protects the subjective belief of an individual', as Lord Nicholls maintained, then this is irrelevant. As the Court of Appeal recognised in *New Testament Church of God* v. *Stewart*,[62] there does not need to be a breach of an 'express tenet' of a religion for Article 9 to be engaged: the only requirement is that there is a conflict with 'religious beliefs'.[63] It must be remembered that religious freedom protects manifestations of religious belief; this is not limited only to manifestations of religious belief which are found to be 'central' or 'obligatory' according to doctrinal texts. To rule otherwise is to assume that all adherents to a certain faith share the same beliefs and is to exclude religious adherents who do not belong to a religious group which has clear religious doctrines. In *Playfoot*, *Eweida* and *Ghai*, there was no need to dismiss the claims in this way: in the future similar disputes should be determined using the question of justification.

---

[59] F. Cranmer, 'Beating People is Wrong: *Campbell and Cosans*, *Williamson* and their Aftermath' (paper delivered at a conference on 'Law, Religion and Education', organised by the Institute of Global Law at UCL (October 2010)).

[60] [2005] UKHL 15 at para. 23.   [61] Para. 22.   [62] [2007] EWCA Civ 1004.   [63] At para. 62.

The tension between the old and the new

The third pressure point is the implicit tension in English law which has developed between the new religion law and older laws protecting religion.[64] These old laws, many still on the statute books, were based upon a different premise. They often sought to protect Christianity in general (or the Church of England in particular) as the norm, while providing some degree of toleration for other faiths. Moreover, the legal regulation of religion was characterised by a lightness of touch. The new religion law is different. It is facilitative, seeking to protect religious freedom mainly as an individual right which needs to be balanced against other rights.[65] No special protection is afforded to any one religion and protection is often afforded to non-religious beliefs. The new legal framework affords utmost importance to the concept of religious equality as the State takes on the role of facilitating the religious marketplace.

This tension between the old and the new laws came to the fore in *McFarlane* v. *Relate Avon Ltd*.[66] Laws LJ surmised Lord Carey's argument to be broadly that 'the courts ought to be more sympathetic to the substance of the Christian beliefs referred to than appears to be the case, and should be readier than they are to uphold and defend them'.[67] Laws LJ addressed this by stressing that while the role of the law was to protect the right to manifest religion, this did not extend to protecting the substance of beliefs:

> The common law and ECHR Article 9 offer vigorous protection of the Christian's right (and every other person's right) to hold and express his or her beliefs. And so they should. By contrast they do not, and should not, offer any protection whatever of the substance or content of those beliefs on the ground only that they are based on religious precepts. . . .
>
> The general law may of course protect a particular social or moral position which is espoused by Christianity, not because of its religious *imprimatur*, but on the footing that in reason its merits commend themselves. So it is with core provisions of the criminal law: the prohibition of violence and dishonesty. The Judaeo-Christian tradition, stretching over many centuries, has no doubt exerted a profound influence upon the judgment of lawmakers as to the objective merits of this or that social policy. And the liturgy and practice of the established Church are to some extent prescribed by law. But the conferment of any legal protection or preference upon a particular substantive moral position on the ground only that it is espoused by the adherents of a particular faith, however long its tradition, however rich its culture, is deeply unprincipled.[68]

---

[64] The following develops an argument first made in R. Sandberg, 'Laws and Religion: Unravelling *McFarlane* v. *Relate Avon Ltd*' (2010) 12 *Ecclesiastical Law Journal* 361.

[65] Often, however, individual religious rights are only protected where the beliefs are shared by a group: see *Eweida* v. *British Airways* [2010] EWCA Civ 80.

[66] [2010] EWCA Civ 880.   [67] Para. 21.   [68] Paras. 22–23.

This is a different argument from saying that Christian ideas have become submerged into general culture. Laws LJ seems to be stating that the law protects certain values not because they are religious values, but by reason of their own merits. This view seems to ignore legal and historical reality. As Chapter 2 made clear, the historical synthesis of law and Christianity means that many laws are the way they are because of clerical fingerprints. And it is difficult to say that these laws are the way they are simply because their 'merits commend themselves', especially as the criteria by which we assess the merits also derives from the same Judaeo-Christian heritage.

Laws LJ's reasoning needs to be understood within the context of the new religion law, which is underpinned by a notion of religious equality that is ahistorical and which does not sit comfortably with legal reality. The importance placed on religious equality has led to the questioning of older laws on religion which begin from the premise that Christianity in general and the Church of England in particular are the norm. This attitude could have wide-ranging effects upon religion law. It has already resulted in the abolition of the offence of blasphemy *after* it had obtained a clear bill of health under the European Convention on Human Rights.[69] It may also question the 'incidents of establishment' and provisions in education law.[70] In modern eyes, many aspects of the way in which the legal system deals with religion may appear 'unprincipled' (to use Laws LJ's term). However, this does not mean that they are necessarily wrong and need to be changed.

As the Strasbourg jurisprudence suggests, the significant factor is whether the provisions disadvantage other religious groups. This should be the focus for those who seek to reform the law. The concept of 'banal discrimination' developed by Beckford may be useful in this regard.[71] Beckford used the work of Billig[72] to contend that English law[73] was characterised by the existence of 'low-level, unthinking, but sometimes institutional discrimination' in favour of 'mainstream Christian churches and against the more marginal' religious communities and organisations. Although Beckford identifies no precise criteria against which banal religiosity can be judged, the concept could be used to identify whether a specific provision disadvantages marginal groups. Banal discrimination could be used to criticise some of the older provisions found in education law as well as aspects

---

[69] See Chapter 7.   [70] See Chapter 8.

[71] J. A. Beckford, 'Banal Discrimination: Equality of Respect for Beliefs and Worldviews in the UK' in D. Davis and G. Besier (eds.), *International Perspectives on Freedom and Equality of Religious Belief* (New York: J. M. Dawson Institute of Church-State Studies, 2002), p. 25.

[72] M. Billig, *Banal Nationalism* (London: Sage, 1995). Billig uses the concept of 'banal nationalism' to describe the ideological habits which enable the established nations of the West to be 'reproduced and constantly perpetuated by everyday habits': *ibid.* p. 6.

[73] Beckford focused upon religious broadcasting, blasphemy law and civic ceremonies. He also made reference to the Human Rights Act 1998 in his introduction.

of the new religion law, such as the judgment in *Eweida* v. *British Airways*[74] and the wording of exceptions in discrimination law.

The three pressure points highlighted suggest that, despite the increase in the number of laws protecting religion, the effectiveness of the law may be questioned. This is to be expected due to the novelty not only of the provisions, but also of the approach of the new legal framework. The new active promotion of religious freedom as an individual right marks a sharp shift in the attitude towards and the regulation of religion in England and Wales. The new laws are expressed in rather abstract ways which make new demands of the judiciary. It is therefore unsurprising that members of the judiciary are 'struggling to find a vocabulary to articulate a consistent and predictable jurisprudence'.[75] Although there has been an expansion in the quantity of regulation affecting religion, the rationale behind this protection remains unclear. Laws LJ's judgment points to the lack of consensus as to why the law ought to protect religion. Unlike previous decisions which suggested that religion was 'something to be encouraged'[76] because of its social functions, Laws LJ seems to be saying that the law will only protect religious values because they have their own merits *despite* being religious. This uncertainty as to *why* the law ought to protect religion has an obvious effect on *how* the law protects religion.

Conclusions

If this book had been written towards the end of the twentieth century, its contents would have been very different. Article 9 of the European Convention on Human Rights was not incorporated into domestic law until 1998, discrimination on grounds of religion or belief was not specifically prohibited and, while the offence of blasphemy existed, English criminal law did not specifically outlaw the stirring up of religious hatred and did not provide tougher sentences for crimes that were religiously aggravated. Admittedly there would have been some similarities, such as the discussion of establishment and the differences between the Church of England and the other non-established religious groups.[77] However, even in relation to those topics, much of the debate, tension and heat would have been missing. Religious courts, schools and dress were not live issues. And litigation concerning religion was a rarity.

---

[74] [2010] EWCA Civ 80.
[75] M. Hill and R. Sandberg, 'Is Nothing Sacred? Clashing Symbols in a Secular World' [2007] *Public Law* 488, 505.
[76] This phrase is used by Munby J, in the quote which began this chapter: *Sulaiman* v. *Juffali* [2002] 2 FCR 427 at para. 47.
[77] See Chapters 2 and 4.

By the end of the first decade of the twenty-first century, this had changed. It is unquestionable that the last ten years have seen a widening and deepening of regulation on religion. This book has sought to provide an exposition and critique of the new legal framework concerning religion, exploring three sets of questions:

1. What has been the effect of the new laws? Have they actually furthered the protection afforded to religious individuals and groups?
2. What has been the significance of the new laws? How do they interact with older laws concerning religion?
3. What affect has this had upon the study of law and religion? To what extent can it now be said that law and religion exists as an academic sub-discipline akin to family law or sports law?

In relation to the first question, the previous chapters have shown how a plethora of laws concerning religion have been enacted, interpreted and administered in the twenty-first century. Some of these provisions have clearly furthered protection, especially in relation to disputes concerning working hours and knowledge of religious rights. However, the effectiveness of other provisions, such as the religious offences and religious exceptions in discrimination law, are open to doubt. And many of the provisions have been interpreted narrowly, especially following *Begum*.

In relation to the second question, it has been shown how these new laws have clashed with older provisions and attitudes. This has notably occurred in relation to blasphemy, education provisions and other 'incidents of establishment'. Whereas many of the older provisions began from the premise that Christianity in general and the Church of England in particular was the norm, the new religion law begins with an expectation of religious equality. Moreover, the way in which the State regulates religion has changed. The juridification of religion has resulted in expectations that the State must facilitate religious freedom. There has been a marked shift towards prescriptive regulation and the active promotion of religious liberty as a right.

In relation to the third question, the substantial increase in legislation, litigation and academic attention concerning religion suggests that law and religion now exists as a legal sub-discipline. Although determining how disciplines and sub-disciplines are formed is by no means straightforward,[78] it would appear that the study of law and religion now possesses many of the characteristics that would be expected of a legal sub-discipline. Law and religion has an institutional presence. There are specialist journals, such as the *Ecclesiastical Law Journal*, *Law & Justice* and *Religion and Human Rights*, and professional associations, such as the Law and Religion Scholars

---

[78] See T. Becher and P. Trowler, *Academic Tribes and Territories*, 2nd edn (Buckingham: Open University Press, 2001), p. 41.

Network (LARSN), the Ecclesiastical Law Society and the number of centres and research clusters developed at individual universities. In addition, a number of academics now identify themselves as being wholly or partly concerned with researching and/or teaching in this area.[79] Moreover, interest in law and religion is not just a fad inspired by the high-profile cases concerning religious rights. There is a 'free standing international community'[80] dedicated to law and religion. It is a well-established sub-discipline in American and continental European universities and there are several important international groupings such as the International Consortium for Law and Religion Studies (ICLARS) and the European Consortium for Church and State Research.

Law and religion also has a clear object of study. Like family law or sports law, it is best understood as 'one of those fields of law which is applied law as opposed to pure or theoretical law'.[81] It does not relate to a clear legal instrument like contract, trust or tort law, but is rather concerned with the recognition and regulation of religious activities.[82] There is an increasing body of law which is concerned with religion. Moreover, it no longer appears that law and religion is only as a Frankenstein-like combination of other legal sub-disciplines rather than a sub-discipline in its own right. Law and religion is no longer simply about the general interaction between law and religion: there is now an identifiable body of religion law.[83]

Laws affecting religion are increasingly cross-referring to one another, developing propositions of religion law. Developments in one part of religion law cannot be understood in isolation from other parts of religion law. This dependence is increasing as the 'two pillars' of the Article 9 and the law on religious discrimination become cemented. Law and religion is fast developing its own vocabulary and culture. Religious disputes are being resolved differently from other disputes. Those advising or commenting upon religious disputes now need to be aware of the general principles of religion law, such as the interpretation of Article 9 and the law prohibiting religious discrimination, as well as the ways in which English law recognises collective religious freedom through the doctrine of consensual compact

---

[79] A. Bradney, 'The Rise and Rise of Legal Education' (1997) 4 *Web Journal of Current Legal Issues*, http://webjcli.ncl.ac.uk/1997/issue4/bradney4.html.

[80] T. Becher and P. Trowler, *Academic Tribes and Territories*, 2nd edn (Buckingham: Open University Press, 2001), p. 41.

[81] Cf. H. Opie, 'Sports Associations and their Legal Environment' in M. McGregor-Lowndes *et al.*, (eds.), *Legal Issues for Non-Profit Associations* (Sydney: LBC, 1996), p. 74, discussed by S. Gardiner *et al.*, *Sports Law*, 3rd edn (London: Cavendish, 2006), pp. 89–90.

[82] Cf. G. Douglas, *An Introduction to Family Law* (Oxford: Claredon Press, 2004), p. 3.

[83] In the same way as there is now a body of sports law in addition to the general interaction between sport and the law: see M. James, *Sports Law* (London: Palgrave Macmillan, 2010), p. 19; and S. Gardiner *et al.*, *Sports Law*, 3rd edn (London: Cavendish, 2006), pp. 88–91, discussed above in Chapter 1.

and the non-interference principle. Discreet doctrines and particular principles are being formed.[84] And the judiciary are beginning to grapple with
questions concerning what is special about religion and 'why it is important
that it is on many occasions treated differently by the law'.[85] The judgments
in *HH Sant Baba Jeet Singh Maharaj* and *McFarlane* are clear steps in this
direction.

Moreover, in addition to being concerned with this distinct body of
religion law, law and religion is also concerned with the study of religious
law. This is by no means unique to law and religion. Other legal sub-
disciplines, most notably sports law, are concerned not only with the effect
of 'external' national and international laws, but also with the 'internal' laws
made as a means of self-regulation. The literature on legal pluralism and
legal typologies suggests that these are and should be a valuable aspect of
legal studies. Moreover, the interaction between religion law and religious
law provides a compelling reason for the development of law and religion
as a sub-discipline. There is a clear need for experts in religious systems of
law to be involved in dialogue with each other and experts in religion law.[86]

In short, this book has sought to demonstrate that law and religion now
possesses the 'academic credibility, intellectual substance and appropriate-
ness of subject matter'[87] to be considered an academic sub-discipline akin
to family law or sports law. On the face of it, addressing this question may
appear to be a spurious exercise in navel-gazing. As Opie points out, 'as new
fields of law emerge it is almost customary for them to undergo this debate
until they have been around long enough to establish themselves'.[88] Yet, it
can be argued that the question is of importance. The further development
of law and religion as a sub-discipline will allow for a common language
to develop and for a disciplinary exchange to occur.[89] This will reduce the
likelihood of academics re-inventing the wheel or failing to see connections between different laws. It will highlight key questions that need to
be researched and orthodoxies that need to be challenged. And an increase

---

[84] Cf. M. Beloff *et al. Sports Law* (Oxford: Hart, 1999), p. 3, discussed by S. Gardiner *et al.*, *Sports Law*, 3rd edn (London: Cavendish, 2006), p. 90.

[85] *Ibid.*

[86] This is the rationale that led to the establishment of the Interfaith Legal Advisers Network (ILAN) by the Centre for Law and Religion at Cardiff University in 2007. See www.law.cf.ac.uk/clr/networks/ilan.

[87] T. Becher and P. Trowler, *Academic Tribes and Territories*, 2nd edn (Buckingham: Open University Press, 2001), p. 41. For Becher and Trowler these are characteristics expected of disciplines; they note that these characteristics 'are less formally recognisable' in 'specialisms' within disciplines: *ibid.*, p. 67.

[88] H. Opie, 'Sports Associations and their Legal Environment' in M. McGregor-Lowndes *et al.*, (eds.), *Legal Issues for Non-Profit Associations* (Sydney: LBC, 1996), p. 74, discussed by S. Gardiner *et al.*, *Sports Law*, 3rd edn (London: Cavendish, 2006), pp. 89–90.

[89] Cf. A. Bradney, 'The Rise and Rise of Legal Education' (1997) 4 *Web Journal of Current Legal Issues*, http://webjcli.ncl.ac.uk/1997/issue4/bradney4.html.

in the reputation of law and religion will also encourage further work in the field.[90] It will not only persuade funding bodies and publishers that the subject is of worth, but will also persuade individual academics to work in the area. To adopt a point made by Bradney, if family law is seen as a sub-discipline and law and religion is not, then it is likely that for career reasons academics would work in family law rather than law and religion.[91] This would mean a reduction in the quantity, and perhaps quality, of research and less awareness of the subject, especially if it were taught to less students.

The development of law and religion as a sub-discipline is required because of the practical importance of the subject-matter of law and religion. There is a need for law students to be aware of these issues;[92] there is a need for dialogue between law and religion scholars themselves; and there is a need for this dialogue to move beyond the Law School to bring in insights from other parts of the academy and beyond. Law and religion has much to gain from and much to contribute within an interdisciplinary climate. There is room for dialogue with theologians, historians, political theorists and social scientists.[93] Moreover, given the popular anxieties that exist in relation to many areas of religion law, there is a need for the dialogue to extend to the public at large and policy-makers. It is easier to make this contribution if law and religion is regarded as a legal sub-discipline. There are, of course, a number of risks inherent in the development of law and religion as a legal sub-discipline. As Bradney has warned, the development of a common language may 'limit the possibilities of argument and conceal the realities of the subject-matter under discussion'.[94] More specifically, an over-reliance upon law may lead to false expectations that there must always be a legal solution. However, although these concerns should be noted, they are soon overcome once the law and religion dialogue extends beyond the Law School.

In twenty-first-century Britain, the interaction between law and religion is rarely far from the headlines. And religious matters are never far from the mind of the legislator and often appear before the judiciary. This has prompted the development of law and religion both as an area of law and as an academic sub-discipline in Law Schools. However, the question of whether legislation, litigation and attention concerning religion will continue to increase is not just a question for lawyers. It also depends upon a host of wider political and social issues. The relationship between religion

---

[90] *Ibid.*   [91] *Ibid.*

[92] W. Menski, 'Law, Religion and Culture in Multicultural Britain' in R. Mehdi *et al.* (eds.), *Law and Religion in Multicultural Societies* (Copenhagen: DJØF Publishing, 2008), pp. 43, 46.

[93] This argument is developed in R. Sandberg, 'Religion, Society and Law: An Analysis of the Interface between the Law on Religion and the Sociology of Religion' (Doctoral Thesis, Cardiff University, 2010).

[94] A. Bradney, 'The Rise and Rise of Legal Education' (1997) 4 *Web Journal of Current Legal Issues*, http://webjcli.ncl.ac.uk/1997/issue4/bradney4.html.

and society in the twenty-first century is characterised by a number of complexities and contradictions. While the secularisation thesis that religion would retreat to the private sphere is now doubted, no convincing narrative has taken its place. Although the numbers sat on church pews have dwindled, the volume of the religious voice has increased. The implications of this for the future interaction between law and religion are unknown. But, for the immediate future at least, it would appear that law and religion will continue to interrelate and collide 'amidst the clash of arms'.[95]

[95] *Sulaiman* v. *Juffali* [2002] 2 FCR 427 at para. 47.

Index